Stephen Bruyant-Langer

The Existential Playbook

How to survive, live and thrive

The Existential Playbook: How to survive, live and thrive
by Stephen Bruyant-Langer
in collaboration with Susanne Sayers

ISBN 978-1-915483-65-2 (paperback)
ISBN 978-1-915483-66-9 (hardback)
ISBN 978-1-915483-67-6 (ebook)
ISBN 978-1-915483-68-3 (audiobook)

Published in 2024 by Right Book Press
Jacket designed by Nick Redeyoff

© Stephen Bruyant-Langer 2024

The right of Stephen Bruyant-Langer to be identified as the author of this work has been asserted in accordance with the Copyright, Designs and Patents Act 1988.

A CIP record of this book is available from the British Library.

All rights reserved. No part of this book may be reproduced, stored in a retrieval system, or transmitted in any form or by any means, electronic, mechanical, photocopying, recording or otherwise, without the prior written permission of the copyright holder.

I thoroughly enjoyed reading this book. It was totally absorbing and fascinating. Eloquent and scholarly, yet still accessible and practical with a lightness of touch – playfulness, even – that allows Stephen's personality to shine through!
– **Mathias Gredal Nørvig, CEO of SYBO Games, creators of *Subway Surfers***

Our notion of self – our identity – inevitably changes as we move through life. What were aspirations for an ambitious future become bleak memories of the past. In addition, the time horizons of past and future change during life as the choices we make for our future often become more concerned with long-term meaning and fulfilment than the short-term wins in a next career move. *The Existential Playbook* puts the reader on a trajectory of opportunities for life choices, reflections and personal insight to inspire how to 'edit the past, curate the present and design the future'. It's a cross-disciplinary view that draws upon established insights from the fields of philosophy, psychology, neurology and strategy, which are combined in compelling ways. The reader is left with plenty of opportunities for informed reflections that may inspire both small changes and bold moves into the future.
– **Majken Schultz, chair of the Carlsberg Foundation, professor at Copenhagen Business School**

Insightful, surprising and engaging – I wish I'd had this book when I turned 40!
– **Jeroen de Flander, co-founder and managing director of The Performance Factory**

This book is essential for anyone seeking to address meaning and purpose in life. Drawing on the very best thinkers, developing powerful models and reflective processes, Bruyant-Langer guides the reader to embrace a deeper sense of self – a real self, an authentic self. It is a must-read for anyone at a crossroads; and who isn't at a crossroads?
– **Peter May, former chief HR officer, Deloitte Global, and former global chief people officer, Baker McKenzie**

A thought-provoking book that draws inspiration from thinkers from Kierkegaard to Camus and from Freud to Frankl. It oscillates in a highly reflective manner between the theoretical and practical; intention and action; mind and body; thoughts and feelings; breakdown and breakthrough; survive and thrive; the personal and the universal; and the successful and the meaningful. Food for existential thought!
– **Morten Albæk, philosopher and founder of Voluntas**

In a world defined by constant change and uncertainty, the ability to navigate transitions with grace and resilience has never been more critical. *The Existential Playbook* is a beacon of wisdom and guidance for those seeking to not only survive but thrive amidst the complexities of life's ever-evolving journey.

Drawing upon a rich tapestry of philosophical insights, psychological principles and real-life 'hacks' and tools, Stephen Bruyant-Langer helps the reader form a comprehensive roadmap for embracing change as an opportunity for growth and transformation.

Through the book's pages, readers will discover real-life case studies, anecdotes, practical strategies, profound truths and empowering exercises to navigate the inevitable transitions of life with courage, clarity and confidence.

At its core it challenges us to reframe our perspectives on change, viewing it not as a threat to be feared but as a catalyst for personal and professional clarity. It furthermore invites us to lean into discomfort, embrace uncertainty and harness the power of resilience to emerge stronger and more fulfilled on the other side.

The Existential Playbook isn't just a book; it is a guide, toolkit and source for those navigating the turbulent waters of change.
– **Richard Leather, chief executive, The Møller Institute, Churchill College, University of Cambridge**

**To my soulmate,
Mette
and to our tribe!**

Contents

Introduction: Your future Self   1

Part 1: Our human condition
1: A new phase in life   11
2: Do you measure success the right way?   37
3: What makes you thrive?   51

Part 2: Transformation
4: The quest for Self   75
5: Show me your friends   93
6: The strategy of reinvention   107

Part 3: Going further
7: Navigating the wider perspective   129
8: How to thrive at work   151
9: Lessons for transformation   175

Epilogue: Ten existential hacks   197

Appendix 1: Scorecard for a meaningful life   201
Appendix 2: Standing on the shoulders of giants   203
Appendix 3: Three existential models   209
Top ten recommended reads   211
Bibliography   212
Acknowledgements   217
Index   219
About the author   231

List of figures, tables and appendices

Figure 1: Your life phases — 18
Figure 2: The four-leaf clover (FLC) — 27
Figure 3: Brain Tuning: the scan of my brain — 62
Figure 4: Brain Tuning: the neuropsychological assessment — 62
Figure 5: The SCARF model — 66
Figure 6: The guiding principle — 70
Figure 7: Levels of social maturity — 79
Figure 8: Stages on life's path — 80
Table 1: How we judge ourselves and others — 81
Table 2: Are you kind to yourself? — 85
Table 3: Our existential questions — 87
Figure 9: The CAR model: Choice, Action, Responsibility — 90
Figure 10: The Meaning 360° model — 101
Figure 11: The Pinocchio model — 108
Figure 12: The growth-plateau-growth relationship — 111
Figure 13: The impact of hormesis — 124
Figure 14: Market crash timeline: growth of $1 — 136
Table 4: Three schools of thought — 141
Table 5: Arendt's key concepts: labour, work and action — 156
Table 6: The Nordic Nine — 161
Figure 15: The Nordic Leadership Model (NLM) — 163
Table 7: The Inner Development Goals — 172

Introduction
Your future Self

Do you sometimes find yourself thinking 'I wish I'd known that it was going to turn out like this when I was younger'? It may be while you're going through a rough time, or it may be that something you spent hours fretting about wasn't so bad or important after all. I know I've found myself in those situations, and from my conversations with coaching clients, I know that most of them have too. So, what if I told you it doesn't have to be like that? While there's no way to know the future with any certainty, it doesn't follow that the future is uncontrollable or a mysterious black box where we have to grope feebly for something familiar in an unknown universe.

This introduction is called 'Your future Self' because this book is about finding your Self (yes, with a capital S). By Self, I mean the essential being that distinguishes you from others, especially in the context of introspection or reflective action. This might seem abstract but trust me, we'll come much closer to a more practical definition soon. If finding your Self was easy, it wouldn't be worth it.

You can prepare for the future without losing your ability to be present in the here and now. You can front-load knowledge. After all, billions of people have lived as humans on this Earth, and millions have lived to tell the tale of many of their experiences, ideas, victories and regrets. We have accumulated wisdom and developed the tools – speech, writing, art, the phone, the internet and generative AI – to share it. And while the past doesn't define the future, the human condition remains recognisable across multiple generations. Our struggles may look different today, and yet when the Roman emperor Marcus Aurelius, in his book *Meditations*, muses upon his struggles and writes notes to himself, his advice is helpful to us today, almost 2,000 years later. For instance, many of us could do with remembering this before attacking perceived opponents on the internet and debates elsewhere: 'Whenever you are about to find fault with someone, ask yourself the following question: what fault of mine most nearly resembles the one I am about to criticise?'

A wealth of philosophers has come before and after Marcus Aurelius. We have much of their advice and thoughts to help us make meaning in our lives today, as well as our ever-growing body of knowledge from the scientific communities, which adds to our understanding of what it means to be human – not just how to survive but to live and thrive. All of this is helpful when you find yourself in one of these moments when you're uncertain about your life, whether you're living it in the way you want to with values and meaning that reflect who you are and who you want to be or to become. You can't change your past but you're the master of how it affects your present and future. Does your history stunt you? Or does it help you grow?

> We humans can edit our past, curate our present and design our future

Throughout the years, I've found that we humans can edit our past, curate our present and design our future. I use the word 'design' rather than 'plan' because it's unlikely that a precise plan will get you where you want to be. Some people object by saying that having a life plan removes spontaneity and surprises. However, I believe in having a design that's sufficiently solid to allow the odd deviation. It's a general direction with guidance tips along the way. I call it 'freedom systematised'. You must have an overall ideal to be aware of what brings you meaning and a sense of fulfilment – and then you can prepare for opportunities and adversity in a way that I usually describe as 'relaxed readiness'. This book isn't about planning every detail but about making you aware of what you want and need in life and how to get your priorities right.

As I've grown older, I feel I've learned a lot from the natural sciences, humanities and social sciences. I'm particularly drawn to existentialist philosophers such as Søren Kierkegaard and Jean-Paul Sartre but I find much to inspire me in the works of other philosophers and schools of thought. I've learned a lot from the people I meet every day, whether they're coaching clients, colleagues, friends, family or more remote connections.

Existentialism is my bedrock and my capstone. By this I mean that it's the culmination of my personal, academic and professional experiences. I've done my best to synthesise, integrate and apply the knowledge of existentialist thought leaders. I'll spend much more time defining existentialism throughout the book but for the time being, I'll simply state that existentialism is about making choices, being authentic and being free. Enticing, isn't it?

I also feel an urge to pass on some of this knowledge. It could, of course, be considered a kind of vanity and to some degree it probably is. But it is, first and foremost, a labour of love and a wish to help people make the most of their lives by sharing knowledge and experience. I meet so many people who wish they knew how to make meaning of their lives, who have in some way lost themselves and are anxious about the future. If you're one of them, I'll try to use this book to get you through that in a way that will make you grow and feel bolder and happier with life, and prepared for the future without fretting about it. Essentially, this book is about awareness, consciousness and knowing yourself. Because once you know what gives you meaning, what makes you thrive mentally and physically, it's easier to choose your way in life.

> We're a social species and we thrive when we collaborate

I was raised in a time when excellence was vital and you had to go it alone. Reaching out for help was to admit failure, that you weren't good enough. New generations have taught me the value of collaboration. We're a social species and we thrive when we collaborate, and our doing so adds value to the result. Thoughts and ideas are debated and tried against different backgrounds and values, and when done correctly, sharing becomes a vetting process.

This book is also an act of collaboration. I've allied myself with four experts who have contributed with wisdom and perspectives from their fields of expertise and personal experiences. This book has emerged due to their willingness to share and discuss ideas across academic areas. Allow me to briefly introduce them.

Tommy Kjær Lassen has a master's degree in theology and used to be the pastor of a small Lutheran church. However, he found the concepts and ideas of philosophy, ethics and existentialism so urgent that he wanted to engage with them more extensively; today, he brings them to the world of business, strategy and management. He works as a business coach, keynote speaker and part-time lecturer at Copenhagen Business School, where he teaches management philosophy, philosophy of science, existentialism and life ethics. Tommy also runs his own company, Stay Human and has authored the book *Philosophy for Leaders* (2020) in which he describes how philosophy, ethics, leadership and self-leadership are connected.

Mikkel Gradert is an organisational psychologist, a much sought-after executive and development coach who's also a master of retention and psychological safety. After spending more than a decade helping people who suffered from burnout, depression, anxiety and other damages inflicted by some of the challenges of modern life, not least everyday work life, he put his energy, skills and knowledge of mental health into prevention rather than treatment. He helps organisations make better and psychologically safe workplaces and coaches individuals on achieving a better quality of life. One of his specialities is decision-making processes, which is highly relevant to this book.

Jens Ole Jarden is a renowned medical doctor specialising in neurology, the author of a long list of articles and studies published in international medical journals and a research fellow at Cornell University and Harvard University. He has been the CEO of a hospital for several years and, since 2019, he's had his own neurology practice, which constantly seeks ways to explore how what we know about the brain can be used to increase our quality of life. Jens Ole is an expert on how our physical brain and hardware affect our psychology and software. He's behind a special assessment, Brain Tuning, where he and a colleague specialising in neuropsychology look at a person's hardware and software and advise on optimising brain health, mental health, cognitive abilities and quality of life.

Claus Maron is a seasoned management consultant and executive advisor who has more than 30 years of work experience within the fields of strategy planning and execution. He's the co-founder of Blue Note Consultants and has an international consulting background working for leading management consultancies. In addition to this, he has many years of leadership experience in top executive positions and boards of directors. Claus is a frequent speaker, writes blogs and articles and has co-authored the book *Promise-Based Execution* (2023). The book combines the latest thinking in leadership psychology with strategy execution.

I'm deeply grateful for their generous and enthusiastic contributions to a book that I hope you'll find helpful as a GPS to your future Self. You'll find questions and themes about identity, meaning, personal growth, choice, action and responsibility. And you'll find old wisdom and new insights from this range of disciplines.

When I began to write this book and collect input from these four experts, I worried that perhaps it would add too much complexity. To my great delight and relief, I found that the opposite turned out to be the case. They cut through the complexity – the conclusions as to what makes us thrive as humans are remarkably similar across their four disciplines. It's neither complicated nor mysterious. However, good advice may feel much more challenging to apply in your everyday life, which you've undoubtedly experienced yourself. This is one of the reasons strategy execution is so important in all of this.

How to read the book

You can read the book from page 1 to the end, including appendices, or you can dive into the chapters that seem most relevant to you. However, I'd advise reading it slowly with time for reflection between each chapter. I've included questions for you to consider at the end of each one. They're an invitation, not a duty. But my experience is that they can help shape an awareness of your true values and what you want to prioritise to give you meaning.

The first part of the book, 'Our human condition', will take you through some background to our human existence in this present day.

Chapter 1 is about those moments of doubt, confusion and desire to do better, which we all get. They can be brief spells but sometimes they become critical inflection points when you begin to doubt whether you're living the life you want to live. How can we use these moments to make them opportunities for growth and a more meaningful future? This chapter is about preparing you in a way that will enable you to face the future in a state of relaxed readiness and with a deep sense of meaning.

Chapter 2 looks at success and how we define it. Humans tend to sacrifice long-term meaning and happiness for short-term proof of our achievements. We tend to measure ourselves and our success by easily recognisable symbols: a lovely house, a smart car, a great qualification, a significant position, expensive clothes. But are these what really matter and will they bring us happiness? Research tells us no. This chapter invites you to reconsider your definition of success and what matters to you.

Chapter 3 will dive into what science tells us contributes to our feelings of happiness and meaning. Philosophy, psychology, neurology and strategy all have essential points to make here, and happily, they all point in the same direction. This chapter explores our biological, physical and mental needs and how we can reconnect with them to lead more fulfilling lives.

The second part of the book, 'Transformation', is about you.

Chapter 4 seeks answers to the eternal philosophical questions, 'Who am I? And who do I want to be?' Knowing yourself is a prerequisite for defining what kind of life you want and what gives you a sense of meaning. Psychology and neurology chime in with their perspectives and will give you an idea of why you are who you are and how you can grow and thrive from there.

Chapter 5 looks at something that too many of us ignore: our relationships. They are critical to a good life, yet many people discover they haven't invested enough energy in them. This chapter will tell you how to increase the quality of your relationships and how we thrive mentally and physically when we have healthy and robust connections.

Chapter 6 gets into the nuts and bolts of how to reinvent yourself and your life. How do you transform? And how do you improve your chances of doing so successfully? This chapter is about applying strategy to your life. Like Pinocchio, most of us have strings that pull us in the wrong direction against our will, making it difficult for us to grow and thrive. In this chapter, you'll learn to identify and cut those strings.

The book's final part, 'Going further', will give you different perspectives on your life.

Chapter 7 discusses paradigm shifts and changing cultural currents and puts them in the context of various philosophical and psychological ideas through the centuries. The 'end times' have always been with us, albeit in a different guise for each generation, who nevertheless survived. My love for philosophy shines through in this chapter and hopefully, you'll also find it of value. Should you wish to know more, I've created two appendices for the real nerds!

Chapter 8 shines a light on the place where most of us spend most of our uptime (at least mentally): the place where we work. How does our work affect us? What's the future of work and, not least, leadership? A new era is emerging with ethics and philosophy as key concepts. Younger generations demand meaning and purpose beyond a pay cheque, while people of all ages are discovering that there's more to life than work. This chapter explores cultural shifts, how they align with your desire to reinvent yourself and how you can lead a meaningful life. It also introduces my brand new Nordic Leadership Model.

Chapter 9 contains advice on transforming yourself and finding a more meaningful and happier life through the lens of philosophy, psychology, neurology and strategy, respectively. This chapter summarises the advice from each of the four disciplines in the book: how to know yourself (philosophy), how to understand yourself (psychology), how to expand yourself (neurology), and how to transform yourself (strategy). I hope you'll emerge with a sense of serenity as well as a stronger sense of yourself, what matters to you, who you are, who you have been and who you want to become.

You'll then find my epilogue in the form of 'ten existential hacks'. This is your fridge door version – ten pieces of advice to be hung on your fridge door to help you stay aware, alert, curious and open to opportunities for the rest of your life. These hacks will help you stay interested and interesting as well as mentally, socially and physically healthy. To implement the hacks, use the scorecard in *Appendix 1* (page 201) to track your progress.

Throughout the book, I mention numerous thinkers whose work I have explored and has fed into my models. I urge you to take your own journey through their thinking. Appendix 2 (page 203) offers a roadmap for you to do this. In the main text, I have marked the first occurrence of names which appear in the *Appendix 2* timeline in **bold**. But just as I observe that 'no human is an island' (Chapter 5), no great thinker's work exists in isolation – so in this appendix I have given examples of cross-fertilisation between these thought leaders and suggested ways in which their insights can be grouped together and be seen to evolve over time.

Finally, *Appendix 3* (page 209) presents my own three existential models – the why, the how, the what – as a framework for thinking about your own self-advancement.

This book has helped me to generate energy in my numerous coaching conversations. It has given me an end goal, answering the question 'What is behind it all?' So, I've felt that each meaningful dialogue I've had over the past many years has contributed to my sense-making. And in that way, I've attached extra importance to each conversation. The essential point here is that it has been meaningful to me. You don't have to agree. You'll find an approach that provides meaning in your life. But in writing this book, I've taken my own medicine. Self-interest often leads to the common good.

Part 1
Our human condition

Chapter 1
A new phase in life

We all get moments of doubt when we sense that we could and should do better. They can be brief spells but sometimes they become critical inflection points when you begin to doubt whether you're living the life you want. Are you getting your priorities right? Have you spent your time on the right things? Those moments can feel lonely but they harbour enormous opportunities for growth and new directions. There's knowledge and wisdom to be found and to help you make the most of them. This book is about preparing you for that moment in a way that will enable you to face the future in a state of relaxed readiness and with a deep sense of meaning.

A CEO of a global advertising agency came to me to find a new perspective on his professional career. He was a highly energetic, self-assured man in his mid-forties but, a couple of years earlier, he'd collapsed at work due to stress. It was a life-and-death situation and he was rushed to hospital.

I have an exercise where I ask coaching clients to go through heaven and hell or, in less dramatic terms, to consider the highs and the lows of their lives so far. The CEO pointed toward this breakdown but I sensed there was more to his story. I asked how his family had reacted. He recalled the family visiting the hospital, including his four-year-old daughter. He told her that maybe he was going to die. Her spontaneous response was to ask 'Could I have a cat, then?' Her father was allergic to pets and had repeatedly denied her a cat when she'd begged for one. His daughter's prompt response and seeming lack of interest in his wellbeing had hurt him deeply.

Now, the daughter probably was concerned. At age four, many children find it challenging to deal with the unthinkable – Dad may die – and much easier to deal with the concrete, in this case, a cat. Childhood is the kingdom in which nobody dies. However, his story of a certain estrangement from his family is repeated in my meetings with other coaching clients and friends. They're beginning to doubt whether they're living the life they want to, whether they're spending time and effort on what matters and is most meaningful. And they're suspecting that the answer is 'no' and that something has to change. But they don't know where to begin.

Let me give you another less dramatic example of this state of mind. This case is about another of my coaching clients, Robert Kledal, who was in his early fifties when I first met him. When he entered, I got the impression that he was used to making decisions and had an aura of solid energy and impatience but also gave off a sense of curiosity and kindness. He was the CEO of a middle-sized international company but had decided to leave his job. He'd given the company and himself plenty of warning: two years, he'd said to the board chair. No more, no less. Then I will be out, no matter what.

Meanwhile, he and his chairman agreed to keep the decision quiet while he did his usual job. He wanted to leave things in good order and was doing so. But he also wanted more from life than the hectic career he'd pursued. His children were growing up and would soon be leaving home. But still, they were dependent on an adult to be there for them. His wife, who was from another continent, usually stayed behind when he travelled with his job, which he did close to 200 days a year. It was beginning to dawn on him that he owed them all more: more presence, more attention, more time. But at the same time, he also knew he liked being a leader. Not the title; he didn't care too much about that. That was one of the reasons he had no problem stepping down as the CEO without having something of similar status to look forward to. But he liked making decisions and wanted to make things happen, succeed and help others succeed.

Like almost any other CEO in the Western world, he'd been through countless coaching and business psychology sessions. Personality tests, 360s... You name it, he'd tried it. And he found the insights, ideas and good conversations interesting. But there seemed to be no way to turn all this knowledge and soul-searching into meaningful action. It was all rather abstract and he was frankly unimpressed with how it seemed to be so much about inward ruminations without any real progress; it was talk and thought and then... nothing.

He knew me from a management society and a talk I'd given on ideas for personal and career development in my top executive coaching system, The Personal Business Plan. At the time, he'd found it fascinating and read the book I wrote about it. He liked that it was about insights and knowledge and how to turn those into action. Now, he hoped I could help him figure out what he wanted to do with the next part of his life – and how to get there. He wanted a sense of meaning, a clearer sense of where he should be going, what should matter in his life.

These two cases aren't unique. Even if the life of these two men may seem quite different from your own and your questions and doubts, we all share something that's part of our human existence: the quest for meaning and how we invest those most precious commodities, time and presence. At some point, most of us will become aware that we have reached a place where our choices matter, not only in the short term. They become existential, defining our future existence. We must decide what's essential, what should take priority, and which values and virtues to use as guiding principles. How to make our lives matter.

> At some point, most of us will become aware that we have reached a place where our choices matter, not only in the short term. They become existential, defining our future existence

It's one of those moments in life where you begin to think about where you've been, where you are now and where you want to go.

These moments can occur at any point in our lives but they tend to be particularly common when we transition from one life phase to another.

We used to talk about 'rites of passage', the formal rituals that would mark many of those occasions, but in a world where things are increasingly fluid and our circumstances are changing considerably and at speed, the transition phases have become less apparent and the rites devoid of much of their original meaning. It's easy to feel lost and alone when dealing with existential doubt. This book will teach you how to look at your life from a vantage point in the future.

When life just happens

Before you read any further, I invite you to consider three fundamental questions:

- What is your next existential choice?
- What is your next existential act?
- Which existential responsibility do you still need to address?

Your initial reaction to these questions might be 'I'm not able to answer those questions without preparation'. However, I've carried out this exercise with many keynote audiences who might have had the same instinctive reaction as you. I then ask them to close their eyes and spend a few minutes thinking about what they still need to do in their lives. Something meaningful always surfaces. We all share a guilty conscience about certain things, for example, broken relationships, dreams not being fulfilled or tasks not being performed. Now is the time to get even with this guilty conscience. Deep down, we all know the right thing to do. The trick is to get these existential issues at arm's length, to be able to treat them like any other task or project. Why is it that we're able to handle external tasks brilliantly but when all of a sudden it's about ourselves, we become a lump of jelly?

If you like, you can write the answers down. Or you can mull them over for as long as you want, or skip them altogether. But these questions are what this book is about. How to choose, how to act and how to be responsible – not as an exercise but as a way of getting your priorities straight. When you know the answers to these three questions, you gain existential clarity, a sense of meaning and the ability to meet the future without unnecessary anxieties, knowing what's important to you. As I mentioned earlier, I call it a state of relaxed readiness. You're ready for the future without being constantly on guard. We'll return to these questions at the end of the book.

When we're busy and everything seems to be going well, we don't spend much time thinking about these existential questions; we usually shove them into the background. We prefer action over reflection and going with the flow over questioning whether the flow is headed in the right direction. Beware of your default behaviour. Only when we reach one of the moments of existential crisis that hit us all from time to time do we begin to doubt the way in which we've lived our lives thus far – sometimes with a feeling of near-panic and a complete lack of control. We tend to become preoccupied with tangible and immediate measures of success. The short-term gains overrule long-term investments and we don't see the consequences until much later. We may think that we're grasping opportunities but if we're not anchored in our virtues, values and what matters to us, we could be squandering them.

I hope this book will inspire you to look at yourself, your life and your goals with a caring but critical eye. Do you know what you want, what truly matters? Or do you sacrifice your long-term sense of meaning for a short-term taste of success? Do you use the correct measurements to judge your life? I wrote this book to help you make existential and conscious decisions about the rest of your life. No matter your age, it will help you achieve a sense of agency in all situations, an awareness that you can steer your life in a direction of your choosing when things aren't going your way. You may not totally control your life but you'll know that you can change it and that your choices and actions matter.

There's joy and meaning to be found in this awareness. Even as you choose more consciously, you'll also find that you're more open to the unforeseen, knowing that you're firmly anchored in your values and meaning and can manoeuvre in unknown waters without losing yourself. However, it takes effort. Getting to know yourself and what's meaningful to you is strenuous but exciting work. And you don't have to wait for any specific moment to get started. When I meet new people on social occasions, I sometimes wear a lapel pin. 'It's Time,' it states, intended to be a conversation starter. 'What does that mean?' people will ask, glass in hand. 'Time to reinvent yourself,' is my answer.

You already know how to transition to the next stage of life

Many psychologists have theorised about life phases. All seem to agree that they exist – we all go through different stages throughout our lifetimes, perhaps most significantly while growing up. However, researchers haven't agreed on precisely what those stages are and to what degree they're universal. One of the most influential theorists, Erik Erikson, a German-born American psychologist and psychoanalyst, believed that we all go through eight psychosocial stages, each defined by a specific challenge or crisis that must be solved before moving on to the next one. The first five deal with the development from infancy to adolescence, while the last three refer to psychosocial challenges in adulthood.

Intimacy vs isolation (young adulthood, 18–40 years): As young adults, we share ourselves and explore and create relationships and commitments to others rather than family members. If we avoid intimacy, fear, obligation and bonds, it can lead to isolation and loneliness. If we succeed, we find happy relationships and a sense of commitment and care. It will lead to the virtue of love.

Generativity vs stagnation (middle adulthood, 40–65 years): Generativity in this context means putting your mark on something and creating something that will outlast you. We do so by giving back to society. We raise our children, are productive at work, get involved with our communities and become part of the bigger picture. When we succeed, we gain a feeling of accomplishment, value and usefulness. If we fail to find a way to contribute, we become stagnant and may feel disconnected. Success will lead to the virtue of care.

Integrity vs despair (late adulthood, >65 years): Older adults reflect on their lives, whether they've achieved what they wanted and led a good life. We become unhappy and perhaps bitter if we don't accomplish our life goals. Suppose we're satisfied with what we see; it will lead to the virtue of wisdom, enabling us to look back with a sense of closure and completeness and an acceptance of death.

The life phases in Figure 1 below are my take on a model based on the works of Rudolf Steiner (1996) and Paul Arden (2003). They are general. One of the criticisms of life phase models is that they're generally based upon the male experience, especially that of middle-class white men in the Western world. Also, not all people experience all the different phases or do so at the proposed time, or in that order. This is even more pronounced these days with so-called mosaic or kaleidoscope careers and fluid identities. You may like to consider it a stage limit and not an age limit.

Therefore you may have found that your phases have been somewhat different, arriving earlier or later or emphasising other questions. After all, we're shaped by our individual circumstances. However, in my experience, these phases fit most people in a society like ours sufficiently to use them as reflection points. But perhaps the most critical point is this: you already know how to transition from being one person to another. You've undoubtedly done it more than once; some schools of thought would argue that you do so constantly. To do it consciously is different from feeling that you're going through some inevitable change but it proves that we're not the same throughout life.

You may know the satirical song 'Les bourgeois' by Jacques Brel. It describes how three friends throughout life gradually change their attitudes. In the beginning, they're disdainful of the bourgeois, the middle-class citizens of small-mindedness, in their point of view. At the end of the song, they end up being exactly that and the target of disdain from younger generations. Well, you don't have to end up being what you despised as a youth but it illustrates the point: we don't remain constant.

Years

0–5	Phase 1: Strong desire to learn
5–15	Phase 2: Critical and rebellious
15–20	Phase 3: Strong need to build an identity and change the world
20–30	Phase 4: Need to settle down and search for maturity
30–40	Phase 5: Ego-driven and hell bent on success
40–45	Phase 6: Repeating success and building a more philosophical perspective
45–50	Phase 7: Trying to keep up with the 25-year-olds and needing to resettle down (mirrors phase 4)
50	**Phase 8: The watershed**
50–60	Phase 9: Strong need to reinvent yourself and re-establish an identity (mirrors phase 3)
60–75	Phase 10: Again, critical and rebellious (mirrors phase 2)
75–85	Phase 11: Again, a strong desire to learn (mirrors phase 1)
85+	Phase 12: Inhibitions lost. Don't give a damn. Me, me, me

Figure 1: Your life phases (my development, based on Rudolf Steiner and Paul Arden)

In the early 20th century, philosopher and educational pioneer Rudolf Steiner conceived a theory of human development based on seven-year cycles. Life expectancy at that time was significantly lower than it is now, so the final cycle was 63–70+. I have therefore combined it with more recent work by advertising executive and author Paul Arden on life's creative circle. I also consider Rudolf Steiner's approach as too Jungian. You may know the work of **Carl Jung**, the Swiss psychoanalyst – if not from anywhere else, then from the Myers–Briggs assessment tool of personalities, which is based on some of his work on archetypes (fundamental ideas and patterns which he held to be common to all humanity).

Fundamentally, I remain somewhat sceptical of psychoanalysis. I sincerely believe that we can shape our existence independently of the cards that life dealt us, and sometimes psychoanalysis seems to be all about how we're defined by past trauma and unfulfilled needs. However, if it helps them move forward and doesn't keep them stuck in their past, I applaud the purpose of making people aware of how they can be tricked and influenced by their unconscious. More on my existentialist premise later in the book.

If you're like most people, you've probably already placed yourself in your age bracket in this overview. But have you also grasped the system behind it? There's a mirroring process taking place.

- Young children (phase 1) have a strong desire to learn. This is also the case for more senior people (in this overview, exemplified by the senior age group, phase 11). That's why grandchildren and grandparents can spend hours together studying a spider or a flower, or building a complicated Lego spaceship. They have the curiosity and the time in common.
- Children (phase 2) are typically critical and rebellious. This attitude is often mirrored in the sixties (phase 10), when people have established their opinions and are willing to fight for them. At this stage, they need to justify that they have made the right choices in life.
- Late teenagers (phase 3) experience a strong need to build an identity and change the world. You probably remember this feeling – the need to break away from your parents and be your own person. You may or may not have experienced the same sense in your fifties (phase 9) but I've observed it numerous times: the strong need to reinvent yourself and re-establish an identity. I've heard people of that age described as 'seenagers', playing with the words senior and teenager, and indeed, these two phases share many similarities. Seniors certainly sometimes act just as foolishly as teenagers!

> *I sincerely believe that we can shape our existence independently of the cards that life dealt us*

Some doors have closed. When we pass 50, we've left youth irrevocably behind us, in the same way that teenagers are acutely aware of the end of childhood. The focus is then on proving that you're valuable in your new life phase – and not only that. When our children become young adults, we regain a sense of freedom, this time combined with a sense of emotional maturity that we didn't possess as teenagers. We may congratulate ourselves on a job well done with the children – or we may find ourselves suffering from 'empty nest' syndrome. No wonder that, for many people, this is a time for reinvention.

One of the most significant differences between us as teenagers and us in phase 9 is the awareness that time isn't unlimited. There's a foreboding of the twilight years approaching. As Bob Dylan says, 'It's not dark yet, but it's gettin' there.' Although our lifespans have lengthened considerably, our mindsets still seem tuned to death, or at least an expectation of being unable to contribute much shortly after retirement. I suspect, though, that this is changing rapidly as the global population ages. We're seeing an increasing number of older people being influential, contributing to their communities and being respected. This, combined with a growing amount of research into healthy ageing, may diminish the sense of finality and increase the need to reinvent yourself and make existential choices for what can now be considered the second half of your life rather than the final years.

Pablo, or in Catalan, Pau, Casals was perhaps our most outstanding cellist. By the time he reached a mature age and had most of his professional career behind him, he continued practising for several hours a day. According to some sources, he'd begin every day by playing all six Bach unaccompanied cello suites. When he was more than 80 years old, a journalist asked him about this. He'd achieved so much, he was famous, he'd won prizes. Why would he still practise? 'I am beginning to notice some improvement,' he answered.

I love this story for the enthusiasm and dedication it shows. But I've also included it here for a different reason. Our concept of what it means to be old is gradually changing. Neuroscience and experts in geriatrics have demonstrated that the ageing brain doesn't need to slip into decay and, indeed, can still improve and learn new skills.

We're beginning to realise that what we once knew about old age was misguided.

In other words, you can no longer use your brain as an excuse not to accept and embrace change! And if you keep practising all your life, you may notice some improvement. People in their twenties (phase 4) must settle down and search for maturity. This need is also felt in the late forties (phase 7) when you try to keep up with the 25-year-olds. You start realising that new trends have developed and you're no longer on top of (all) things. Some examples could be digitisation, social media, sustainability or generative AI. Or it could be cultural shifts, such as the present emphasis on diversity, equity and inclusion, to name a few.

Many people in their thirties (phase 5) are ego-driven and hell-bent on success: 'Been there, seen that, done that!' They need to prove themselves, to perform, to be acknowledged. In terms of energy levels, most people peak in their thirties. This combination of energy and experience culminates between 35 and 40, usually leading to a professional peak in this life phase. But again, this may be a male-centric point of view. At this time in life, many women have, by culture and tradition, spent a lot of their energy bringing up children and being responsible for most tasks in the family, even when they've had careers. And they may have more energy to pour into their professional lives some years later, becoming late bloomers. This is an excellent example of the fact that some of these phases are also defined by culture and not solely by biological or psychosocial necessity.

> *You enter the second half of your life, and for the first time, you experience a feeling of counting down*

In the early forties (phase 6), you've probably found a formula that works for you and you begin to press the repeat button. But you also start to think that there must be more to life than endless repetition.

The point in time when you turn 50 may be the one that many feel to be the most poignant. Many experience this as an inflection point. You enter the second half of your life, and for the first time, you experience a feeling of counting down. Up to now, the central theme of your story has been achievement. But now you begin to think in terms of preservation. How do I maintain what I've got? And not only that – how do I move forward from here? How do I keep feeling that my life has meaning, that I can make a difference when I've already achieved so much (or, for some, a sense of too little)? How do I shape a legacy?

The camel, the lion and the child

The German philosopher **Friedrich Nietzsche** describes two metamorphoses that I find endearing and wise: we go from camel to lion to child.

The camel is a beast of burden, not through obeisance but through taking deep pride in its strength – collecting burdens, conquering hardships and showing its worth by carrying as much as possible. However, in time this becomes more of a duty than a joy. The camel finds itself in the deepest and loneliest desert. Here, it can either be weighed down by bitterness or despair, or it can transform into a lion.

The lion discovers the joy of freedom. No more burdens! What glory to be the lord of its own world. 'I will,' roars the lion, and tries to bend the world to its liking. But however mighty the lion is, it can't reign supreme. It meets a dragon with 'Thou shalt!' written on its scales – the norms of society are not to be ignored. 'Holy no!' replies the lion. The lion and the dragon engage in combat and now the lion must transform to avoid being completely overwhelmed by the dragon.

So, the lion turns into… a child – according to Nietzsche, a curious, playful human being who paradoxically is at the highest level of maturity. The child doesn't fight society but meets it with a 'holy yes!' exploring, creating and celebrating life. With maturity comes a lightness of being that isn't indifference or foolishness but the same seriousness we can sometimes appreciate when we watch a child deeply engaged in play. Discovery, play, exploration and being open and curious as a child is how Nietzsche sees us as our best and most mature.

Life choices are rarely for life

Many of us alive today will survive to be 100 years old. At 50, we no longer need to think that we're looking back on the best part of our lives. We can allow ourselves to believe that we're looking forward to it. The concept of late bloomers has gained traction in recent years, describing how many of us seem to thrive well past our youth, both professionally and personally. Talent was considered a young person's field but today, we're increasingly aware that many people begin to unfold their potential later in life. Children are growing up and no longer need the same amount of physical presence and nurturing from their parents, and that leaves time and energy to use all the knowledge and experiences we've gathered differently. It leaves time to develop new skills, gather new experiences and set new goals. The answer to the question 'When do you peak in life?' should be 'Never!' We all have the potential for continuous growth and development and tickets to the future haven't been sold out.

Life isn't a race or a zero-sum game

This sense of opportunity, regardless of age, should also relieve pressure from people in earlier life phases. You don't have to achieve everything by the age of 35 and it's never too late to change direction. When you're young, it feels as if everything in the future hinges on your decision regarding what to study and how to make a living. There should be comfort in knowing that you can allow yourself to feel as if you made a mistake and you want your life to go in another direction from now on. You should take your life choices seriously but without feeling overwhelmed. Life choices are rarely for life, though the best may be.

Life isn't a race or a zero-sum game. You don't have to win anything or be better than others. You must be the best and most meaningful version of yourself.

I come across coaching clients who are as taut as a bowstring, constantly anxious about the future and how to be prepared for it and stay on top. They usually feel adrift, with no clear sense of meaning or values. This, in turn, means that they're left with an overwhelming number of possibilities and scenarios. You could call it analysis paralysis. They find it a crushing burden; it would be for any of us.

So, when I think and talk about the future, about your future, it isn't in the sense of an infinite space of endless opportunities that you jump between and try to catch up with. You need to know who you are, what gives you meaning and energy and what you want to achieve. You may call it your guiding principle. Then you can relax, knowing you're ready to grasp the right opportunities. That sense of awareness and connectedness will help you navigate your life when everything is up in the air. I describe it as 'Edit the past, curate the present and design the future'.

And despite what may be the most common experience, it's once again important to stress that moments of existential doubt can always hit us. Teenagers frequently feel it acutely. From my conversations with young people, I know that many of them feel intense pressure to make all the right decisions. They don't have the luxury of experience, which makes older generations less concerned. We know there are many ways to live a meaningful and fulfilling life but, to many young people, it seems as if they must get it right from the beginning or all is lost. No wonder so many are anxious.

> I aim to increase your chances of setting and achieving the right goals

I often provide initial comfort to my coaching clients by presenting a scenario tool called the BMW framework. It consists of establishing the Best, the Most likely and the Worst outcome of a situation. Suddenly, the future seems less threatening and the path ahead more straightforward. Consider that there's always the zero scenario, which consists of doing nothing. Sometimes, that pathway ends up looking like the worst outcome. As the American poet Robert Frost put it: 'The best way out is always through.'

One mission of this book is to provide you, regardless of age, with implementable and actionable practices and solutions to help you secure the quality of your future life, to help you fill it up with exceptional experiences and relationships and a deep sense of meaning. I aim to increase your chances of setting and achieving the right goals. You may see it as a transition from rational efficiency towards existential resilience. But more importantly, it's a question of direction. Let me quote Antoine de Saint-Exupéry from *The Little Prince*: 'If you want to build a ship, don't drum up people to collect wood and don't assign them tasks and work, but rather teach them to long for the endless immensity of the sea.'

Like so many ageing people before me, I think I have some knowledge and experience, solemnly described as a certain amount of wisdom, to pass on. Some life lessons can be helpful to other people, so they don't need to feel so confused and alone when they enter these existential moments. We've all been there. And though the future is unknown to all of us, it's possible to be prepared for it, to anticipate some of these life phases, what we want from them, and how we may tackle them. In other words, to become future fit.

When you begin to think of your life in terms of phases, you can front-load some of them, gaining a sense of existential clarity. You'll have a good idea of what life has in store for you. As the proverb goes, 'The best time to plant a tree is 20 years ago.' Hopefully, being more aware of your desired future will help you grow those trees in the present.

I'll also provide you with theory and knowledge from several academic fields. This isn't a 'how to reinvent yourself step by step' book, although you'll also get that. It's an attempt to condense our collective knowledge on human thriving and meaning and to invite you to apply that to your life. So, you'll read theories and ideas from philosophy, psychology, neurology and strategy before I dig into how you can use them to transform yourself. The intention is to provide you with knowledge and insights from different fields and a perspective of the world, because in order to decide where you want to go, you need to know where you are.

My own reinvention

Having met existential inflection points, I've had to reinvent myself several times. Some choices have been voluntary but circumstances forced others. In 1996, I worked as chief marketing officer at Coca-Cola. One day, two gentlemen in dark suits flew in from company headquarters in Atlanta and told me, 'We're sorry to inform you that you're no longer with the company – it's not personal.' This is a sentence that most, if not all, people who are fired come to hate. It may not be personal but it sure feels like it.

From that day on, I decided on freedom and independence as my fundamental values. I spent 20 years as a top headhunter. Since 2014, my wife (who has had a career as a business lawyer and vice president of finance) and I have focused on building a global top executive coaching company. In parallel, I've built an academic career. I often say that this keeps me on my toes by connecting me to trends and youth – my students always stay the same age! Demography is the mother of all trends, just as repetition is the mother of all skills. Along the way, I discovered that teaching is the leadership of learning. It connects beautifully with my leadership perspective and my sincere wish to support the growth of others. My ambition is to help you create a truly exponential life. The starting point, however, was that, back in 1996, I needed the money. It's always possible to retrofit the story of your life! Please try this for yourself. Position yourself solidly in the future and then retrofit. Explain how everything in your life points directly to the situation in which you now find yourself. If you can't convince yourself, you can't convince anybody. You probably know the popular saying, 'Fake it till you make it.' However, I prefer social psychologist Amy Cuddy's version: 'Fake it till you become it.'

> *Some of my most profound changes have come from learning from my family, caring for them and being cared for in return*

In my private life, there have been several inflection points. My wife and I have raised four children and now have nine grandchildren. In the business world, we rarely talk about how family can reinvent you but some of my most profound changes have come from learning from my family, caring for them and being cared for in return. You realise that, despite what society may try to tell you, you can't always put yourself first, and neither should you. Being of value to others is genuinely and profoundly meaningful and family life, frustrating as it can also be, drives that lesson home.

It's these experiences, both private and professional, and many more that I draw on in my practice and in this book. My signature model (to be read clockwise from the top) is a four-leaf clover. It represents two infinity loops and multiple directions. It's a symbol of life. You choose your path, your goals and your means. Sometimes, you cross your tracks, pivot or persevere, and sometimes life simply happens. Once you know where you are in life and where you're going, you will have obtained existential clarity and won't feel lost or that life is meaningless.

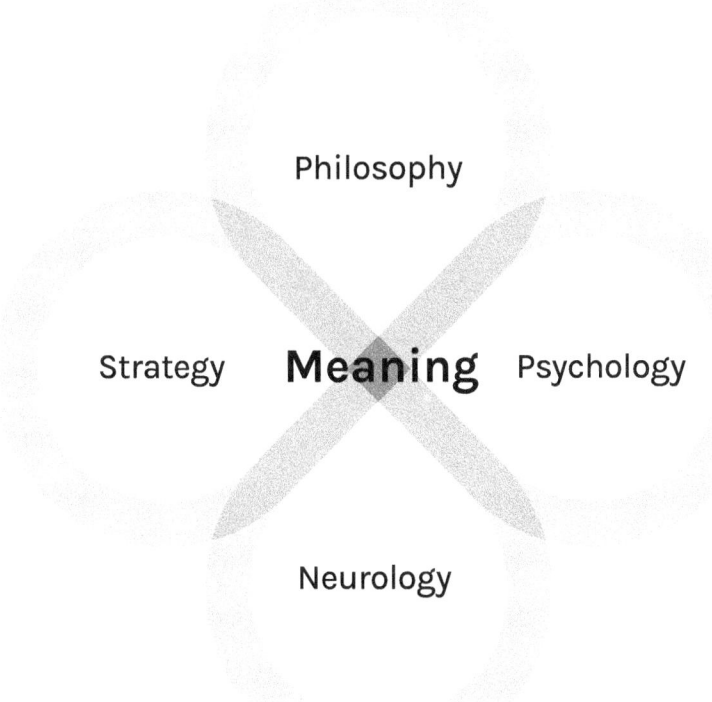

Figure 2: The four-leaf clover

You'll still feel doubts and pains. Clarity isn't about being above those feelings or avoiding them. With awareness also comes responsibility. Awareness is, in this sense, a loss of innocence. You can't pretend that your choices and actions have no consequences. You're responsible for your choices and actions. But you'll be better prepared to make choices that lead in the direction you intend, to act in the way you want. And that will make responsibility less heavy – there's a meaning behind it all. It's your meaning – it doesn't matter if others see the same picture or agree with it.

We need multiple perspectives

This book won't tell you which path to choose but it aims to help you choose your path wisely in a way that's meaningful to you. To do so, I'll include my practical experience and add knowledge from the four disciplines I've referred to.

I found an intriguing video on YouTube (Aqel 2019) that illustrated how one point of view doesn't show the whole picture. It begins with a point on a two-dimensional graphical curve but then shifts the perspective to 3D, which makes you sense the larger view and context that expands from that point of view. It was an apt reminder that there's almost always more to the story than the immediate surface and that we need different perspectives to grasp the complete picture. Life is complex and so are we. If you look for simple solutions, you'll often find the wrong ones.

As I wrote in the introduction to this book, I've allied myself with some of the best brains in these disciplines to extract the knowledge and perspectives inherent in philosophy, psychology, neurology and strategy, which will allow us to grasp at least a fuller picture of our existence. I chose these four disciplines specifically because they have a common denominator: at their core, they're about awareness. To choose and act consciously, you need to be aware of yourself, your mind, your brain, your capabilities, your situation, your relationships, how you're connected to other people and the world, how your actions are reflected and how they reverberate and how, in turn, you're affected by others and their thoughts and deeds. I've already presented each of the experts, so here are a few words on each of the disciplines. You can also see an illustration of the three existential models in Appendix 3 (page 209).

Philosophy is the WHY

Scientifically speaking, philosophy is the oldest of the four disciplines. It has a story going back to the dawn of humanity and keeps developing. Philosophy offers us divergent insights into our existence and our connection to others. It debates ideals and clarifies and lays out different models of the individual and the world that can help us gather new perspectives and greater awareness. It can teach us empathy and an understanding of others through our knowledge of ourselves and provide us with the kind of critical thinking that makes us able to progress, question old truths and suggest new ideas and ideals.

Philosophy is a broad concept. The schools of thought vary, and this book will explore some of the differences and interactions between them, specifically defining three schools of thought: the rational school, the emotional school and the existential school. Or, as they could be called, head, heart and hands. You think, you feel, you grab your future. Philosophy is about asking yourself the right questions – to find the answers and your resulting life choices. In the words of Christian van Nieuwerburgh, executive coach and professor of coaching and positive psychology at the University of East London, 'If coaching is the answer, then what is the question?'

Psychology is the WHAT

It's a much younger discipline (psychology was a part of philosophy until around 150 years ago) but psychology focuses on the same questions from a different starting point. It's less concerned with ideals; instead, it focuses on our minds, how they function and how they affect our behaviours, relationships and lives. Psychology helps us to be aware of our specific circumstances, how they have shaped us and continue to do so, and how we can use that awareness to change them and be more fulfilled.

In psychology, different schools have emerged as well. The original psychotherapy of **Sigmund Freud** has been expanded. Some of his original ideas have been questioned, and areas such as cognitive psychology, with its emphasis on scientific studies of our mental processes and how we use language and reason, solve problems and what and how we remember, have become increasingly popular. The present trend goes towards metacognitive therapy, pointing at the belief systems that hold people back. With the enormous leaps that neurology has made in understanding the brain, neuropsychology is gaining ground, bridging neurology and psychology.

Neurology is also the WHAT

Together with its brainchild neuropsychology, neurology takes a more direct physiological approach to our personalities and possibilities. How do our brain and nervous system affect us and our lives? It's a discipline mainly known in the context of disease, when the brain has been damaged, often due to trauma. But it's increasingly acknowledged that it can also help us improve our abilities and chances of succeeding with what we want.

Specific centres of the brain are associated with particular abilities and neurology teaches us that we can enhance our capabilities throughout our lives. We used to believe that the brain would peak at some point, and from then on, it was all downhill. Today, we know that this is not the case. The brain changes as we mature and grow older but it keeps being able to learn and improve. This should be cause for optimism in all of us.

Neurology also shows us the potential dangers of being unaware. According to many researchers, including the psychologist **Daniel Kahneman**, author of the bestseller *Thinking, Fast and Slow* (2012), as much as 80 per cent of our decisions and actions are governed by the autopilot of our brain. They simply happen, which is inherently intelligent because otherwise we would constantly be hit by analysis paralysis. But it also means that biases and other preconceptions influence our decisions without us noticing and we find it difficult to change what has already become a habit.

Neuropsychology translates these insights into behaviour and cognitive development, combining the physical knowledge of neurology with our mental wellbeing. I like to say that neurology focuses on the hardware and neuropsychology deals with the software inside your head. Neurophilosophy has begun to emerge more recently, integrating the insights from neurology into philosophy.

Strategy is the HOW

Strategy differs because it's less concerned with the why and what of existence. It focuses on the how. How do you plan a strategy that gets you where you want to go? How do you apply it in your life? How do you execute it? The awareness here is all about choices. The small, everyday choices should lead towards the big decisions about where you want to go and what you want to achieve. Strategy is about making conscious choices between available options. It's about taking charge of your destiny and path to a meaningful life.

Somehow, as we age, many of us forget the big goals. We often strive for a specific job or situation that we've now achieved, and instead of setting a new goal, we optimise our current situation. This can be OK, but when you reach that watershed moment, you become aware that it's no longer enough. By setting goals for who you want to be in 10 or 20 years' time, you'll become more aware of your everyday decisions and whether they'll help you on the road to where you want to go.

Of course, as disciplines, they differ. But they all share this quest for the human condition and how to improve it. When you combine them, there are a lot of synergies, which I realised back in 2016 when I read the following passage in the book *Strategy That Works* by Paul Leinwand and Cesare Mainardi with Art Kleiner (2016): '[Our theory of strategy] suggests that the path to sustainable success, as the companies in this book have found, is through developing an identity all your own, grounded in your way of capturing and delivering value and in your most distinctive capabilities. This identity is expressed as who you are and what you are great at doing, rather than where you are going and what you sell.'

This text could just as easily have been written in a psychology book. Just change the focus from companies to individuals. The leap to philosophy, with its emphasis on identity, isn't big either. As I began to look, I found this to be accurate. Whether looking into strategy, psychology or philosophy, much of the content is true across disciplines. This made me wonder about the professional silos we all work in, one echo chamber unaware of what's happening in the other. I want to bring to life the collective wisdom from these bodies of science and offer you the condensed version.

Fundamentally, we're all the same

In these turbulent times, it can feel as if our problems and challenges and their possible solutions are something new and, of course, to some extent, they are. Some aspects of our lives are founded thoroughly in our specific times and circumstances. But underneath the surface, these questions remain the same. How do I make the most of my existence? How should I live? How do I leave a legacy I'll feel proud of? How should I measure my worth? These are questions that humans seem to have pondered throughout our evolution. They're all based on one fundamental truth: life is a one-way street – you can't go back!

It's easy to feel lost, especially when everything moves fast. What was true yesterday may not be true tomorrow. Hierarchies are broken down, privileges are debated and conventional wisdom is questioned. And yet again, this has always been the case. Consider the sighs from ancient scholars and philosophers about the sorry state of their times and the lack of respect from younger generations. *O tempora, o mores*! ('Oh the times, oh the customs!') This doesn't mean that the sense of disorientation and the quest for meaning that can punch us in the solar plexus with the force of an iron fist or keep us awake and anxious at night are in any way banal or trivial. But it does mean we're not alone when we reach these transitional phases. We have extensive literature and knowledge that can help us. Some of it has been passed down through the centuries and is still relevant because the human condition hasn't changed significantly, even if the times have.

Through my work as a top executive coach, I've had delightful dialogues with thousands of competent leaders. I've had the privilege of exploring ideas, challenging identities and helping them gain control of their lives. Our shared objective is to find meaning in life and experience existential clarity. We're all the same. We share the same doubts and the same fears. We even share the same secrets. As Carl R Rogers, one of the founders of humanistic psychology, famously said in his book *On Becoming a Person* (1961): 'What is most personal is most general.' He'd found that, when he shared his most profound, private thoughts and feelings, they resonated with others who recognised similar thoughts and feelings in themselves. You may have had the same experience. You share a deeply personal story, probably somewhat timidly and perhaps with a fear of being condemned or ridiculed, only to find that others have similar stories to share.

There's nothing to be afraid of. Don't fear your secrets or your doubts; they may be personal but they're also universal. Moments of doubt and despair can lead to moments of great clarity. With this book, I hope to help you make the most of them. As the title says, it's not a rulebook, it's a playbook. You'll find nothing in it about what you can't do or which rules to adhere to. But it will strive to make you aware of yourself and your values, enable you to define meaningful goals, analyse which choices, actions and responsibilities will lead to them, and navigate life's watersheds confidently.

The subtitle of this book, 'How to Survive, Live and Thrive', may sound pretentious. I'm not suggesting I know how you should live your life. However, I'm sure that you want to thrive and live a rich, fulfilling life that gives you energy and to which you devote your energy. A sense of meaning and agency is the foundation of thriving. Thriving isn't the same as perpetual bliss or happiness. Instead, it's a state of inner confidence that whatever life throws at you, you'll be ready for it and ready to create something good with it because you're anchored in your values. After all, you're connected to yourself and others because your life provides meaning. I will return to the idea of relaxed readiness in more detail later in the book. Going through life, it might be worth remembering the words of T S Eliot ('Little Gidding', 1942): 'What we call the beginning is often the end. And to make an end is to make a beginning. The end is where we start from.'

You are responsible

I was born in Denmark, a modern egalitarian country that emphasises community and trust and, like the other Scandinavian countries, tries to balance the common good with respect for the rights of the individual. It's also highly competitive, which many see as a paradox. How can you be competitive when you have high taxes, a high degree of safety and a work–life balance that allows people to take several weeks off for holidays? The answer is that the modern state, with its tax-paid education and healthcare, has allowed companies to thrive and invest in innovation and digitisation. In Latin, 'compete' translates as 'strive together'.

Denmark is usually known for being among the happiest countries in the world, for *hygge* – the art of making small moments into memorable cosiness, even when it's dark, wet and cold outside – and for the fairy tale writer Hans Christian Andersen, as well as television series and novels that are surprisingly noir in an otherwise seemingly idyllic country. There also seems to be a trend for Scandi chic. These days, Denmark is also a country that enjoys having some of the world's best restaurants alongside green and clean surroundings. Politically, it's a stable democracy. Denmark's King Frederik X stems from the same bloodline that has occupied the Danish throne for almost 1,100 years. Polarisation is limited; there's a large degree of collaboration and consensus across political divides. Digitisation is extremely high and there's generally a high degree of trust in other people and public administration. In many ways Denmark is a country punching above its weight. As one of the Danish researchers on trust, Professor Gert Tinggaard from Aarhus University, paraphrases a Lenin quote: 'Control is good; trust is cheaper.' Society runs smoother and cheaper when you don't have to spend financial and human resources on control.

Those are the upsides and, of course, there are downsides. But I feel that Denmark, to a large extent, has achieved the quality of life that people from many other countries long for. Denmark is also the birthplace of Søren Kierkegaard, widely considered to be the first existentialist philosopher. His works are vast and complex but among his key ideas is an emphasis on choice – either/or – as well as action and responsibility, which are at the core of this book and the three key factors that will lead to meaning and agency in your life. According to Kierkegaard, you can't 'think out' your existential choices. You must act on them and face the responsibility that comes with them.

Having a French mother, I was also raised in French culture, with **Jean-Paul Sartre** being the rock star and **Albert Camus** the James Dean of contemporary philosophy. This has given me a double view of both cultures, with their inherent differences. The Danish egalitarian viewpoint and celebration of collaboration and trust, among other things, are countered by the French intellectual prism, abstract approach, elitist view and a striving for excellence. Both views are present in this book. They have their strengths and weaknesses, just like everything else that shapes us and our attitudes towards life. But they are part of knowing where I come from and how that will likely influence my choices. As a reader, you'll probably have a different background affecting your life and ideals. The practices and solutions in this book won't try to sway you to a particular point of view but rather encourage you to consider what influences you and what place you should have in your life. Again, this is a playbook, not a rulebook.

Along the way, you'll meet some of my executive coaching clients and, based on my long career, I'll suggest some points to consider and steps to take. It's up to you whether you want to apply them or save them for that watershed moment when you realise something has to change. Either way, the experience of my coaching clients is that they work. I intend to leave you with a sense of meaning and clarity as well as a trust in the future and the knowledge that you're not alone, nor are you helpless. You can get your priorities right. This is, at its core, a life-affirming and fundamentally optimistic book. But it also stresses that you are responsible for your own life. So, I invite you again to consider: what's the absolute imperative existential choice you must make now? And because a choice is hardly a choice without action, how do you need to act to make the choice significant? And by what means do you hold yourself responsible and accountable?

Questions to ask yourself

- When you reflect on your life, which have been the most fulfilling and meaningful years?
- What made them stand out?
- What lessons can you apply from those periods to your future Self to make the rest of your life fulfilling and meaningful?
- What is holding you back?

Chapter 2

Do you measure success in the right way?

Humans tend to sacrifice long-term meaning and happiness for more short-term proof of our achievements. We tend to measure ourselves and our success by easily recognisable symbols: a lovely house, a smart car, a great qualification, a significant position in a renowned company, expensive clothes and accessories. But are these really what matters and will they bring you happiness? Research tells us no. This chapter invites you to reconsider your definition of success and what matters to you. And if you didn't already know, failure can be good for you. We're all bound to fail occasionally, so this is good news.

'You get what you measure' is part of a saying attributed to H Thomas Johnson, the American accounting historian and professor of business administration. The full quote is: 'Perhaps what you measure is what you get. More likely, what you measure is all you'll get. What you don't (or can't) measure is lost.' It's a case for measuring and keeping track of significant progress but it's also a case for measuring the right things and using the right measure.

You may have seen the TED talk that Harvard Business School professor **Clayton Christensen** presented in 2012, entitled 'How will you measure your life?' Christensen was, at least until that point, primarily known as the father of disruption. He wrote the ground-breaking book *The Innovator's Dilemma* (1997) about why old companies find it hard to survive new technologies and new and disruptive business models. A brilliant example of true disruption is when Sam Altman, the founder of OpenAI, was asked, 'How will OpenAI ever become profitable?' He answered, 'Honestly, we don't know. First, we will build it. And then we will ask it.'

In later years, Christensen realised that much of what he'd dedicated to teaching the business world could be applied to our personal lives. He taught his students, 'If you study the root cause of business disasters, over and over you will find a predisposition towards endeavours that offer immediate gratification.' And the overall message in his TED talk was this: we measure the wrong things.

> We seem particularly concerned with individual achievement and self-fulfilment as a measurement of success in the Western world

Based on lifelong experience and conversations with coaching clients and friends, I tend to agree. We're so concerned with apparent success and how to prove we've been successful that we forget whether our measurements make us thrive.

Christensen describes how, after five years, his own Harvard Executive MBA class reunion was a happy one: people are doing well, they have spouses that are better-looking than they are, children on their way, and their careers seem to be on track. But something happens. Fast-forward 20 years and the picture is very different. Now, most people are miserable. They may be successful in the eyes of the world but they're divorced, other people are raising their children and they're lonely.

We seem particularly concerned with individual achievement and self-fulfilment as a measurement of success in the Western world. We fundamentally believe that, at least to some extent, you're responsible for your own life and that we essentially live in a meritocracy where you get what you deserve, or nearly so. We've more or less killed off God and fate as viable excuses for not being successful.

Now, it's all up to us.

But we aren't born with equal opportunities, and fate does play a hand. A talented young football player may be hit by a bus. A bright student may suffer a brain injury. They may never reach the achievement that would make us define them as successful at first glance. Perhaps their back story would make us reconsider our initial judgement. I do, however, believe that despite inequality in opportunities, we can all be successful; but you'll have to find a meaningful definition. It boils down to being true to yourself and your values, and those will shift through life. And know this: you can't be successful at everything. If you put effort into one area of life, others can and must get less attention. Your priorities will undoubtedly change as life changes. Youthful success is different to success later in life. And you're not successful once and for all. It's a transitional phase where you gradually change your goals. According to Christensen, we have limited minds and they tend to be concerned with a short-term horizon. Immediate and tangible evidence of achievement is prioritised over long-term meaning and fulfilment. A great car, a beautiful house… tangible and visible symbols of success but meaningless in the long run. They don't make us happy.

Numerous studies have shown that poverty is associated with a significantly raised risk of depression, anxiety, early death and suicide. However, once you get above a comfortable baseline – mainly having enough money to pay your bills and take care of responsibilities – there's no significantly increased happiness in earning more money. Thinking in hierarchies and worrying about whether you're the top dog and able to prove it just creates more anxiety.

We're concerned with how much money we make, what positions we hold and how others perceive it precisely because we think in hierarchies. But at the end of your life, it was never about what cars you drove or what houses you lived in but how you felt about your life and how you helped others be better people, whether it's your children, your partner, your colleagues or members of your community. Our choice of measurement is, says Christensen, a big deal.

He also published the book *How Will You Measure Your Life?* (2012) and expanded on several subjects from his talk. But the overall message was the same: we tend to sacrifice long-term happiness and meaning for short-term satisfaction. We tend to optimise continuously but this chain of optimised short-term decisions seldom leads to overall, long-term satisfaction. Christensen's Harvard class consisted of the best and brightest. Why did they seemingly continue making the right decisions but all end up between a rock and a hard place? It takes 20 years to raise children and be able to, as he says, finally, hands on hips, congratulate yourself on bringing up great people. It's an investment to nurture relationships and give back to your community and it may not provide you with any visible signs of success. You'll only have your deep sense of meaning and achievement in return, but that's worth more than flashing an expensive watch or a prestigious title.

Who is successful?

If you want something to feel like a success, it must feel meaningful. Meaning and success aren't the same for all of us. One way of answering what people see as providing meaning is to look at different types of meaning. McKinsey & Company did that back in 2020. They identified nine types:

1. **Achievement** – status, power, authority, high income
2. **Conservation** – working to preserve the environment and caring for it
3. **Caring** – helping other people, your loved ones, your family and friends
4. **Freedom** – forming your own opinion, choosing your own goals, learning things for yourself
5. **Respect** – avoiding humiliation, not being shamed in front of others
6. **Tradition** – respecting your culture's history, feeling part of it, practising the rituals of your culture or religion
7. **Enjoyment** – new experiences, adventure, excitement
8. **Stability** – order, rules, respecting authority figures
9. **Equality and justice** – listening to different people, trying to understand others (even if you disagree with them) and fair treatment.

In my opinion, legacy is missing. I want to add that type of meaning:

10. **Legacy** – leave something behind, contribute to the greater good, do what only you can do.

Looking at the list, you'll see that what's usually used as the primary measure of success, finding meaning in status, is just a tiny part of something much more complex and compelling. For example, I'll return to Robert Kledal, a business leader and one of my coaching clients, who asked for help while going through a life transition. One of his characteristics is that he's uninterested in status, at least in how most of us understand status as a title, the place we live and what we can afford. This disinterest allowed him to let go of his title as a CEO. He didn't feel that losing that title made him worth less. It's an excellent position to be in. Many of us hold back because of our definitions of success and inability to let go of them. We may not even be aware that we harbour them. Robert explained to me how he'd been surprised to find that many of his friends and contacts were preoccupied with their status and whether they were perceived to be successful.

Meaning and success aren't the same for all of us

We all share some bias as to what success looks like. Just think about it: if I were to ask you over for lunch and said I'd bring someone very successful with me, what kind of person would you imagine I'd have invited? You'd likely picture someone with visible success in professional life: an entrepreneur, an accomplished artist or athlete, or a CEO. But what if I brought along a grandmother, a little old lady with a face as wrinkled as an apple in March, the matriarch of her family – a woman who'd raised several children with care and love and helped their children along with care and love, who'd never been anything but a housewife? Would she not be a successful person?

Success is highly personal. Yet, when we speak about success, it's frequently associated with status. In Latin, status means condition, position or rank. Somebody successful is someone climbing the social ladder eloquently and admirably. As Clayton Christensen says, there's more to being successful than status. In the superficial sense of the word, you could achieve status through plain luck, such as winning the lottery or being the child of wealthy parents. So, we sense a striving in the word success – a lot of hard work, maybe ruthless decisions, perhaps sacrifices.

We're social beings and want to be appreciated by our friends, family and society. And yet we have, at least in the business world, tried to distance ourselves from those emotional bonds to others. 'You don't have to be loved; you have to be respected' has been one of the *bons mots* among CEOs, as if love and respect were opposites. We've nurtured values that reflect ruthlessness and willpower and fighting for a place at the top of the hierarchy. You're successful as long as you're on your way up and willing to do what it takes to get there. As some say, 'If you don't have a seat at the table, you're on the menu.'

When you coach highly successful business people and discover how many have had to cut themselves off from their deeper values and emotions to emulate this narrow definition of success, it makes you reflective. This is why you must consider and define what success is to you before you can change and grow into the person you want to become. No matter which ideal of success you subscribe to, mediocrity won't get you to where you want to be. Whatever your definition, you must strive for it and invest in it.

I talk about maximising and sufficing as two different mindsets – two different attitudes towards life. By the very definition of maximising, you can't maximise two things if they're trade-offs. Limitation is built into the human condition. Some people strive constantly; they're never satisfied but reach higher all the time. Other people can be content with little; if they have what they want and can't imagine why they would need more, they may never want to strive. In my experience, most people are a mix, leaning to one side or the other. I truly admire one of my daughters, a business lawyer who succeeds in prioritising her time. She delivers adequately in all circumstances, not too much, not too little. Her favourite quote is from Sheryl Sandberg, the former COO of Facebook (now Meta): 'Done is better than perfect.'

Both mindsets have their value. It's a pity to go through life and never feel satisfied and experience balanced calm. But it's also a pity never to believe that things could be better or, more importantly, that you could improve and be a better version of yourself. But you have to realise that sometimes enough *is* enough. In economics, we'd call it the law of diminishing marginal returns – that there's no point in continuing further down the same pathway. The difference may, again, be how you measure what enough is, what makes you satisfied and what gives your life meaning. If it's wealth and a way to show it, enough may never be enough. There will always be someone more prosperous and more powerful than you. Do you ever compare your inner Self with the outer of others? We all have a tendency to do that. But it's an unfair comparison. Even the most successful individuals have the same doubts and uncertainties as you, perhaps even at a larger scale. But these doubts and uncertainties don't show in the outer world.

In my opinion, too much time is spent dwelling on and ruminating about past experiences. It's never too late to have a happy childhood. It simply depends on the memories you decide to focus on. If we choose to, we can all recollect positive memorable moments. The actor Halle Berry puts it this way in an article from the *New York Times Style Magazine* (Maynard 2012): 'My mother helped me identify myself the way the world would identify me. Bloodlines didn't matter as much as how I would be perceived.' She underwent a transformation after a tough childhood (involving diabetes, racism and an alcoholic father, who abused her mother and sister but not her) and achieved global stardom. The actor Tom Hanks describes her in this way: 'She's got this way of looking at the camera. Very deep and still. There's a calm about her, and that comes through in her performances. She's a peaceful pond on a late summer's day.'

The most exclusive thing in this modern world is calm.

> *There will always be someone more prosperous and more powerful than you*

The ancient virtues

In the Greek philosopher Plato's best-known work, *The Republic*, he describes how his master, Socrates, debates with the citizens of Athens. They argue the principles for a virtuous life and Socrates comes up with four cardinal virtues: prudence (or wisdom), justice, fortitude (or courage) and temperance (or moderation). Those are the virtues upon which all others hinge. In the view of many Greek philosophers, the definition of success is to live a virtuous life. There are several philosophical schools and directions but philosophy is always concerned with what constitutes a good life and which values should direct it.

Four cardinal virtues: prudence (or wisdom), justice, fortitude (or courage) and temperance (or moderation)

The Stoics agreed with Plato and Socrates on the cardinal virtues but were perhaps especially concerned with temperance and fortitude. The Stoic will say that you can't change what has happened but you can choose how to deal with it. Success is living the life you were meant to live and to make good of even the worst experiences. It's often misunderstood. Some people think stoicism is about suppressing feelings and trying to feel nothing. But it's more about emotional alchemy: transforming negative emotions into constructive ones. To make good of something terrible and to accept what's inevitable. The Stoic school of thought is getting a lot of traction these days, perhaps because so many things are outside our influence. But how we think and react should not be.

I subscribe to existentialism, to choice, action and responsibility. Success is living a life where you can control what you choose, have the agency and freedom to act, and have the will and conscience to be responsible. You may not really be in control of all things – you can still get hit by a bus – but you should feel sufficiently in control to live up to your own rules and values. It gives you resilience, it gives you energy and commitment and it roots you in your being while you feel part of something bigger. Drive, willpower – all of this is enhanced when you live according to your rules and values. It gives you the agency to choose, act and be responsible.

Did you fail? Or grow?

If we define success in that way – as striving for what you believe in and what's meaningful to you – we also define failure as something you specify, regardless of other people's opinions. You'll know whether you've lived up to your ideals and will realise that you can be successful even though your business goes bankrupt, your latest experiment didn't work out or you live a life with limited finances. This is important because we'll inevitably fail in other ways. Learning and growing are all about trying and practising – initially being bad and gradually getting better. You have to fail in order to learn and grow. If we define success only as being good at something, how would we dare to try something that we may be miserable at? If we become afraid of failure, we limit ourselves. There's a significant difference between fighting to win and fighting to avoid losing.

I subscribe to existentialism, to choice, action and responsibility

Let me give you a few practical examples. I practise boxing and most of the training sessions start with skipping rope. If you haven't tried skipping rope before, you'll look ridiculous in the beginning, while trying to learn. Of course, this shouldn't hold you back. You'll eventually become better. And you can rest assured that everyone else looked ridiculous when they started.

Another example comes from my barber, whom I brought to boxing training. He didn't want to start exercising until he'd lost some weight. Not very logical, is it? If you define success as staying true to yourself and your values, there are no limits to what you can try and fail at, learning along the way and growing as you improve. And then, you can succeed at achieving your goals. This is slightly different, although related to success at large and your perception of being able to choose, act and be responsible, as existentialism stresses. We need skills and knowledge to choose and act competently; we need values to be willing to be held accountable and to assume responsibility.

It's not easy to look at failure in that way. In today's society, individuals are almost always to blame if they don't reach the goal they've set for themselves. They should've worked harder. They should've been smarter. They shouldn't have given up; they weren't sufficiently persistent. As the saying goes, 'Persistence prevails when all else fails.' No wonder many people try so hard to keep at a task, even if it was clear from an earlier point that it was futile. Psychologists work with a concept called 'creeping ambition'. It means that when you've reached your objective, your ambition will have increased and you're therefore not yet satisfied. You've probably experienced that several times in your life. Or we can get pushed to work towards something that was never meaningful. For instance, our parents' wishes can push us in directions we never really wanted to go, defining success in a way that isn't truly consistent with our desires.

My father died when I was only 12, but I went to business school quite a few years later because – according to my mother – it had been his strong wish to have a merchant or trader in the family. That I primarily used my mercantile background in the first part of my career is probably just as well. I transformed my business school experience into something meaningful to me. That's how I frame it, but I often see others refusing to let go because they view it as a personal failure to do so rather than recognising that the goal is the wrong one for them.

A recent example stems from when my wife and I built the online toolkit for our Personal Business Plan executive coaching system. Our ambition was to create a huge software as a service (SaaS) business, becoming a dominant global player in the personal development market. OK, we now have users in 94 countries, which isn't bad. But we didn't achieve global dominance! The point is that at some point along the way, I gradually accepted that our dream would not become reality. And much to my surprise, this realisation brought instant relief. A feeling of satisfaction slowly crept in, replacing my feeling of frustration. A burden fell off my shoulders. I remembered what our son-in-law, a serial entrepreneur, told us when we started building our business: 'Remember that what you're doing is difficult. Be happy for what you achieve and not unhappy for what you don't achieve.'

If you consider myths and the ancient Greek philosophers, failure wasn't always such a lonely thing. Greek plays and stories are sprawling with tragic heroes who remained heroes even if they failed. In his work *The Poetics*, Aristotle defines the tragic hero as somebody of virtue, a decent person, but also somebody who makes mistakes occasionally, even if they may not seem like mistakes to begin with. Thanks to a flaw in their character – Aristotle's word is *hamartia* – amplified by a twist of fate or the hand of one or several of the gods, small mistakes begin to have grave consequences, ending in catastrophe. But we still sympathise with our hero, even though he can't be considered successful in a traditional understanding of the world.

Why do we do that? Perhaps because we realise that even though we've killed our gods, there's more to success than the individual. Circumstances can be cruel. The Greeks poetically showed this through the tragedies. We may not believe in fate or gods but we recognise that humans sometimes fail through no fault of their own, or at least only partly so. Our small mistakes can become catastrophes through a chain of events we don't fully control.

The highway of life is littered with flat squirrels that couldn't make up their minds

Small and wise decisions can become huge successes through the same kind of halfway incidental process. We don't talk about that so often. It's a more pleasant thought that our successes are entirely our creations. Aristotle found that tragedies should inspire pity and fear, as well as compassion for the hero who, despite striving, ended up in a bad situation through an unhappy chain of events. We might fear that it could happen to us – and develop an understanding that easy judgement of another person is frequently only easy, not just.

Success isn't only a question of having sufficient will and making the right choices. And failure *is* an option. However, you decide what you want to make of it. It doesn't have to define you as a failure. The highway of life is littered with flat squirrels that couldn't make up their minds.

Mr Toilet and the millionaires

One thing we miss when we focus on success and failure as solely individual responsibilities is how much we depend on other people and how we're all interconnected and dependent on each other. Problem solving is a team sport. Instead of measuring success in terms of individual achievements, sometimes we should consider measuring our success by the quality of our relationships. Do we have people we can rely on, no matter our status, and are we equally reliable to our close connections?

An increasing number of people, including those in the business world, are redefining success. The quest for a sustainable world has forced us to acknowledge that you're not successful in achieving your goals if you do it at a considerable cost to society in terms of the climate crisis, depletion of resources and increasing inequality and social injustice. You could say that the world has gone from egocentric to ecocentric. Neither is it successful to cut yourself off from the most important and meaningful relationships in your life to prove a point about success. Where, just a few decades ago, striving to make the world a better place would be met with derision across the board, it's now becoming increasingly common and not just to greenwash or whitewash business.

> *Sometimes we should consider measuring our success by the quality of our relationships*

One example of a successful person who knew how to transform himself in time is Jack Sim from Singapore. He's a highly successful entrepreneur who, by the time he turned 40, had realised that he'd accumulated more wealth than he could ever spend. Jack is a good businessman. He put his energy into something he wouldn't profit from. More wealth was meaningless; he'd be prioritising his time on something useless to him. Instead, he decided to make a difference in the world. He found his cause: sanitisation. A vast number of people on the planet still have no toilet facilities. It's a severe problem in several ways; the spreading of diseases is just one of them. So, Jack became Mr Toilet, spreading the gospel of good sanitisation, building an organisation that could help build toilet facilities. It hasn't made him richer financially but has given his life new direction and meaning.

Jack pointed out that, when discussing millionaires, maybe we shouldn't measure them by their wealth. Perhaps a millionaire should be someone who has helped a million people, not someone who has made a million dollars. He's far from the only one. Globally, people realise that success is more about helping others than reaching a goal measured by your wealth or position. And no matter your status, you can make the world better for others. It could be helping your neighbour with groceries or volunteering to help your nephew with his maths.

We don't all have the power to help a million people. But when you define what success is to you and what you want to achieve, you may also want to consider how your success can lead to a better world for others. My cause is homelessness. When I meet homeless people in shelters around Denmark, I realise that the difference between a good and materially safe life and a life on the street is smaller than most think. Some of the people I've met used to be in good positions, in steady jobs, with a family. Some life events pushed them off course – a divorce, getting fired, mental illness, substance abuse – and in a frighteningly short amount of time, sometimes just a couple of years, they ended up on the street. It gives me a deep sense of meaning to help improve their conditions.

> *Perhaps a millionaire should be someone who has helped a million people, not someone who has made a million dollars*

Again, in the words of Clayton Christensen, how will you measure your life? What makes you feel genuinely happy? What will you reflect on when you reach a ripe old age as your true legacy? What will people think about you? Or, more importantly, if you were to look back on your life at the end of it and write about it, what would you like to be able to write?

Be careful how you measure your life. And be sure that your goals are indeed your own and not just something superficial that you thought would bring you happiness.

Questions to ask yourself

- In which way would you define yourself as successful?
- Which is the best failure you have had so far? And what did it give you?
- Which new goals have you set for yourself?
- Is it time to let go of some of your old ones?

Chapter 3
What makes you thrive?

Today, we know a lot about what makes us thrive. Philosophy, psychology and neurology have lessons to pass on. However, we sometimes forget to heed them. This chapter explores our biological, physical and mental needs and how we can reconnect with them to lead more fulfilling lives. There's plenty of cause for optimism in these findings. It turns out that most of what we enjoy as humans – being with others, playing, not working too hard, challenges, love, new experiences, feeling appreciated, contributing, to name a few – is precisely what we need.

Most of us are concerned with current events, the debates that shape our society and the numerous challenges piling up in front of us. But they can be distractions from our essential human condition. We imagine ourselves way beyond our primitive ancestors and believe we've progressed to an extent where we can ignore our origins. Science, not least neurology and psychology, will inform us that we're fooling ourselves. Fields such as modern archaeology and DNA techniques have also added a deeper understanding of how we remain the same as when the first modern humans traversed the plains of Africa and spread into neighbouring continents nearly half a million years ago.

This is still relevant today. In the following chapters, I'll detail how to approach the situation that most of my coaching clients are in. They want to make the next phases of their lives meaningful and to live fulfilling lives. To thrive. They need to know their priorities, values, what they want to achieve and what they want to let go of. But it's equally helpful to know where we come from and what still shapes how we feel, think, act and react, mentally and physically. And for that, we need to return to humanity's hazy dawn.

The popular story has been this: our ancestors lived a dangerous and usually brief life, brutally ended by either beast or man. They'd be hunting vicious animals, with the strongest surviving and in control and the weak submissive or dead. Life was a struggle for survival; there was time for little else. We imagine cave dwellers in wars against fellow humans from competing tribes, or tribe members competing for dominance. Maybe all this was part of their lives to some extent. But modern sciences, including neurology, tell us a completely different story about the life they likely lived.

So, let's travel back some 100,000 years to our hunter-gatherer ancestors. That's what we've been for between 98 and 99 per cent of our evolutionary history as a species and our biology hasn't had enough time to evolve to adapt to the times we now live in. Agriculture is only about 10,000 years old, the equivalent of a blink of an eye in our development. As biological beings, we're physically and mentally adapted to a completely different life than the one we live. A growing number of researchers from both social and natural sciences find that this dissonance between the life that most of us live and the life that we're biologically suited to may be the cause of a large amount of the current ailments in terms of stress, anxiety, depression and many physical diseases.

Our understanding of ancient hunter-gatherer societies isn't complete but scientists from different academic disciplines have been able to change our view of those early modern humans in a remarkable way. Contrary to popular belief, their existence was much less strenuous than ours in terms of time spent surviving – if you

As biological beings, we're physically and mentally adapted to a completely different life than the one we live

consider survival a question of getting enough to eat and a safe place to sleep, procreate and bring up your children. The few remaining hunter-gatherer tribes live in some of the world's harshest environments. And yet, they spend less than half the time working for survival than we do in even the most advanced Western economies. And though hunting plays an important role, gathering food is the foundation of survival.

The Hadza people, who mainly live in the Rift Valley in Tanzania, have preserved their way of life as hunter-gatherers through centuries, perhaps millennia. They've been studied extensively and the time they spend gathering food and on what we'd consider household duties is negligible compared to what most families in our societies face. Instead, they're preoccupied with gambling, playing and socialising. Their society is egalitarian and collaborative rather than competitive. Women and men have equal status. Children are brought up not only by their parents but by a larger group; they're the responsibility of the whole tribe. Arguments are frequent, just as they are in any group of humans. Fights, however, are not.

Although the Hadza don't spend as much time providing for themselves as most of us do, their lives include plenty of physical exercise. Both hunting and gathering require covering large distances and, as humans, we have the 'Swiss Army knife' of mammalian bodies. We can crawl and walk both forwards and backwards; we can climb, bend, stretch, run, skip, jump, swim... we're physical jacks of all trades, all of which most likely reflects a lifestyle similar to that of the Hadza people and our ancestors and how they need to move to get enough to eat. This matters! Because this is the kind of life that our brains, minds and bodies have adapted to through hundreds of thousands of years. Agriculture changed that. With growing crops and raising animals came requirements for land; with land came ownership; with ownership came hierarchies; with hierarchies came inequality and an emphasis on competition rather than coexistence and collaboration.

With the industrial revolution, this deviation from our evolutionary background was enhanced. The day became divided into even, logical time slots for valuable activities. Relationships were still essential, not necessarily because of their inherent bonds of love and affection but as useful connections and signs of status. Philosophy and its close cousin religion have stressed duty, virtue and hard work rather than joy and playfulness as the meaning of life – all of which have brought wealth and scientific progress at a price.

All of this is not to idealise a hunter-gatherer existence. It comes with challenges, and hardly any of us would be willing to trade places. But it's essential knowledge because what makes us function and thrive reflects that kind of life. Our evolutionary history may seem remote to us but it's present in our biology and how we react. We need a life with time for relationships, playing and raising children and a physically active life in a natural environment. And we ignore this at our peril. We risk feeling disconnected from our deepest Self, others, relationships and life.

> We need a life with time for relationships, playing and raising children

Body, mind – and brain

Several disciplines are concerned with defining what humans are, what defines us, what defines our world, what gives our lives meaning, how we differ from other animals and how we do not. It simplifies complicated scientific and philosophical quests but at the core across different disciplines is defining a Self. 'Know thyself' is the goal of philosophy, according to Socrates. The Chinese philosopher Laozi, the founder of philosophical Taoism, says in his book *Tao Te Ching* that 'Knowing others is wisdom. Knowing the Self is enlightenment. Mastering others requires force. Mastering the Self requires strength.' Later, psychology, anthropology, physiology and archaeology have been preoccupied with the same question: who are we? And why?

Ancient philosophers such as Aristotle and Plato divided body and soul. The soul, the psyche, according to them, is the essence of being human – something beyond and above the body. The body is mainly seen as a tool or a vehicle for the true identity, the psyche. This dualism has persisted in our thinking, although we've also believed that the body reflects the mind. A physically ugly person would also be ugly on the inside; a maimed body would be a sign of a maimed soul. But the body was always secondary: mind over matter.

In this line of thought, the body is mainly a biological machine, something of inferior importance to the mind. The Persian philosopher Ibn Sina, a genuinely brilliant polymath excelling in astronomy and medicine, among other subjects, wrote about how it would feel to be suspended in the air with no sensations whatsoever. He argued that the mind would still be able to think and be self-conscious. Thus, physical sensations weren't part of our true selves.

René Descartes (1596–1650) was a French philosopher, scientist and mathematician, widely considered to be a seminal figure in the emergence of modern philosophy and science. The importance of the mind is also behind his statement, 'Cogito, ergo sum' (I think, therefore I am). This heralded the rational school of thought, which holds that reason should be the judge when deciding right or wrong and good or bad. Our human cognitive powers provide us with sufficient rational insight to choose.

The body is a distraction, something to be controlled. The same goes for many emotions that are considered unwanted and should be suppressed or at least not trusted. The cardinal sins, also known as the seven deadly sins, reflect this: pride, greed, wrath, envy, lust, gluttony and sloth. They're pitted against the cardinal virtues: prudence, justice, temperance, fortitude, faith, hope and charity, which aren't feelings but somewhat conscious actions and therefore virtuous. Feelings are actual physical sensations in our bodies – we feel them. We don't think them. They cause bodily reactions such as a faster heartbeat or a release of certain chemicals, such as adrenaline, into our bloodstream.

> The cardinal sins, also known as the seven deadly sins, reflect this: pride, greed, wrath, envy, lust, gluttony and sloth

This mind–body dualism has mainly been disputed by more recent philosophers and increasingly by psychologists and neuroscientists. Body and mind aren't separate entities but feed and affect each other. When we use our bodies and senses, our brain is remodelled, new connections are made and fresh understandings are shaped. We grasp the world with our hands; they're an extension of our brain. And yet this dualism persists because it has been so pervasive in almost all of our spheres of life. Disease, for instance, has been seen as a deviation from biological norms, not as something natural – something that can and should be treated like repairing a car with a defective mechanical part. Until fairly recently, health has been defined in terms of disease. After the Second World War, the World Health Organization defined health as 'a state of complete physical, mental and social wellbeing and not merely the absence of disease or infirmity'. This definition respects that thriving is the core aspect of health. And we need to consider both body and mind to arrive at a meaningful description of what it means to be healthy.

Today, we have a much better understanding of how the mind and body aren't separate but mutually dependent. Early psychology was mainly concerned with the mind but this has changed in recent decades. In the postwar years, the French philosopher **Maurice Merleau-Ponty** was one of France's leading proponents of existentialism. Still, his main contribution may be in the field of phenomenology, the study of structures of consciousness, how we experience things and how we make meaning of them. He described the 'lived body', in which bodies should be understood to be 'multiphasic, experimental beings of finite freedom'. He stressed how the body and its sensations and experiences shape our perceptions.

Advances in neuroscience and nervous system investigation have further accelerated a movement towards rejecting the mind–body dualism in psychology. Neuroscience tells us that our brains are at the very core of our existence. What happens in our brains is reflected in our wellbeing and our personalities, and vice versa: what happens to us, what we feel and experience physically and emotionally, is reflected in our brains. So, our selves, whatever they are, are both body and mind and not only mind in the psychological and philosophical understanding of the concept. It's the brain and our nervous system. We're shaped by whatever our bodies experience and can use our bodies to shape our environment and circumstances. It would be too far reaching to conclude the exact relationship in this book while scientists and other academics are still making fascinating discoveries. The crucial point is that body and mind can't be separated in any meaningful way.

Get to know your brain

Let's look closer at the brain, where the body and mind coexist in unison. Neuroscience studies the anatomy of the brain and nervous system. This has been advanced by technologies such as QEEG (quantitative electroencephalography), fMRI (functional magnetic resonance imaging) and PET (positron emission tomography), and this has helped researchers link the physical brain with the psychological mind, how we think, act, feel and understand the world around us.

Some of the most essential areas of the brain are as follows.

The prefrontal cortex – your working memory

This is a part of the brain located at the front of the frontal lobe. It involves many higher cognitive functions, including decision making, problem solving, planning and social behaviour. It will engage when you encounter new situations, ideas and assumptions. It will compare them with what you already know. It could be that you find a new brand of muesli on your supermarket shelf. The brain will then rationally try to compare the advantages and disadvantages of the new kind of muesli compared to your usual brand. But it could also be a new way of thinking, for instance, that there are more than two genders, which the brain will match with what you already know.

Receiving new information and comparing it with old data is energy consuming. The brain is only responsible for about 2 per cent of our body weight but 20 per cent of our energy use. Neurons (brain cells) are highly active cells that require constant energy to maintain their electrical activity and communication with other neurons.

The prefrontal cortex is incredibly well developed in humans compared to other mammals. In terms of our evolutionary history, it's a young part of our brain and can become drained – you've probably noticed how difficult it can be to make good choices and act constructively at the end of a very long and challenging day. More on this a bit further on.

The basal ganglia – your automatic transmission

These are responsible for your routine actions and habits. It could be putting your favourite muesli brand in the supermarket basket without thinking about it. You may not even remember having done so; it just happens. You could compare it to driving an automatic instead of a car with manual gears. You don't have to think; transitioning from one gear to another just happens. The basal ganglia are placed in the central part of the brain, close to neural circuits of a more permanent character. Compared to the prefrontal cortex, this part of the brain is much less energy intensive. It enables you to live your life without having to ponder every single act and to make routine decisions.

The brain is only responsible for about 2 per cent of our body weight but 20 per cent of our energy use

When we begin to learn something new, we have to spend a lot of energy in the prefrontal cortex. It could be driving a car. There's a lot to remember and be aware of. However, after just a few months, it becomes routine. The prefrontal cortex no longer needs to be involved and can push the task to the basal ganglia, freeing capacity in the energy-consuming prefrontal cortex. Only when you have to drive in a new way – if you go to a country where they drive on the other side of the road, for instance – will the prefrontal cortex have to become involved again.

The psychologist Daniel Kahneman described these two functions in his book *Thinking, Fast and Slow* and popularised them as System 1 (the fast and automatic basal ganglia) and System 2 (the slower but conscious prefrontal cortex). He described how we could get decisions wrong when we designate a task that should be given to the prefrontal cortex to the basal ganglia, when we act on instinct instead of considering a subject more carefully. This reaction is understandable – evolution has taught us to conserve energy – but it also makes us prone to being caught unawares by bias and assumptions. This affects our ability to choose, act and be responsible. If we try to avoid the more energy-consuming processes in the prefrontal cortex, we may find it unpleasant to get involved in strategic thinking or make decisions that require us to think and rethink what we thought we knew. This is, by the way, one of the reasons why paradigm shifts and reinventing yourself can be challenging to handle. It's not only a question of values and ideas; you have to switch from the basal ganglia to the prefrontal cortex.

Orbitofrontal cortex and the amygdala – your error and threat detection centre

There's another reason why we find it difficult to change or adapt to new ways of thinking and doing things. The human brain has a vast capacity for discovering what the neurosciences label 'errors', a discrepancy between what you expect and what you experience. You may have reached for your mug, hoping to sip tea, only to spit it out when you taste coffee. Or you thought that sugar was salt and reacted with the same kind of disgust as it hit your taste buds. It's not necessarily that you find coffee or sugar repulsive, but the brain responds to these discrepancies by sending out neural solid signals that are costly in terms of brain energy.

These error signals are shaped by the part of the brain known as the orbitofrontal cortex, which you can find just above your eyes. It collaborates closely with the amygdala, a tiny, almond-shaped region commonly known as the brain's fear network. It regulates the overwhelming anger or fear we may encounter when faced with something we perceive as a threat. It's among the oldest parts of our brain and has probably evolved as a survival mechanism early in our evolutionary history. We share it with other mammals.

When the orbitofrontal cortex and the amygdala are activated, they drain energy from the prefrontal cortex – the region responsible for our rational choices and actions. These error and threat detection signals can, in other words, cause us to become less rational and more emotional and impulsive. We respond more like animals and with a focus that's purely on short-sighted survival. The good news is that you don't have to let the older and more impulsive part of your brain overrule the more rational prefrontal cortex and become a green Hulk of rage and fear when faced with the unexpected or threatening. There are ways to strengthen your conscious and analytical brain. Meditation is one way. Spending time in nature is another. You can engage in cognitive training such as solving puzzles and crosswords or learning new skills, whether it's a language or how to play the piano. Physical exercise and healthy sleeping habits will help you keep the prefrontal cortex online when the fear network would otherwise overtake you.

> There are ways to strengthen your conscious and analytical brain

Can you predict your wellbeing?

Research has made it increasingly clear that we can measure and predict thriving by studying the brain. Different personality traits are reflected in how the brain is shaped and working. However, this isn't a one-way street; your brain structure doesn't mean that you have to be a certain way. Contrary to what used to be considered the case, the brain develops and is highly plastic. When you change your habits or do something else that is new, the brain will grow new neural connections and change.

While it's true that the brain's nerve cells don't regenerate in the same way that cells regenerate in the rest of the body, they're constantly looking for new connections or changing their relationship with existing connections, weakening or strengthening them. If you suffer a stroke or a concussion, the surviving nerve cells will try to compensate for any loss of cells by reconnecting to other cells and finding new byways. This is why we can frequently recover from this kind of incident, although it may take time and not always get back to the way it was – the new road may be more of a path, whereas the old one was a highway. But the physical training after, for instance, a stroke, be it relearning how to walk or talk, is helping these nerve cells to find new connections.

Increasingly, neurology is about what makes both the brain and the mind thrive, what enables us to live long, happy lives with maximum wellbeing. And what helps the injured brain – physical exercise, new experiences, stimulating the senses and natural surroundings – also turns out to be beneficial for the healthy brain. We're largely dependent on our genetics – longevity and avoidance of debilitating diseases such as Alzheimer's seem to be the general rule in some families, while not in others. However, being predisposed to certain conditions isn't the same as being unable to increase or decrease the likelihood of something. You may be genetically favoured towards avoiding dementia but accidents or a damaging lifestyle could still override that. You can also increase your chances of good brain health well into old age by living a life that gives your brain and therefore your mind the maximum chance of thriving.

You can also increase your chances of good brain health well into old age

A personal wake-up call

My fascination with neurology goes way back but it has increased recently. My life changed on 27 February 2017. As part of my coaching work with clients, I was introduced to a brilliant neurologist, Jens Ole Jarden, who was interested in working with healthy people (and is among the experts contributing to this book). He was used to scanning patients who had suffered trauma and wanted to spread his competence to people not considered to be ill. Together with a neuropsychologist, he developed a Brain Tuning programme consisting of a neurological assessment and a neuropsychological assessment.

The neurological assessment consists of a brain scan. This one is mine:

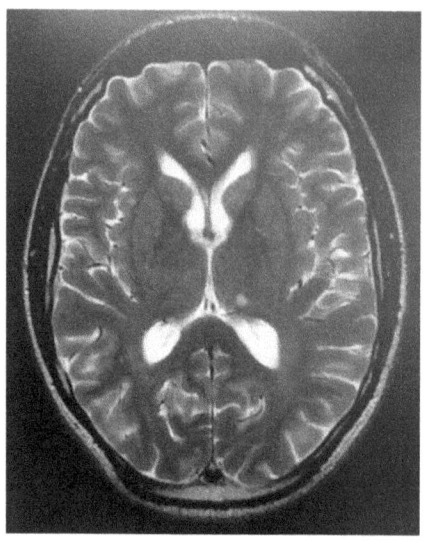

Figure 3: Brain tuning: the scan of my brain

The neuropsychological assessment consists of a large battery of cognitive tests such as these:

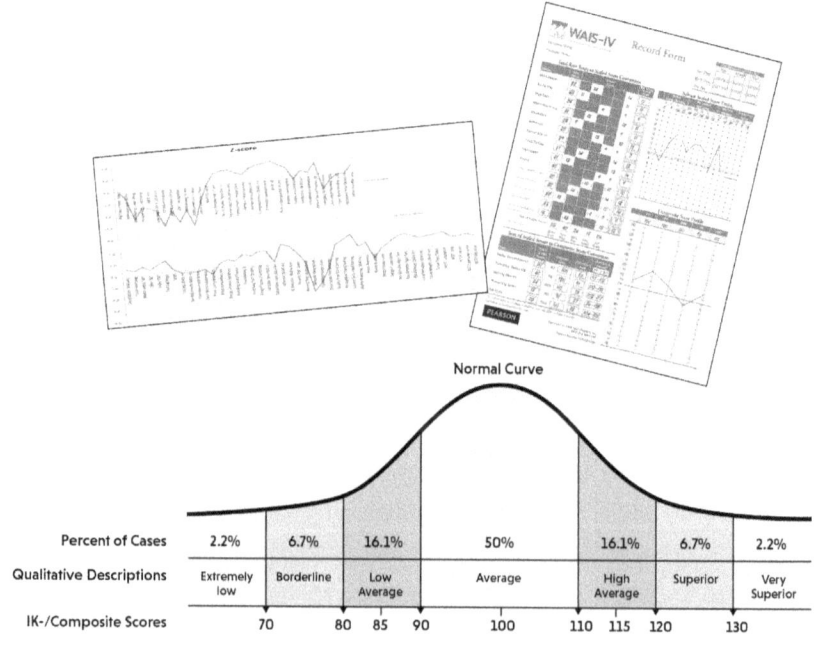

Figure 4: Brain tuning: the neuropsychological assessment

Together, they'll give you a picture of your brain, its cognitive abilities and how they influence your behaviours, intellectual capabilities and other aspects of your life.

Let me, in order to be completely correct, quote Vibeke Elise Brønniche, the co-creator of the Brain Tuning programme: 'A neuropsychological profile gives an objective presentation of the person's abilities and helps understand the person's potential, career preferences, hemisphere-dominant intelligence and personality. Knowing your abilities brings you closer to a realistic sense of Self and allows you to use your abilities better in relation to your surroundings, make the right decisions and have a more satisfying life.'

A neuropsychological profile can be created after hours-long individual testing and subsequent analysis. For most people, it's a positive experience to have their cognitive abilities challenged and it feels like a form of brain fitness. The brain's cognitive domains are precisely mapped with strengths and weaknesses, including linguistic and pictorial mentalising abilities, pace, attention, concentration, inculcation and memory overview and creative, constructive and problem-free abilities, as well as certain emotional and social cognitive abilities. The analysis gives a score of the different cognitive domains in relation to the age norm. The report explains the results and presents the neuropsychological profile graphically, comparing the performances converted to Z-scores – ie in terms of how far away the figures are from the average. Positive Z-score is above average for age and negative Z-score is below average for age. Z+1 corresponds to the 84th percentile and Z+2 corresponds to the 97th percentile. Repetition of a pattern can confirm a trend in the brain's geographic structures and the report can provide suggestions on how to further work with them.

Z-scores are illustrated in units in the normal distribution shown in Figure 4. If you rank the performance (eg IQ) of 100 random people, most will rank in the normal range (typically IQ between 85 and 115), fewer as high or low talented. The highly talented (IQ over 130) rank in the top 3 per cent, the talented (IQ over 120) in the top 10 per cent, and the bright (IQ over 110) in the top 30 per cent. Most people have an idea of what their intelligence is, without this ever being measured properly.

Being successful requires interaction between abilities, career, courage and the social field. Even with average skills, you can achieve success by playing your cards well. However, knowing what your cards are provides a big advantage. Knowing and understanding one's cognitive profile can have a significant role in terms of where and in which contexts to achieve success. My wife and I served as guinea pigs as part of this development. So, we underwent a Brain Tuning programme, described as a brain scan (the hardware) and a neuropsychological assessment (the software). The thesis was that since the brain is essential to our being, we had better take care of it. We've learned a lot from these programmes, both from our own and from those of my clients. Let me summarise some key learnings:

- Even though you think you're bad at something, eg face recognition, you might still be above average. But your performance on other dimensions might simply be even better, compared to the average.
- Your short-term memory sometimes can't cope with the speed of your thoughts, which has been calculated to 432 km/h. So, reducing the speed of your speech, pausing a little longer, will significantly enhance your communication.
- Most of my clients are highly intelligent. Based on the neuropsychological assessments, this is a fact. But here comes my most interesting finding. When asked about the reason for their success, my clients tend to say 'I've been lucky', 'I was at the right place at the right time', 'Things have come to me', 'It has been easy', 'I've always taken on challenges' or 'I've had more energy than most'. There's no doubt that all these answers are true but the common denominator behind these answers is *intelligence*.

Somehow there's a taboo around intelligence. Socially, you're not allowed to say about yourself, 'I'm intelligent'. But, objectively, this could simply be a fact, just like the statement 'I'm a good runner'. Makes you think, doesn't it? There's another interesting taboo. A former CEO of a company specialising in brain diseases once told me that research into the brain is severely restricted by the notion that the brain is different from all other organs. This has resulted in all sorts of protective legislation and regulation.

Most of us know what to do when it comes to our bodies. We try to eat well, avoid too many stimulants, sleep well and exercise. But when it comes to the brain, it's like a black box to many. How do we take care of our brain as well as we take care of the rest of our body? And how does it influence us? This is one of the reasons why I chose to include neurology as a dimension of thriving in this book. Several of my clients have gone through the Brain Tuning process. They get an understanding of how their brains influence their memory and their risk for dementia and disease. The reason why my clients engage in this process may be that they worry about dementia. They may have parents suffering from dementia and wonder whether they're predisposed to this illness. Others have had a not-so-healthy lifestyle with perhaps too much alcohol or smoking and they wonder whether this has affected their future brain functionality. Some just want a brain hack and to learn how to preserve their cognitive abilities.

Strokes happened to other people, not to me

Back to 27 February 2017. This was the day that I received a phone call from Jens Ole Jarden. He told me that his examination of my brain scan had revealed two small blood clots. In other words, I'd suffered the precondition of a stroke. This was kind of unreal. Strokes happened to other people, not to me. And I hadn't had any symptoms whatsoever. But it led to a series of analyses of my whole organism: heart, veins, organs and nerves. And for that, I'm deeply grateful. It gave me a more extensive awareness of how to care for myself and my abilities. I know that I can influence both my body and mind. This event also provoked some deep reflection about my life and the potential end of it. I started writing this book in 2016 and gave myself ten years to finish it. Slow and steady wins the race.

I'd long been fascinated by the works of **Irvin D Yalom**, primarily his book *Existential Psychotherapy* (1980). In this seminal work, he defines existential psychotherapy as a dynamic approach to therapy that focuses on issues deeply rooted in human existence. His defining dimensions are death, freedom, isolation and meaninglessness. All of a sudden, these concepts resonated at a much more personal level. Most therapists are conscious that recognising one's finality can often catalyse a significant inner perspective shift. And that was precisely what happened to me. All of a sudden, I felt vulnerable. Even though I felt no physical change, the simple fact that a potential risk of a stroke was present sharpened my focus on healthy living – both physically and mentally.

This is something I work on with clients in a systematic way. With the help of specialists, they get their brains scanned, combined with a battery of cognitive testing to better understand how their brains work. This, in turn, enables the client to get specific advice on performing better and put this new awareness of their brain into action and growth. But even without such a scan, there's a lot of knowledge that you can apply to your life to increase your feelings of wellbeing. Connections are also hugely important in brain health, not just how the nerve cells of the brain connect. Our social relationships, trust in ourselves and others and a feeling of psychological safety play a crucial role.

Dr David Rock, who holds a professional doctorate in the neuroscience of leadership and is the CEO and founder of the NeuroLeadership Institute, has developed the SCARF model of psychological safety:

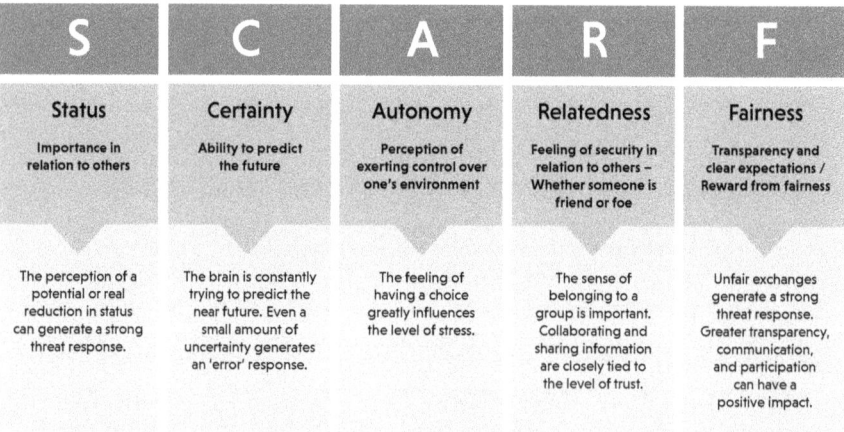

Figure 5: The SCARF model. Source: David Rock

Now, this may look a lot like psychology, and it is. But behind it, the brain is at work. Nerve cells communicate by so-called neurotransmitters and chemical packages and those chemicals make the body and mind react in specific ways. Some are increased by stress, which can be beneficial in the short run, but feeling constantly stressed and alert to dangers will deteriorate your brain in the long run. When stressed, try to spell the word stressed backwards. What does it say? Desserts, right? Doesn't that sound better? And doesn't that make you feel better?

The feeling of psychological safety, with its emphasis on positive connections to yourself, others and the world at large, as presented in the SCARF model, has shown itself to be one of the main predictors of thriving. And though this is also dependent on your environment, you can train your brain to perceive the world differently and help it shape connections that are better for you. When you take your brain health seriously, you'll have much fewer stressful moments and more moments of joy.

When you take your brain health seriously, you'll have much fewer stressful moments and more moments of joy

The power of good relationships

To feel connected to your Self, you must allow for your evolutionary and biological needs. Time to play, new experiences, being present, time in nature, time for movement – all this helps lower stress levels and gives you the energy to live and thrive. It will help you feel connected to yourself. This is already a lot, but it's not enough. You also need to feel connected to others. Your relationships are vital.

In psychology, it has always been well known that your relationships shape and define you. The smallest social entity is two, not one. It may be popular to say that we're born alone and die alone but that doesn't make it accurate. We're born out of someone, connected to our mothers in some ways and perhaps to more than them. The mind of an unborn child is already beginning to be shaped by the impressions that reach it in the womb. It's true that some people die without others around them. However, they are few and their deaths affect others.

A person may be absent. Yet you'll get a good idea of their personality through the descriptions from other people, how they've been affected by that person.

Several studies demonstrate the power of good relationships. Loneliness, defined as an unmet need for social connections and relationships, is a killer, especially if the feelings of isolation are persistent. A meta-analytic review entitled 'Loneliness and social isolation as risk factors for mortality' by Holt-Lunstad et al (2015) found that loneliness is associated with a 25 per cent increased risk of early death. Social isolation leads to mental problems and increases the risk of substance abuse, self-neglect and accidents. Good relationships seem to be the most critical factor in studies about which factors determine our quality of life – good connections with the people closest to us, family and friends and the wider world. One example is the world's longest-running study on thriving, the Harvard Study of Adult Development. It began in 1938 and, for nearly 90 years, the original participants and their descendants through three generations have been studied to find out what makes us healthy and happy. The number one factor is good relationships.

> We seem to have evolved to become more compassionate and collaborative in our quest to survive

We're social creatures. Darwin never said anything about the survival of the fittest, which, in Danish (somewhat catastrophically in terms of understanding his theories), has been translated into 'survival of the strongest'. In the book *The Descent of Man* (1871) he did, however, write that 'sympathy is our strongest instinct, sometimes stronger than self-interest'. He argued that sympathy would spread through natural selection because 'the most sympathetic members would flourish best and rear the greatest number of offspring'. Darwin used the word sympathy because 'empathy' wasn't used in his time but we can perhaps dare to assume that he'd have used it today. A growing body of evidence supports his claim. We seem to have evolved to become more compassionate and collaborative in our quest to survive and thrive. A group of scientists at the University of California, Berkeley, has called it 'survival of the kindest'. We seem to be genetically predisposed to be empathetic.

And yet, many of us tend to neglect our relationships. Work seems more important because it gives us status and provides us with our material needs. This has perhaps been especially true for men, who tend to have nurtured fewer relationships outside the workplace than women. If they lose their jobs, many face a crisis when having to look for a new job; or when they retire, they find it hard to adapt to their new circumstances. They will also lose some of their closest and most meaningful connections – their colleagues.

This is one of the most important secrets behind successful retirement. You must establish a base of new playmates before leaving the job market. Establishing a new network that will catch you and lift you takes time to develop. Relationships are built in times of peace. So, you must front-load new friendships and make yourself available in new and exciting contexts. Sports clubs, cultural events, voluntary work and group travel represent only a few opportunities. It's all about getting out of your comfort zone. But you need to make a conscious decision. It represents a pivotal investment in your future. I'm not telling you it's going to be easy – I'm telling you that it's going to be worth it. Our human condition needs physical connections. Our bodies need the warmth of other bodies. Strange and beautiful things happen when we look into each other's eyes or put our smartphones and screens away to be present, listen, share and empathise.

We need connections. Our brains need them in a very physical sense. New pathways and connection points are built when we engage with people, new experiences and new challenges. Our minds need them. Some researchers believe that our feelings of loneliness are a warning siren to warn us of the danger of being alone and disconnected, much like feeling hunger is a warning siren to warn us of the risks of not getting food. And we need connections to figure out who we are and, not least, who we want to be. Relationships are not means; they're end goals. A purpose in life is to achieve quality time with your loved ones. However, in our hectic lives filled with short-term duties, relationships are sometimes perceived as interrupting a continuous stream of activities.

My guiding principle model is a reflection on these aspects.

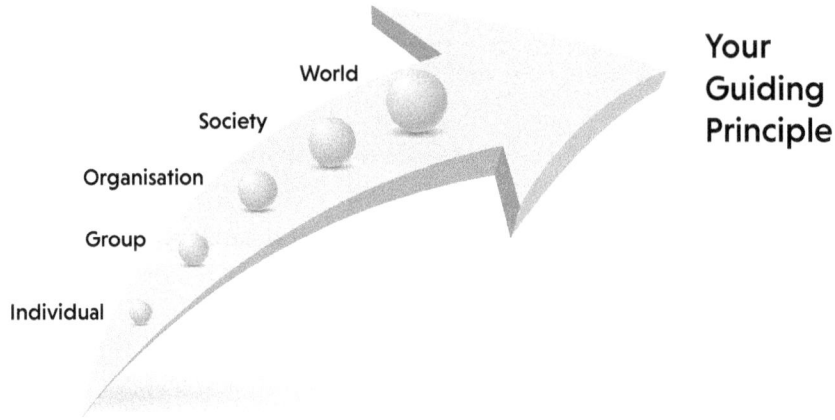

Figure 6: The guiding principle

To thrive, you have to feel connected to yourself, to a peer or reference group such as colleagues and friends, to the organisation you're part of, to society and eventually, to the world. When you feel connected and present, you'll become more tolerant of others who may have different ideas about themselves and their connections. You can accept the winds of change because you're firmly connected to what makes you thrive and feel you can move your world. Archimedes is quoted as saying, 'Give me a place to stand and a lever long enough and I shall move the Earth.'

Your guiding principle also creates direction. Instead of all the noise created by contradictory messages on social media and divergent information from the news, you're able to pick up the items that create meaning for you. It's a convergent, sense-making process. You attach more importance to the facts that are aligned with your goals and prioritise the activities that add value to your future.

Questions to ask yourself

- Do you have time enough to play and have fun?
- Do you have time set aside for reflection and contemplation? If not, how can you get playfulness and meditation into your life?
- Which new activity will you learn that you don't (yet) know how to do?
- Which skill would you love to possess? When will you start to learn?

Part 2
Transformation

Chapter 4
The quest for Self

Who am I? And who do I want to be? These existential questions have been with us since the dawn of humanity. Philosophers have tried to answer them for nearly as long, and though their answers differ, they all agree that it's essential that you know yourself, your values and your relationship with the rest of the world. Psychology and neurology chime in with their perspectives and will give you an idea of why you are who you are and how you can grow and thrive from there. When you're rooted in yourself and what's important to you, how to make the most of your life becomes clearer.

One night, as one of my clients, Lasse Rich Henningsen, drove home from work in his new car, he suddenly lost his sight. He had been driving fast but somehow managed to slow down and pull into the side of the road. Then he called his mother and cried his eyes out, overcome by what was happening to him. Everything had been going well. His company knew him as 'the King of Execution'; if you wanted to get things done, he was your man. He was going fast, and not just in his car. He was just 32 years old, already the father of two children with a third on the way. He loved his wife and family, his job and his high-flying career. But something had got out of hand. He'd been working too hard for too long. He'd lost touch with himself, with what mattered, what gave him energy, what drained him.

His sight returned just after his heartbroken conversation with his mother but he knew that something had to change. He had to get in contact with himself again. Today, one of his key takeaways is that you can't be one person at work and another in your private life. You have to stay true to your Self. This is a lesson that has helped him numerous times when things have been rough. I'll get back to one of these occasions later but in this chapter, I'll focus on how to stay connected to your Self.

Throughout my coaching sessions and conversations, I've found that most, if not all, of us have been in similar situations to Lasse's, even if they're rarely as dramatic. But this kind of existential doubt, where you find yourself anxious, disconnected and exhausted, is common, especially when you approach or enter a new life phase and have worked beyond your limits to achieve success and not spent time staying connected. Being connected to yourself shouldn't be difficult. After all, you live with yourself every second of your life. But it can be so. We're busy beings who often forget to check in with our thoughts and emotions.

> We're busy beings who often forget to check in with our thoughts and emotions

As I mentioned earlier, defining a Self can be tricky. To some, it's a solid core; to others, it's constantly changing. Perhaps that distinction isn't so crucial when you begin to define your Self, but there are insights to be found from different approaches. In philosophy, the Self is often defined as the individual consciousness or the subject of our experience. This is the sense in which we think of ourselves as unique individuals with our thoughts, feelings, experiences and understanding of how we fit into the world. In psychology, the Self is often considered to be the collection of beliefs, attitudes and other mental constructs we have about ourselves, which are shaped by our upbringing and our subconscious. This includes our sense of identity, personal goals and values, and relationships with others.

In neurology, the concept of Self refers to our subjective experience of identity and individuality. Neurology sees the Self as a combination of cognitive, emotional and physical experiences processed by the brain. The exact neural mechanisms involved in forming the Self aren't fully understood. Still, research suggests that several areas of our brain, including the prefrontal cortex, are part of our self-awareness and perception of the Self. As you can see, each discipline approaches the question of Self and consciousness from different perspectives but they share similarities.

The Self and Søren Kierkegaard

The search for this definition has led to one of my most significant breakthroughs. While I was searching for the Self, I came across this quote from the Danish existentialist philosopher **Søren Kierkegaard** in his book *The Sickness unto Death*, which was published in 1849: 'The Self is a relation which relates itself to itself, or it is in the relation that the relation relates itself to itself; the Self is not the relation but that the relation relates itself to itself.'

At first sight, this may seem like pure gibberish or at least extremely confusing. What was that dude smoking, anyway? I was hardly impressed. However, it grew on me. It felt like a riddle, something that had to be solved, and my brain wouldn't let go of it. And eventually, it did make sense. It means that the Self isn't an object or a substance. It's a process, something that happens rather than something that is.

> The Self isn't an object or a substance. It's a process, something that happens rather than something that is

Jean-Paul Sartre explicitly shared his famous three-word formula 'Existence precedes essence' in his 1945 lecture 'Existentialism is a Humanism', based on Kierkegaard's foundation. To existentialists, human beings can, through their consciousness, relate themselves to their Self, create their values and determine a meaning for their lives. It's not predestined or set in stone. This indicates that the search for Self is futile. It can't be found. Why, then, do we use concepts such as myself, yourself, self-awareness, self-leadership, self-help and self-worth? Because even though the Self may be a volatile process, we're still individuals with values and meanings. It doesn't arrive wholesale shipped in by Amazon but it is something that we create through all our relationships, experiences and connections.

I interpret Self as the process of relating profoundly and subjectively while at the same time observing one's own behaviour and thought processes as if from an external vantage point. I am my surveillance camera, so to speak, monitoring what's happening. Not everyone does this consciously, especially not when very young, so the Self isn't reliant on that. But it will add to your perception of Self and allow you to be present and engaged in yourself while at the same time being – at least to some extent – detached and curious about yourself.

My understanding is that the Self is represented by the relationship between us, both internally and externally. I often sit with coaching clients and have a dialogue. Simultaneously, I know what's happening inside me, inside my client and the process. So, there are two internal lenses and one external lens, providing a holistic perspective. I register the conversation from an external perspective, the view from above. Hinduism and Buddhism would consider this to be the 'third eye perspective'. The three dimensions can also be viewed as three sources of communication: the sender, the receiver and the situation in which the communication is sent. You can add a fourth dimension: the meaning of the communication, which is less relevant in this context. If we stick with the idea of how the view of ourselves relates to communication, we may describe it as an outside-in versus an inside-out approach. At the micro level, communication is individual. At the macro level, communication is relational. And at the meta level, communication is cultural. (For more reflections on a similar three-dimensional approach, see Appendix 3, page 209.)

A favourite quote of mine is 'Culture is what remains when all else is forgotten', which is often attributed to the French politician Édouard Herriot but has roots going back to Ezra Pound. It was my (French) mother who, in the early stages of dementia, mentioned this quote to me. Touching, isn't it?

Levels of maturity

In the book *The Evolving Self* (1983), Robert Kegan describes this development. He differentiates between 'focus on me' and 'focus on others'.

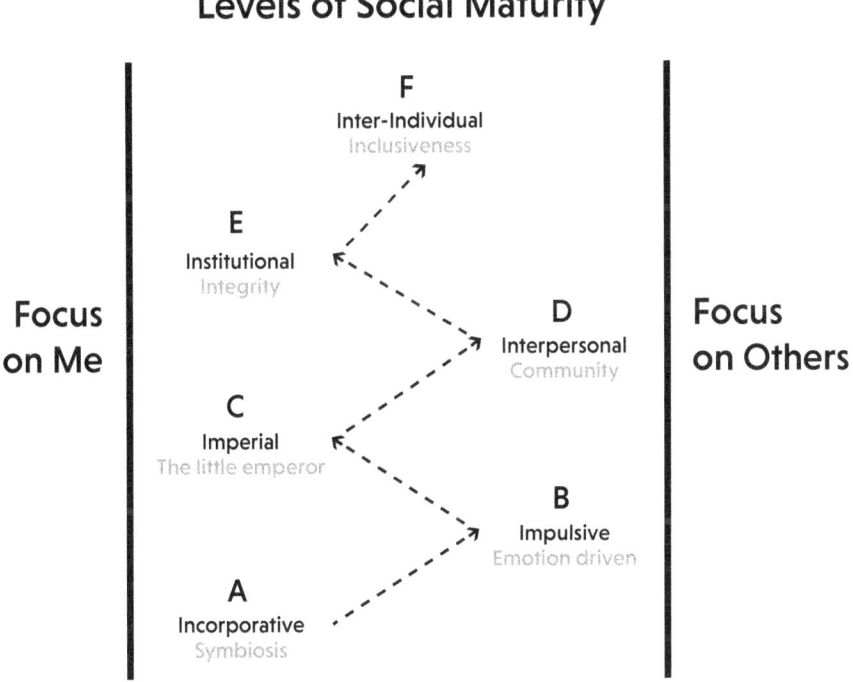

Figure 7: Levels of social maturity

When you're born, you're in perfect symbiosis with your mother. At the next level of social maturity, you're impulsive and driven by emotions. Then comes an imperial phase where you act as 'the little emperor' (any parent will recognise this phase). You then reach the interpersonal level at which you focus on community. The next level, the institutional/cultural level, has integrity at its core. It refers to the Self being in line with the collective values of a society. And then, finally, comes the inter-individual level, where inclusiveness is at the centre and which has to integrate all sorts of conflicting interests and strategic priorities. At this level, you'll have perfected the ability to go meta – to observe yourself as you act. It's as if you're constantly self-monitoring. It's a 'both–and' ability that requires an excellent overview. Some call this fluid attention; others call it situational awareness or intuition. Whatever the name, you have this monitor switched on and running in the background. It allows you to foresee multiple alternative outcomes of a situation or a conversation. You may argue that being in this self-monitoring mode reduces your ability to be present with genuine emotions and full attention. And yes, this is a risk. However, it doesn't have to be. I've met many people who can manage to be fully and genuinely present while monitoring the situation and themselves.

Looking back at my career path, I can now see how it has taken time to develop this capability. I realise that I used to follow excellence as my guiding principle. Over time, this has evolved into presence. Even though I know where I want to go and what I want to achieve, I've become much more aware of the moment instead of focusing solely on the result. Each of us along the way needs to define our superpower. So what's yours?

Returning to Kierkegaard, he introduced four stages on the path of life. In a slightly edited and updated form, they look like this:

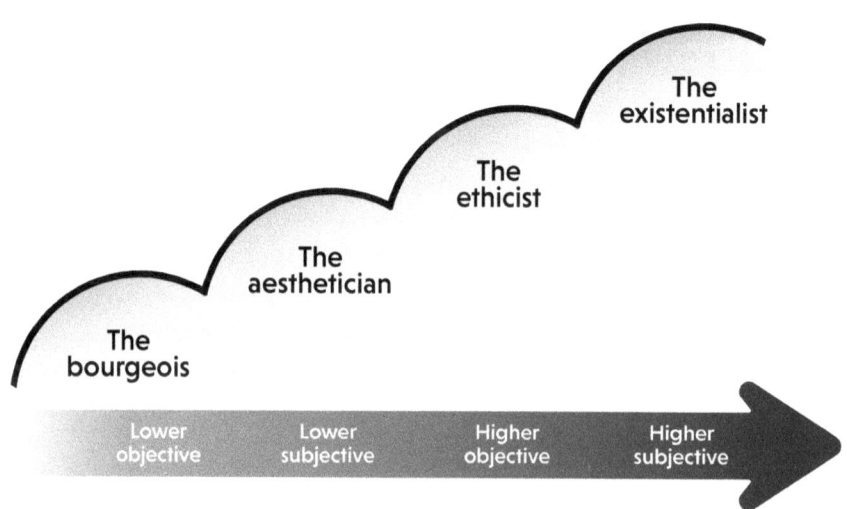

Figure 8: Stages on life's path. Source: Adapted from Tommy Kjær Lassen, Philosophy for Leaders *(in Danish)*

Of course, the theory is based on a 19th-century Danish world view. The bourgeois (leading citizens) become aestheticians because one day, they discover they've been living life on autopilot and haven't been present. The aestheticians become ethicists when they take up far too much time in their life projects and may have grown tired of many, sometimes extreme attempts at self-realisation. The ethicists become existentialists when they discover that they're living a reasonable and predictable life without courage and inner passion. So, our sense of Self is something that's gradually maturing, changed by us and our relationships and experiences and at the same time changing us as we become more aware.

As that overview from the monitor mentioned above kicks into gear, it allows us a better understanding of how we feel, think and act on our own and in our relationships with others. Without this kind of monitor, we're easily misled by our assumptions and how we judge ourselves and others, as the table below shows.

How we judge	Ourselves	Others
	Intentions	Actions
	Thoughts and feelings	Appearance
	Situation	Personality

Table 1: How we judge ourselves and others

We know our intentions, and the saying 'It's the thought that counts' reflects that your intentions are more important than your actions. You may not have been able to do as you intended but at least your intentions were good. However, we're prone to judge others by their actions rather than their intentions. So, if somebody doesn't deliver, you'll be less likely to think that good intentions alone were enough. You want meaningful action, never mind the intentions. In the same way, we know how we feel and think. We may feel that we're good at nothing while looking at other seemingly more successful people on social media. They have it all. We see their outside but, inside, they most likely harbour the same doubts and feelings of vulnerability as we do.

We may be late for an important meeting or act in a mean way. The traffic was horrific; you had a stressful day at work and didn't get enough sleep. In other words, the situation made you behave in a specific way. Whereas others who are late or mean probably have a lousy personality. You see somebody racing along a busy road and judge their hazardous driving. But what if they're speeding because they're rushing somebody to the hospital? When you develop your monitor, you can judge yourself and others more fairly and consistently, becoming perhaps less self-indulgent and more tolerant of others.

Flow in chemicals

As a reader, you may wonder where all of this is going. The critical point is that you can become more connected to the Self and that the Self is something that isn't unchangeable. But neither is it random and fluid. As we're born and growing up, our relationships with others and our environment shape us. We have certain biological traits that will also shape our experiences. But we can will ourselves to be the best possible version of ourselves. And I assume that this is what you're aiming for – not a completely 'new you', but a life where you take the best of your skills and use them to the best of your abilities and where you can feel that your existence has meaning and is valuable to yourself and others.

We can will ourselves to be the best possible version of ourselves

This is, first of all, a question of awareness and attention. As American author and coach Tony Robbins says, where focus goes, energy flows. There are many approaches to achieving the balance necessary for this kind of state, a sense of relaxed readiness, because you're grounded in your Self and your values. It's a relaxed mental and physiological state favouring resilience. You could call it a baseline.

Like any other organism, we function optimally when we assign just the right amount of energy to each activity. This contradicts the common belief that this is achieved by being hyper-tense and pumped up with adrenaline. Flow is often described as a low-energy, high-yield process. We all recognise being in the zone when our whole brain-body system seems alert and genuinely feels alive. A fundamental prerequisite for this thriving state of mind is feeling secure and safe. It's a combination of physical safety, psychological safety and social safety. When these conditions are met, a collaborative, inclusive and interconnected relationship with your surroundings, whether family, friends, workplace or other organisations, is possible.

There are a whole bunch of chemicals that help us thrive, flow and feel connected to ourselves and others. Specific activities release them and they can help you build resilience. Deep breathing, meditation and mindfulness activities can trigger some, while playing with other people – hugging, exercising, being in nature and being in the sun – can release others.

Dopamine is usually dubbed the reward hormone. That's too simple but it does enhance the good feeling we get when we begin to cope with a task and can tick off items on our to-do list. Eating and celebrating little wins will also release dopamine.

Oxytocin is called the love hormone. It's the warm, happy feeling you get for caring for your loved ones, stroking your favourite pet, hugging and making others feel good.

Endorphins work as painkillers. You've undoubtedly heard of 'runner's high', which occurs when the endorphins kick in and wash away tiredness and pain. But laughing – and eating dark chocolate – can also activate endorphins.

Serotonin stabilises you and your mental state. It's the calm feeling that meditation can give you – but so can being in a beautiful garden, walking in nature or basking in the sun.

Talk kindly to yourself

However, feeling connected to Self is also a question of being aware of your values and ideals. What motivates you? What makes you happy? What kind of person do you want to be in five years, in ten years, in twenty years? One of my clients put it this way: 'My hero should be myself as I am in ten years.' In Chapter 5, I will get into more practical and concrete advice on initiating this kind of process but again, awareness is vital and it's easier to reach this kind of awareness when you feel safe.

Feeling safe is also about which kind of conversation you have with yourself. We all have this inner voice that tells us how we should feel about ourselves. This isn't to be confused with the monitoring of Self that I described earlier. That monitor is a more objective observer of yourself, your relationships and your situations. Our inner voice tends to have a point of view and gets it across in our emotions. Consider Jiminy Cricket, who's constantly helping Pinocchio discover what's right and wrong. Or, from comics, the devil on one shoulder and the angel on the other, tempting or censoring us. One of my friends, a business psychologist, once asked me, 'Are you friendly?' Surprised, I answered, 'Yes, I am a friendly person.' However, as I should've guessed, that wasn't what he was talking about. In general, he was talking about the critical-friendly dimension. At first, I thought that this was nothing new. I knew perfectly well that there are two attitudes in life: friendly and critical. Some people are predominantly optimistic; others tend to be pessimistic. But he was talking about our conversations with ourselves, whether critical or friendly towards ourselves. Is your inner voice on Team You, or is it trying to make you feel unworthy or inferior?

Is your inner voice on Team You, or is it trying to make you feel unworthy or inferior?

This made me think of a list I've been preparing for years. Even though I've refined this list through many of my Personal Business Plan coaching programmes, it's still incomplete. But to give you an example, see Table 2.

You can probably continue the list based on your own experience. The key is to be able to decipher your inner dialogue. Do you tend to use moods and emotions mainly from the critical or friendly columns? Do you sometimes stop all activities and simply enjoy the moment? Have an ice cream? Breathe deeply? Express gratitude? Get wowed by a sunset or the starlit winter sky? Allow yourself to be happy with what you've accomplished?

CRITICAL	FRIENDLY
Provide	Enjoy
Must	Want
Duty	Desire
Calvinist	Hedonist
Pessimist	Optimist
Sow	Harvest
Seriousness	Joy
Pain	Gain
Forsaking	Gratifying
Denigrating	Appreciative
Produce	Obtain
Give	Receive
Excusing	Assertive

Table 2: Are you kind to yourself?

I've coached thousands of ambitious individuals. They're often characterised by having a large bandwidth. This means that they have the ability to reduce complexity and create clarity in their surroundings as well as in their own lives (see also the discussion of 'pattern recognition minds' in Chapter 7). But most of them are also quite hard on themselves. They feel they should always be a little better and do more. This provides a certain inner drive. They're proud but not satisfied. However, being able to enjoy the moment and let go a little doesn't mean you have to lose that drive.

Our inner dialogue is shaped by our experiences, going back to early childhood. If your internal dialogue is mainly critical, it can severely affect your connection to yourself and others. Turning a hostile self-conversation into a friendly one doesn't mean letting go of your conscience, which is something else entirely. Neither will it make you a bragging bighead. Humility comes not from feeling inferior but from having a healthy relationship with yourself where you can also appreciate others, your luck, your privileges, your failings and your less flattering sides without getting defensive because you feel threatened. It will enable you to find a place to monitor your Self safely and allow yourself to grow and transition in a relaxed and ready way.

Existential questions throughout life

Let's focus on the existential questions that most people pose around the ages of 39, 49, 59 and 69 years, which I touched upon in Chapter 1. These ages happen to be points in life when my clients frequently approach me for executive coaching. At one of my keynote speeches, a partner in one of the world's largest professional services firms came up to me and said that she was happy with her situation, but somehow it didn't satisfy her anymore, and she didn't know why. I asked her, 'How old are you?' She answered '49', to which I replied, 'There you are!'

But, of course, these turning points are not carved in stone, as mentioned before. They may occur at any time. People mature differently, so take them as a guideline, not as an absolute. However, on the brink of a new decade, we usually feel the need to ponder life. Each new decade brings a sensation of transition coupled with reflection and emotions – a step towards a new chapter in life with renewed opportunities for change and new beginnings. It's like an enhanced feeling of the new year – time to make new decade resolutions!

So, take a look at the matrix in Table 3. Do any of the questions resonate with you? Do you recognise yourself in your current phase? Do you remember your experiences and emotions in the past stages? And do the questions in future stages match your expectations? It resembles the life phase figure from Chapter 1 but goes a bit deeper into the key questions of some of our decades.

The future has an interesting aspect. Our empathy is unable to engage with it. For somebody aged 59, it's still possible to have a good idea of what youth is like today. We've all been young and recognise moods and actions, even if we decide to disapprove (as our elders frequently disapprove of us). We also understand the pressures of being a new parent, landing an important job, etc. But we can't honestly imagine what it means to be older than we are. We can look at older people, listen to them and be inspired by them – but we still have no clear picture until we get there. Mick Jagger, at more than 80, still touring as the singer of the Rolling Stones, famously once said, 'I'd rather be dead than sing "Satisfaction" when I'm 45.'

Age	Personal	Work	Financial	Physical
39	How can I get the most out of my situation?	How can I keep up with the 25-year-olds?	How can I secure my family?	What? Is that a grey hair?
49	How can I best live the second half of my life?	How can I reinvent myself and redefine my identity?	Do I have enough for the rest of my life?	How can I compensate for my loss of body functionality?
59	How can I create meaning for myself?	How can I best use my experience to create value for others?	I've done well, so now what?	What did you say? And where are my glasses?
69	What legacy can I leave?	How can I best stay relevant?	How can I give back?	How can I best stay alive?

Table 3: Our existential questions

However, we can do our best to front-load and be prepared for our future Self. This is why I like the idea of my client, who decided he wanted to be his own hero in ten years' time. You can't shape everything. But if you have a clear picture of what and where you want to be, chances are you'll go in that direction.

Choice, action, responsibility

As I have mentioned, my philosophical understanding is anchored in French existentialism. My mother's aunt had an apartment just across from the brasserie La Coupole on Boulevard Montparnasse in Paris. From the balcony, I could look over at this iconic art deco temple.

More importantly, La Coupole is widely considered to be the spiritual headquarters of French existentialism. Jean-Paul Sartre, the high priest of existentialism, sat at table 149 near the cloakroom, where he could observe the young girls (this was long before the #MeToo movement). In October 1957, Albert Camus, author of *The Stranger* (1942), celebrated his Nobel Prize for Literature here.

So, I grew up with the myth of La Coupole with its soundtrack to the hard-living, free-loving lifestyle of the student followers of Sartre and his acolytes. At school, my philosophy teachers were existentialists – freedom-seeking, intelligent, modern, provocative, liberated intellectuals. Some of their ways would be unacceptable today, not least the grooming of young girls. But their existentialist thoughts are still highly relevant. From a 21st-century vantage point, the culture of French existentialism – like most faded youth subcultures – can now seem out of date. But let's re-examine existentialism as a way of thinking that can transform reality, that is separate from more abstract philosophies.

> Existentialism, at its core, is about making choices

In her brilliant book *At the Existentialist Café* (2016), Sarah Bakewell begins with the old undergraduate chestnut about whether existentialism is a mood or a philosophy. The correct answer is, of course, that it's both, often at the same time. More to the point, behind the subculture, the sensationalism and jokes, existentialist philosophy was inspired by the recent and real crises of war and occupation in France in the mid-20th century. Seeing the rise of irrationality on all sides, Bakewell asks whether freedom may be the great puzzle of the 21st century. That's why she's so right when she wonders if, in the new age of bad faith, 'we need the existentialists more than we thought'.

Existentialism, at its core, is about making choices. The concept of choice is fundamental. While the supreme value of existentialist thought is commonly acknowledged to be freedom, its primary virtue is authenticity. How to live? How to be free? How to be an 'authentic' human being? When I work with my clients, I often come back to my strong family values, which are also the foundation of my work: life ambition, personal reinvention, learning agility and courage to commit.

- *Life ambition* deals with doing as much as possible to attain a meaningful life. Behind every frustration lies an unfulfilled ambition. Aim high.
- *Personal reinvention* is a prerequisite for evolving in this direction. We all need to develop on the one-way street that is life. Life is not a rehearsal.
- *Learning agility* is about knowing what to do when you don't know what to do. We all need a set of guiding principles to help us overcome challenges and lead us toward the ambitions we've set for ourselves. Keep moving with the times.
- *Courage to commit* corresponds to the concept of choice. My wife and I have taught our children to get an education, a partner, a job and a place to live without continuously waiting for an even better opportunity. Act and take responsibility instead of stalling.

All of this is part of my cornerstone CAR model:

- **C**hoice: you always have a choice
- **A**ction: you need to act on your choices
- **R**esponsibility: you need to take responsibility for your actions.

The CAR model

In this circular model, value lies in the gaps. To paraphrase Leonard Cohen, there is a gap in everything, which is how the light comes in. By performing gap analysis you need to focus on the following:

- Choice–Action Gap: Choice without Action lacks impact.
- Action–Responsibility Gap: Action without Responsibility lacks integrity.
- Responsibility–Choice Gap: Responsibility without Choice lacks courage.

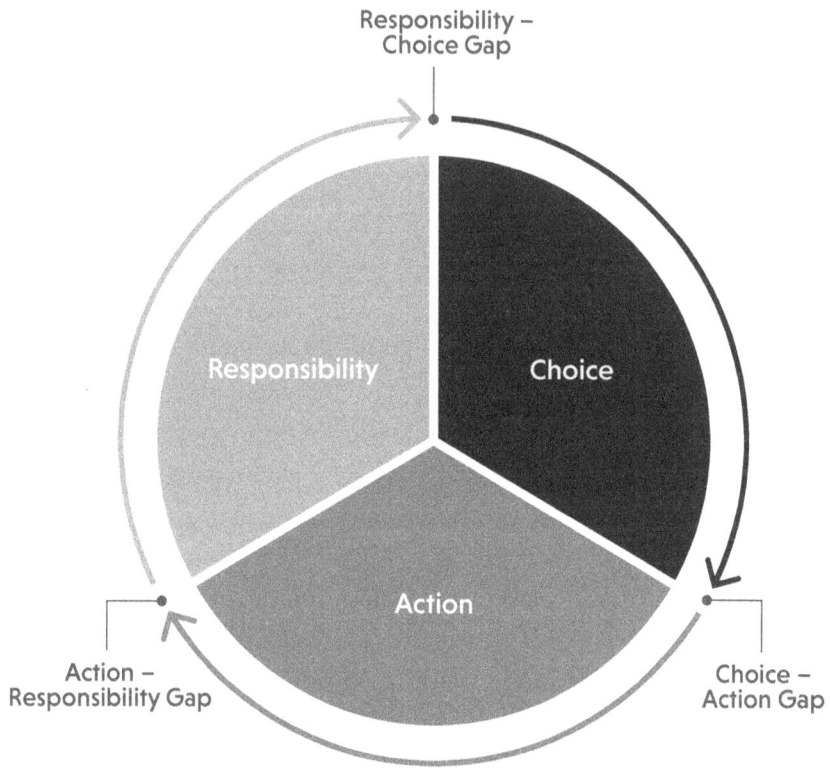

Figure 9: The CAR model: Choice, Action, Responsibility. Source: Inspired by Schultz & Hatch

Most of us have experienced the Choice–Action Gap. It's called procrastination. There's a Spanish proverb: 'Tomorrow is often the busiest day of the week.' Stop trusting your future Self to get stuff done. Do it now.

We also all experience the Action–Responsibility Gap. It's called blame-shifting: 'It wasn't me.' Many of us instinctively react defensively when confronted with potential criticism. Try to keep the issue at arm's length. It's not about you.

Last but not least, we also all experience the Responsibility–Choice Gap. It's called worrying or ruminating without making a choice. How many nights have you spent mulling over issues that you feel responsible for but can't really influence?

When you have learned instinctively to go through this circle then you will have reached total accountability.

Do you remember the existential questions I posed at the beginning of the book?

- What is your next existential choice?
- What is your next existential act?
- Which existential responsibility do you still need to address?

I trust that they have now become easier for you to answer. Please give them another shot.

This circular approach has helped me find my roots – my intellectual platform – and connect with my most profound identity. These reflections give me an exuberant feeling of youth, limitlessness, mystery and freedom, coupled with an acute sense of nostalgia, reflection, understanding and meaning. I hope, through this book, to be able to give you the same.

Questions to ask yourself

- Which negative inner dialogue do you want to get rid of?
- Which action have you not yet held yourself responsible for? When will you do it?
- What do you want to stand for?
- If others should judge you only by your deeds, what would their judgement be?

Chapter 5
Show me your friends

It's all about relationships and connections. No human is an island. We're deeply interdependent, yet when we get caught up in our careers and need to feel successful we tend to neglect friends and family. We often think collaboration and reaching out are less worthy than doing everything ourselves. But we thrive mentally and physically with healthy and robust connections, as does our brain. In this chapter, you'll find inspiration about assessing your relationships and, if necessary, how to strengthen them.

I recently participated in the Copenhagen Marathon, a much-loved event with thousands of participants. To me, it was a special day. It was my 100th official race and I'd pinned a note on my back saying so. It was self-congratulatory, of course, but it was, first and foremost, a way of inviting comments and conversations. The invitation was well received. Many people congratulated me or asked about my experiences, both veterans like me and first-time participants. It added to the sense of community and comradeship I always feel in those circumstances. When he strolled around Copenhagen each day, Kierkegaard talked about 'my daily people bath'.

Seeking new goals meant that I needed to identify a new ambition for my running. This has now become 'I want to complete a marathon when I'm 80 years old'. This ambition should certainly keep me on my toes. There's another truth behind this. You probably know one of the secrets behind sports such as tennis, golf or boxing. In short, it's this: 'Don't stop the swing!' If you start holding back at the point where you hit the ball or the boxing bag, you've already lost significant momentum. Your brain automatically discounts the effort and diminishes the energy spent. My boxing coach says it clearly: 'You need to aim for the other side of the boxing bag!'

Let me draw a few leadership conclusions from my 100th race:

- The message on my back: 'This is my official race #100' generated many conversations along the route. It's up to you to start the conversation!
- Some of the runners passing me offered their congratulations. When I met them further along the route, it was my turn to encourage them. We all meet again!
- Pain is temporary; quitting lasts forever. Keep on runnin'!
- It's a collective effort. We're all in this together. With a little help from my friends!
- It's just a finish line, not the end. Seek new goals!
- Let's run and have fun. Don't forget to enjoy the ride!
- Finally, a quote from Haruki Murakami's *What I Talk about When I Talk about Running* (2007): 'At least he never walked!'

From an existential point of view, this means that we always need to have an overarching aim, one that's nearly unattainable. This will give you escape velocity. Many of my coaching clients have reached a point in life where they've become financially independent. An inspiring existential goal for many of them is to give to charity. Having amassed enough wealth to take care of their extended family, they now want to help others. It certainly adds meaning to their effort. I'm blessed with strong relationships with friends, family, colleagues and professional acquaintances. And still, I need to feel connected to society in the larger sense of the word. It's one of the reasons I'm still enjoying the yearly Roskilde rock festival, one of Europe's largest, in a tent camp housing more than 40 men. The feeling of sharing this kind of experience is intense. People from all walks of life come together, united in their love of running or live music, letting their hair down (well, at my age, it's usually in the symbolic sense of the word) and feeling part of something bigger. These brief and glowingly glorious bursts of having something in common are essential, as are all relationships. And yet, many of us tend to neglect our relationships, even with those who are vital to us and whom we love more than anything.

Many of my clients admit that their relationships have suffered, at least to some degree. Work and career have taken the front seat. They may have been attentive parents and partners but, more often than not, they feel guilty towards their families. Business has turned into busyness. They've usually failed to prioritise the larger family, such as parents or siblings, not to mention friends. This is especially true for men in leading positions but it's not unique to them. Across countries in Europe and North America, people in surveys tend to worry about their work–life balance, although the percentage varies widely, depending on how the questions are asked. Negative stress and burnout are widespread.

I often use an exercise where I ask a client a question and follow up with 'Why?' each time they reply. I'll do this five times while trying to understand the root cause of what's happening. My first question might be:

'What's making you unhappy right now?'
The answer could be: 'I feel that I don't have enough time.'
'Why is that a problem?'
'Because it makes me feel stressed.'
'Why is that a problem?'
'I don't have time for things that I enjoy.'
'Why is that a problem?'
'It drains me. I can't recharge.'
'Why is that a problem?'
'I become angry fast and I'm not fun to be around.'
'Why is that a problem?'
'I'm lonely.'

It's remarkable how often loneliness creeps in at the last 'Why?'. At the same time, we've nurtured a culture where it's difficult to reach out for help. I've talked about the changing paradigms and one of the most notable is the change from hierarchical, linear thinking to network and circular thinking.

Before we continue, let me ask you a couple of questions. Who can you rely on? When you need encouragement, when you need a frank yet friendly assessment, when you feel down, when you're happy and want to share the good news – who can you reach out to?

Most people of my generation have been accustomed to thinking that you have to put effort into climbing the career ladder and then even more effort into staying on top. If that took long hours, that was the price you had to pay. It would be seen as a sign of weakness if you found it difficult and the weak didn't reach the pinnacle. 'It's lonely at the top' is one of those sayings that demonstrate linear thinking. There's a top, and if you get there, don't expect to have any friends. And if you find company up there, be prepared to push the next person off the cliff.

That isn't to say that we haven't had networks. We have, and they have been and remain valuable. But they've also been characterised by a limited amount of diversity. To some extent, they've been more like closed clubs where you can help each other but where the social jockeying for position has still been keen and where a sign of weakness could mean that you'd find it harder to get somebody to recommend you for a position, such as a place on a board or a new job. Some of us have put more value in 'deal friends' than 'dear friends'. In the proposed friendship hierarchy of Aristotle, utilitarian friendships are at the lowest level, yet they're frequently prioritised for the advantages they can give us.

This picture is, of course, too bleak. But these kinds of networks are not, as a general rule, where you can share existential doubts, show insecurity or talk about the pressures you feel. On the highest level of Aristotle's hierarchy is 'perfect friendship', where friends value each other's existence without expecting profitability, which defines utilitarian friendships. You undoubtedly know the old proverb 'Show me your friends and I will tell you who you are'. Scientific research shows us that there's more truth to that than we may have realised. Our relationships shape us and their quality dramatically affects whether or not we thrive. As mentioned before, we're social, playful and inherently helpful beings, and we ignore this at our peril.

Psychologists were initially occupied mainly with the relationship between parents and children and, to a lesser extent, siblings – the dynamics of the close family. This is hardly surprising, given that the academic field grew from a middle-class, mid-European society where the immediate family was the central social unit. It remains so in many places, especially Scandinavia, northern Europe and North America. Had psychology originated in, say, an African, Asian or even a southern European context, it would probably have emphasised other relationship dynamics.

As psychology has developed, so has our understanding of how hugely important our relationships are and to what extent they're reflected directly in our mental and physical health. Research shows that loneliness, defined as an involuntary lack of meaningful relationships rather than simply being alone for a duration you've chosen, could be more lethal than smoking or inactivity. No death certificate will have 'loneliness' written on it but prolonged periods of loneliness have increased the risk of a range of deadly diseases and conditions, whereas healthy and strong relationships are associated with a significantly lower risk of disease and early death.

Some of this is psychological. Loneliness may make you more prone to behaviours that increase your risk of diseases and accidents, such as substance abuse. But neurology and particularly neurochemistry also show that good relationships increase the output of beneficial chemicals such as oxytocin while keeping stress hormones such as cortisol at healthy levels. You'll find researchers who argue that improving relationships and psychological safety across society would significantly lower the number of people suffering from different physical diseases. Heart disease is the biggest killer worldwide and having good relationships decreases the emotions and conditions that boost heart disease risk, such as anger, depression, anxiety and hostility. During the Covid-19 pandemic, the Danes coined the concept of 'skin starvation', meaning a deep need and hunger for being physically close, to hug and to touch.

I mentioned chemical hacks earlier. Certain practices can trigger your happiness chemicals and help you feel better. But hacks or no hacks, relationships remain fundamental to our wellbeing. Even

> We need to believe that we contribute and that our contributions are meaningful and valued

though we've progressed tremendously technologically and are no longer as dependent on other people for our immediate survival, we're still psychologically hardwired to need relationships. We need to feel included, wanted and appreciated. We need to believe that we contribute and that our contributions are meaningful and valued.

Humans learn from each other. I've been fortunate to have had brilliant clients, friends, family and teachers who have taught me truths, some of them harrowing, the majority inspiring. Those are the lessons on life transitions and existential questions that we can share and pass on. I grew up in a Harry Potter-like environment, at a Danish boarding school where my father was a teacher. The hallway leading to our apartment was flanked by sculptures of ancient Greek and Roman philosophers and it was hard not to feel a certain awe and appreciation, not to mention the weight of the accumulated wisdom when you passed through it. Some people had strived to make humanity wiser and kinder in ancient times and their words and thoughts are still with us today to help us find meaning and clarity. We learn, we teach and we hope to make a difference.

We're all individuals leading unique lives. But luckily for us all, most of us have similar wishes for life. While we're highly different, we're also very much alike. Across cultures and spans of time, we remain social beings who want to be loved and appreciated for who we are. Almost all wishes are aspects of that, as well as having basic needs for physical safety taken care of, such as a place to live, food to eat, etc. But the aspects differ, depending on the person and the situation. Some researchers have described the almost physical pain that a sense of loneliness can give us as similar to hunger pangs or feeling thirsty. It's a survival mechanism, telling us that we're in danger if we don't do something about our situation, whether it's lack of water, food or other people. Psychology, neurology and most philosophical schools will confirm that relationships are part of whoever you are. And though some branches of philosophy are more concerned with the individual, others emphasise the relationship between the individual Self and society.

Who can you count on?

Most of my coaching clients are not alone. They tend to have close relatives – spouses, children or somebody they can rely on. But they haven't always been good at maintaining relationships or prioritising them. When invited to consider this question, some are surprised to realise that they don't have close friends. So, let's have a look at your relationships. How many names appear if I ask you to name all your friends? Use the broadest sense of the term to include people you don't see regularly but whom you consider friends.

Now, if I ask you to name the people – friends, family, neighbours – to whom you can reach out, no matter what, and whom you trust to help you regardless of the circumstances, how many reappear? This isn't a numbers game. There's a limit to how many close friendships you can maintain, and relationships are also about having people you can share a common interest with, be it a choir, biking, cooking class, discussing books or the ancient art of calligraphy. But we need people we can confide in and trust to be honest in their response and love us, even when we make mistakes.

The next question is, would you reach out if you needed help? If you're like me and most of my clients, you'd usually prefer not to reach out but rather try to solve whatever the problem is yourself, because you'd be accustomed to perceiving that asking for help is a sign of weakness. My advice is: get over it. You need other people. It's not a weakness; it's a human strength to seek and give help. This is how we've progressed as a species. Success isn't a zero-sum game. Just consider how you feel when somebody you like asks you for advice or comes to you for help. Does it make you feel annoyed? Do you perceive that person as weak? Or is it more likely that you'll feel happy to help? Research tells us that most people like helping others. Not everyone, and not all the time, but even strangers can usually count on people to help them if they're in need. So, if you don't feel annoyed or consider somebody coming to you for help as weak and even feel pleased – why should others think differently when you go to them?

Lasse Rich Henningsen also mentioned this. Others were vital when he was going through a crisis. Without them, he'd have felt much more at a loss. He also added something noteworthy: even when you're down and feeling low, there's strength and energy to be found in helping others. He told me: 'I still had to be able to hug my children, to give something back to the family. This is also something to consider when you've been through a tough patch and others have supported you. Remember to fill up the relationship account. Even in tough times, you should never resort to self-pity. It has a narcissistic tinge and doesn't help you, either.'

Also, build relationships in peacetime. It's too late to reach out when there's a crisis. It takes time to build up mutual trust.

Ride the Ferris wheel

Even when you're down and feeling low, there's strength and energy to be found in helping others

I usually do this exercise with my coaching clients. Take a look at Figure 10.

This is a kind of 360-degree scan of your relationships and networks. I've made it look like a Ferris wheel because some gondolas will be closer to the ground and some higher up as the wheel turns, just like it is with your relationships. At different points in life, some spheres of relationships will feel closer and more critical to you but they're all part of what makes the wheel go round and are all necessary for balance. As you can see, relationships come in all sorts of packages. Some are people you share a life with, at least for some time. Others are more like acquaintances than friends; they're networks, people whose lives you become part of in a different and less attached sense but who nevertheless are meaningful to you.

While you look at your Ferris wheel, I also invite you to consider the quality of your relationships. How do they make you feel about yourself? Are they primarily consisting of people you don't feel connected to and who make you feel as if you have to pretend to be something you're not to please them? Do they make you feel good or bad about yourself and your life? I once told my wife, 'You make a better person out of me.' Her reply was, 'Isn't that the point of marriage?'

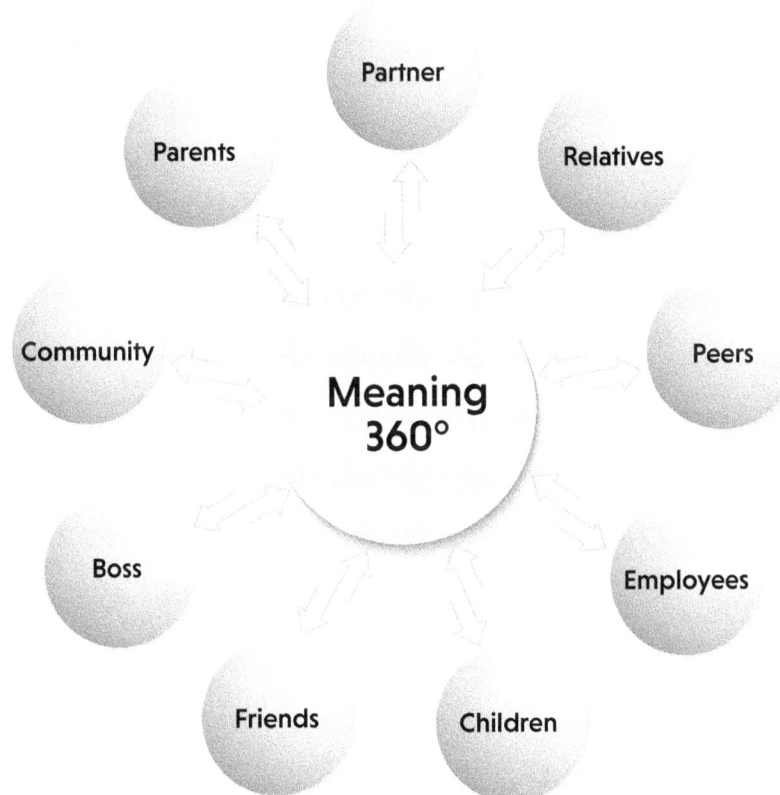

Figure 10: The Meaning 360° model

I've already mentioned the deep and meaningful relationships with the people closest to us. Networking is something that many people look at with a kind of scepticism or even a sense of disdain: small talk is for other people. I have more important matters to debate. What some people don't get is that small talk can be a helpful initial process where all involved are trying to scan a number of subjects to find out what they have in common and what could be interesting to talk about, and which might then lead to something more solid and lasting.

One of my clients whom I mentioned before, Robert Kledal, told me that he hated these kinds of 'mix and mingle' events where you have to balance floppy plates with dainty smoked salmon sandwiches and a glass of tepid white wine while talking to other people, who'll then leave you the minute they discover somebody they perceive as more interesting. It left him decidedly anti-networking, as he said. But networking doesn't have to be like that. Networking simply means meeting new people; a network is nothing more mysterious than your connections to other people in a specific context, whether inside or outside work.

I suggested that Robert might consider cultivating and building on his networks in other circumstances, making it a personal one-on-one conversation about a subject that both had agreed on in advance and that both enjoyed. Networking doesn't have to involve large social gatherings, especially if they make you feel like hiding in the shadows, close to the exit, hoping for the first acceptable excuse to leave. However, networks are worth investing your time in. And it's worth mapping your relationships and connections to discover how your Ferris wheel is running. Why? Because we need other people; not to exploit them but because our connections give our lives meaning. They provide us with a sense of social wellbeing, give us confidence and enable us to exchange ideas and thoughts and get new perspectives from people we trust and respect.

Good networking isn't about trading favours but about sharing opportunities, knowledge, experiences and energy

Networking is often seen as a somewhat cynical 'you scratch my back, I'll scratch yours' approach to people you know. But that misses the point about a sense of responsibility between network members, be it formal or informal. Good networking isn't about trading favours but about sharing opportunities, knowledge, experiences and energy. There's no denying, though, and nothing wrong with the fact that networks can also be beneficial when you need an extra hand. The numbers vary between countries but in most places, networks play a huge role when companies recruit or coveted positions are open. Or it may be that you need knowledge and insights from a less familiar field and can reach out to someone you know and trust in one of your networks. Networks are helpful and will boost your ability to succeed – as long as you know that it has to be mutual. You must make yourself available to others and be considered a valuable part of the network based on who you are. The golden rule of networking is to give without expecting anything in return. But don't be afraid to reach out when you need something.

A colleague of mine used to cohabit with seven other people. One of the others wisely said that it would only work if each of them did one-sixth of whatever needed to be done around the place. I like that idea. Everything works better when each of us provides a little bit more than our fair share.

You're better connected than you think

To many of us, it can seem that everybody else is better connected and has more friends and relationships than we do. Social media plays a role here; we're quick to share our successes and much more reluctant regarding hardships. My experience is that we're usually much better connected than we think.

The Ferris wheel is an invitation to map your network. We all have several networks in different contexts and the funny thing is that we usually find it difficult to look beyond the specific context. Suppose you know Aysha as one of the parents from your children's school. In that case, you may not realise or remember that she's also the senior advisor in a company that specialises in the circular economy and how to apply it. Or if you think about your oldest nephew, sometimes it's hard to remember that he's not just a family member but a grown-up with a career in AI, with his own networks. We tend to keep people we know in a specific sphere and forget that they have other roles in other contexts.

If you look at the Ferris wheel, some gondolas are self-explanatory. You know who your partner, children and parents are. But what about their networks? How well do you know them? Are there people it may be an idea for you to reach out to? You may have employees, you may have a boss, or both. You've probably had several of those throughout the years, some of whom you'll remember fondly, and that feeling tends to be mutual. Where are they today? Are they part of networks you could also contribute to and participate in? Look at each of the gondolas, map the networks involved and then map the possible network associated with them – for instance, the partners of your children or their parents or your nieces, etc. Ask yourself how you could contribute.

Mapping your networks like this takes time but also reveals whether you have the social connections you want and, if not, where there's a lack. And then you can do something about it. Sometimes, all it takes is to ask a question. Next time you watch your daughter's basketball game, ask one of the other parents what they do. Or ask your colleagues at work what they like to do in their spare time. Sometimes, people show very different sides of themselves when invited to share something they care about – and you may find yourself a new friend.

> *We tend to keep people we know in a specific sphere and forget that they have other roles in other contexts*

Just a final comment on networking. If nothing else works, the strategy is: go personal. Don't be afraid to give a spontaneous compliment or, say, comment on how much the person in front of you likes dogs. We all want to be seen and heard and everybody likes talking about themselves. The closer to themselves the conversation is, the more the person in front of you will feel appreciated and engaged. The more they've spoken about themselves, the better a conversation they'll feel they have had.

Questions to ask yourself

- If you list the five people that you take the most care of, who are they?
- Do you have people you can rely on no matter what? And who can rely on you?
- Do you know people outside your own social circle and from different backgrounds and values?
- Did you remember to include yourself in the list of five people that you take care of?

Chapter 6:
The strategy of reinvention

You may feel that you know yourself by now. But do you know who you want to be? And what holds you back? Like Pinocchio, most of us have strings that pull us in the wrong direction against our will, making it difficult for us to grow and thrive. In this chapter, you'll learn to identify and cut those strings. And you'll get some practical and concrete advice on how to set your goals – and reach them. You'll also get ideas on how to face and use adversity, obstacles and stressful periods as opportunities for personal growth.

I know from my coaching clients that most of them already know, at least to some degree, that they want to and need to change, grow and progress. They're usually happy with their achievements but the answer to the question 'What should I do with the rest of my life?' can no longer be 'More of the same'. They need to find a different answer, one that's meaningful to them.

Remember the life phases? We change as we grow in years and knowledge. As described in previous chapters, it's debatable what our Self is, how crystallised or fluid it is. We may have specific characteristics that have remained constant throughout many years but if we look deeper into our values and ways of thinking, most of us will find profound change along the way. We may have been rebellious in youth and complacent in our current situation.

We are, in other words, not unable to reinvent ourselves. But to do it consciously is an entirely different process. To reinvent yourself and your meaning can feel overwhelming. Where to begin? Hopefully, the previous chapters have made you more aware of yourself and how we're all shaped by our emotions, our experiences, knowledge and, not least, our relationships. Now is the time to put that knowledge into play. Your self-awareness is at the centre of your ability to transition yourself. Who have you been? Who are you now? And who do you want to become? You can't let go of your past but when you're aware of how it has shaped you, it no longer has the power to tackle you from behind.

Cut the strings

To get to that point with my clients, I use a straightforward exercise that I call Pinocchio, named after the wooden puppet who dreams of becoming a real boy. Puppets can't move unless somebody pulls their strings. Pinocchio wants to be able to move by himself, choose his fate, be loved, play, act and be alive, just like we all do. But like the puppet Pinocchio, we also have strings that pull us and make us do things we don't want to do.

So, take a look at the figure below.

Past   Future

Figure 11: The Pinocchio model

To the left, you see yourself burdened by the strings of your history. I aim to set you free and provide you with a better sense of control over your life by:

- editing your past
- curating your present
- designing your future.

Look thoroughly at your life right now, your professional and your private life. Identify the five most constraining characteristics you currently carry in your baggage. It can be anything from specific reactions to events or circumstances. In some cases, some of them may have been useful previously but have served their purpose. You know best. Think of your inner dialogue. When was the last time you said to yourself, 'Oh no, not again!'? You may want to write a much more extensive list than five but, in the end, you should narrow it down, otherwise you lose focus and the ability to devote your energy to this transition.

Let me use an example from Robert Kledal, who I've mentioned a couple of times and who has been generous enough to let me use his example here. He came to me because he knew he wanted something different from life than his present career, even if it looked spectacularly successful by traditional measures. He'd lived across China, Hong Kong, the US and Europe, worked in the Middle East and considered himself a global citizen with a keen understanding of cultural differences and a high tolerance for ambiguity.

The strings of the past and present that were holding Pinocchio back were, in his words:

- overloaded
- less interested in operations
- loyal to a fault
- overweight
- rebellious.

All in all, his old foundation contained a large amount of self-doubt. But the words he chose also illustrated characteristics he could do something about, such as being overloaded – or put into use more constructively. Loyalty is a virtue when placed where it's deserved and doesn't turn into unquestioning devotion to a cause or person. Rebelliousness can nurture independent thinking and lead to new ideas and actions when it's reined in by an ability to listen to reason and acknowledge the perspective of others.

After that, I invited him to write down five characteristics he'd like to define his future Self. This is probably not something that you can do within a few minutes but consider what you want. It's usually not a specific goal, such as 'being the CEO of a larger company within three years' or 'having found a life partner'. Instead, it's often capabilities and life attitudes that you want to embrace.

These are Robert's choices:

- embrace the elitist
- intelligence
- networker
- aesthetics
- interesting and interested.

His new foundation? He described it as 'a very kind bulldozer'! For the past nine years, he had been the CEO of a private equity-owned global supplier to the maritime industry and was now looking for new opportunities. He was much more excited about finding meaning than anxious about what to do next. And so, he quit his job to do something about feeling overloaded and began to transition into the new, defining characteristics. He spent three years living out some of his dreams: entrepreneurship, being with his loved ones, getting fitter by taking long walks with his wife and meeting people. Three years later, he's found his new home as… the CEO of a private equity-owned global supplier to the maritime industry. But he has a new foundation and feels much more at ease with himself and the job. He knows he has to avoid the overload that tied him down in his previous position. And, during his initial talks with the company, he was able to stress precisely what they were getting and perhaps even more what they were not getting. He no longer wanted to 'sell' himself or paint a flattering picture. If they wanted him as the CEO, they should want him as he had come to know himself.

With my clients, I very often see this pattern:

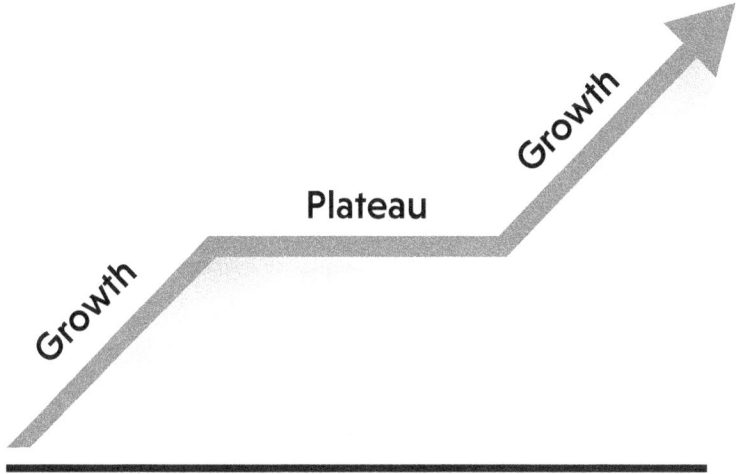

Figure 12: The growth-plateau-growth relationship

After a period of personal development comes an inflection point. Then comes a plateau where you must disentangle yourself from your past and work on cutting those strings. There's no rule for how long that should take – but don't expect this to be something that happens in a hurry. Typically, it will be about two years, after which you're ready to accelerate and provoke a new inflection point. Working in executive search, I've seen this pattern repeatedly. You must distance yourself from your former situation to progress towards a new and improved identity. As Robert illustrated, transitioning doesn't have to be about turning your whole life upside down. He returned to a position that looked much like the one he was no longer happy with. The change was within himself, his foundation and understanding of what mattered to him.

How to apply strategy to your life

Let's return to Pinocchio. You've noted the five characteristics that are currently holding you back. You've identified the five characteristics you want to define your future Self. And you've figured out what you want to do with your life, what matters to you, your values, what success means to you. Now what? If you come from the business world, you probably already know a lot about setting goals. In this case, you also know that setting them and reaching them are two different things. Execution is difficult.

Studies and researchers tell us that strategies frequently fail for many reasons. One of them is that the strategy is unclear or purposeless to those who have to execute it through their daily choices. Another is that the organisation and the day-to-day operations don't support or may not even be connected to the overall goals and strategy. If you take this to a more personal level, one aspect is that whatever your goal, it has to be meaningful to you. We've been through that but it illustrates the importance of this particular aspect. You have to know not only what you're doing but especially why you're doing it.

One of the strategists I work with and who has contributed to this book, Claus Maron from Blue Note Consultants, uses an approach called 'promise-based execution'. It has been designed for businesses but he stresses that it can also be used at a personal level. His message is in so many ways similar to the one from Clayton Christensen: take care not to optimise your chances of success in the short term by sacrificing meaning and your idea of success in the long term.

At a personal level, this promise-based execution strategy would look something like this:

- *Set an ambitious goal for yourself.* As the author Diana Sharf-Hunt says, goals are dreams with deadlines. If you only adjust based on where you are, you won't make any fundamental changes. It has to be an ambitious and meaningful goal to motivate you, challenging enough to transform your actions and choices yet reachable and relevant.
- *Promise yourself that you'll do all it takes* to get there based

on your values, your sense of Self and what's important to you. It isn't a question of being ruthless but authentic to yourself. If you don't feel ready to do everything it takes, ask yourself why. Is the goal not as meaningful as you thought? If so, adjust until you find something worth striving sufficiently hard towards.

- *Identify which factors are critical* for your success. Are you dependent on others to get there, for instance, your family or business partners? You have to make sure they're aware of that and you should ask whether they can contribute or align until you agree on what should happen. You'll probably have to check those factors at least once a year. Do they remain the same, or are there new ones?
- *Share your goal with others*. It doesn't have to be the whole world but the minute you make your plan public, it becomes more of a commitment to yourself and others.
- *Keep your overall goal* for your future Self in mind when you make small everyday decisions and choices. Which life circumstances are facilitating your goal? Which are putting the brakes on it? When you pursue your goal, you may have to make essential choices about the path you choose to get there. Strategising is all about making the bigger conscious choices that will guide your smaller execution ones. Remember to be mindful of your options; don't simply choose the most obvious one ahead of you. When making such choices from different options – they may be existential by nature, such as changing career path or giving up an exciting job to spend more time with your family – consider whether they're in accordance with your values (what's important to you), your interest profile (what you find motivating) and your strengths (what you learn quickly or where you already have unique capabilities).
- *Create short-term targets*. For instance, one month or six months – and milestones between the short-term targets and your overall ambition, for example, what you want to have achieved or changed in two years. Just like you need both the high beam and the low beam in a car, you need to be able to

see far ahead while keeping an eye on the road immediately in front of you. Remember to celebrate and pat yourself on your back when you reach them. Adjust them to ensure they're still relevant to you and what you want to achieve. Maybe you're now in a place where you can be even more ambitious. Or perhaps circumstances have changed. When a goal is ambitious enough and you're motivated enough to reach it, it will have transformative power. You'll align your activities in a way that works towards the goal for yourself instead of just steering through life on autopilot.

Revisit your Pinocchio repeatedly, just as you revisit your goals and targets. New strings could replace old ones. Or you may wish to redefine who you want to be as you grow, learn and strengthen your relationships. You may even discover that your potential for change was larger than expected. When you've figured out where you want to go and what you want to let go of, it's time to double check. How motivated are you? Does the thought of your future Self seem engaging and energising enough for you to put the necessary effort into it? When you've reached your point of no return, you'll feel a strong pull and not feel the burden of push any more – you won't be able *not* to do what you've chosen. Otherwise, please continue with the process of identifying what you want to become until you're excited enough about it to begin. This may take time.

It's also important to remember that a strategy is about an ambitious choice – in this case, a life transition – that defines all the small choices and everyday decisions. Making the big choice isn't easy but it is the easiest part. It's the day-to-day decisions that will make the difference. Or, as Tony Robbins has put it, a decision isn't a decision until it's implemented. Until then, it's a plan.

We are back at choice, action and responsibility. You have to put your intentions into everyday action and take responsibility for doing that. A practical way of doing this is to set specific, small goals that lead toward the bigger goal. If, like Robert Kledal, you want to be more of a networker, set the goal of having at least two coffee meetings every week for the next four weeks with people you'd like to connect or reconnect with. It's a good idea to keep a log of your progress. When you encounter setbacks – which you will do – it's helpful to go back to see how far you've come.

The best of both worlds

Who you are, who you want to become and why you want to do it is at the core of reinventing yourself. The precise 'how' of it is where you can be flexible. You'll find that there are usually more ways than one to go about your goals. Yet the how of it is frequently the point that will lead to arguments, confusion and sometimes difficult choices. This is where the big plans have to be translated into smaller and more specific actions and decisions and it's rarely straightforward. According to common wisdom, most decisions imply that you miss out on alternatives. As the saying goes, you can't have your cake and eat it, too. But is that true? Or could you find a way to have the best of both worlds?

My wife and I have a saying: when in doubt about what to choose, choose both. It's not always possible, of course. But many choices are not as binary as they seem when you study them from a different level and angle. If you try to figure out how you can have the advantages of both options, you may find that there are alternatives that will allow you to combine seemingly incompatible choices. To some extent, you can compare it to standing at a crossroads and deciding to make a new path instead of choosing between the existing ones. 'There are no paths until somebody begins to walk,' as I saw written on the wall as graffiti somewhere.

> *When in doubt about what to choose, choose both*

The strategist and bestselling author **Roger Martin** discusses using design thinking in strategy (Martin & Lafley 2013). He says that, when two, both attractive but from the outset alternative options occur, you have to develop a pro–pro chart. By this, he means:

1. list the two options
2. identify the pros and cons related to each option

3. mark the pros you'd like to see materialise and use this list to design a new solution containing pros from both options.

I see design thinking as a way to translate the call to action implicit in existentialism into practical solutions that are fair and encompass divergent views. It's a way to look at problems from different angles, a human-centric approach that involves empathising with others and seeing the situation from their point of view. Solving problems becomes a collaborative and ongoing process that constantly aims to make it easier to do the right thing. Initially a method developed for technological design, it has nevertheless reverberated through other fields and offers a lens through which we can sometimes find unexpected ways to deal with dilemmas and problems and create win–win scenarios. An example is choosing between full-time employment with a company or a professional life as an independent. Pro of the company: colleagues and shared purpose. Con: having to take orders from others. Pro of being independent: being your own boss. Con: missing out on the energy and wisdom of good colleagues. Possible solution: design a future career as an independent but part of a group of peers working together.

Focus on the why and what of your goal, not the how

Many of my clients want to do well at work and be good parents, partners and friends – and they want time to learn new things and experience new places. This usually ends up in a compromise where everybody gains something without feeling truly satisfied or happy. The way of dealing with this is to focus on the why and what of your goal, not the how. Why does it matter? What should it lead to? What is success to you? Leave the how and the possible obstacles; for now, they'll only cloud the picture. You must be aware of your virtues and values and what matters most to you. It's an approach to solutions that can be immensely effective. When you look at the choices before you, try to look at them differently. Is the problem what you think it is? Or could you see it in a different way that allows you to make a win–win solution where you get the best of both worlds? It would help if you began to look into the how only when you're clear on the why and the what. Be open towards solutions you hadn't considered before. Maybe there are ways to combine being a present and devoted parent and being successful professionally. Still, it may mean you have to go about it differently than what you initially imagined.

Suffer well

It's one thing to put a strategy down on paper. It's quite a different thing to pursue it and succeed. You'll undoubtedly face adversity and obstacles, sometimes so severe that they seem impossible to overcome. This can be difficult to cope with but both philosophy, psychology and neurology have lessons about that and they all boil down to one, perhaps surprising, fact: adversity and stress can be good for you as long as they arrive at manageable levels and intervals that allow you to rest in between.

If you look back on your life, try to think about one or two periods when you felt that you learned something which positively shaped who you are today. Were those periods characterised by lazy days in the sun or other kinds of bliss? Or would you think back on them as rather stressful?

Behind every break-through lies a breakdown

Most clients would agree that those days weren't easy to get through. But they usually wouldn't be without them. As Erik Kjær, one of my mentors – and a renowned business psychologist – taught me, behind every breakthrough lies a breakdown. It's the breakdown of your habits and mental constructs. In Chapter 7 we will look at paradigms. A breakdown leads to a new paradigm being formed, which again leads to more existential clarity.

I once learned a saying from a friend, who is also a Stoic: 'Suffer well,' he said. This doesn't sound uplifting. Whom among us wants to suffer? Nevertheless, suffering is part of the human condition. We all face adversity, setbacks and the tragedies of life. While you go on to transform yourself, you'll undoubtedly meet obstacles and unexpected resistance; you'll have moments of doubt and confusion.

If you remember your 'why', those moments are likely to be fewer and shorter than if you go through life without feeling this inner meaning. But they're bound to occur and you may occasionally find yourself in the rougher whirlwinds of life. All of this is an opportunity for growth. As another Stoic, Seneca the Younger, said a couple of thousand years ago, you learn to know a (ship's) pilot in a storm. Seneca pitied people who'd never experienced adversity. They hadn't learned how to prove themselves.

To suffer well doesn't mean you should enjoy suffering but that you should strive to bear the suffering in a way that will contribute to your growth as a human and your understanding of yourself. It's not the suffering itself that will teach you but the acceptance of it. The famous Soviet dissident and author Alexandr Solzhenitsyn, who was awarded the Nobel Prize in literature, wrote in his book *The Gulag Archipelago* (1973) about his experiences in the horrific prison camp where he spent several years, deprived of everything, subject to forced labour and humiliation. But he found a sense of meaning. He came to understand that the object of life isn't prosperity but the maturity of the human soul – and that the line separating good and evil isn't a question of nations, ideologies or classes but a line through the human heart. 'And that is why I turn back to the years of my imprisonment and say, sometimes to the astonishment of those around me, "Bless you, prison, for having been part of my life."'

> As long as I stay true to my values, I can prevail

It's a highly Stoic approach – finding meaning while living in meaningless cruelty, finding freedom in a prison and wisdom in the barbaric confinements of human folly. Hopefully, you'll never have to face that kind of suffering but the Stoics are a great source of inspiration whenever you face adversity. Sometimes they're misunderstood. Stoicism isn't about being unemotional but about controlling what is within your power to control and letting go of the rest. It's a valuable strategy, especially when you're dealing with headwinds. It's easy to become wound up in resentment, envy and perhaps even bitterness when you look at your circumstances and the hand life has dealt you. But focusing on where you can make a difference usually makes what you have to deal with less overwhelming.

Lasse Rich Henningsen, who I described earlier, was the CEO of a well-known cultural centre when he and his organisation were confronted with hard criticism in the media. For months, the headlines were almost constantly negative and some criticism became personal.

Lasse has always found adversity energising but this was different. It wasn't so much about solving a problem as facing something unfair and destructive. And yet he managed to stay and weather the crisis. Here's his explanation: 'I know myself and what I stand for. And I hadn't compromised on that. Looking at myself in the mirror, I didn't need to feel doubt or shame. As long as I stay true to my values, I can prevail. That isn't to say I have no faults or can do nothing wrong. We all have faults and do wrong and it's important to acknowledge that and hold yourself accountable, even if it could mean losing your position. But once you start to undermine your values, you begin to lose yourself. And that's fatal.'

Like the Stoic philosophers, Lasse is trying to focus on what he can influence and let go of what isn't within his power. He can control his thoughts and actions. It also helps him, he says, that he has a firm belief in God and the values and ethics that go with that – but he stresses that this doesn't have to be about religious faith: 'As long as you acknowledge that you're accountable to more than yourself, you'll know when you stray from your values. To me, it's God. It could be a set of ethics or a certain way of life to someone else.'

The Stoic way

Marcus Aurelius was a Roman emperor known as the last of the 'five good emperors' and, at the same time, a Stoic philosopher. His most famous work, *Meditations*, is a collection of quotes and 'notes to self' rather than comprehensive philosophical teachings. They were his reminders of how to live stoically when faced with the numerous challenges and stresses he faced as the head of an empire dealing with numerous rebellions while trying to be just and act for the greater good of all humanity. You can sometimes feel how he sternly reminds himself not to moan when he has to take up the burden of his office:

'At dawn, when you have trouble getting out of bed, tell yourself, I have to go to work – as a human being. What do I have to complain about if I'm going to do what I was born for – the things I was brought into the world to do? Or is this what I was created for? To huddle under the blankets and stay warm? So, you were born to feel 'nice'? Instead of doing things and experiencing them? Don't you see the plants, the birds, the ants and spiders and bees going about their individual tasks, putting the world in order as best they can? And you're not willing to do your job as a human being? Why aren't you running to do what your nature demands?'

The Stoics have become increasingly popular, perhaps because their teachings are more about how to face life as an individual in practical terms than about society. Don't go to the Stoics for inspiration about how to change society. They're concerned with how you change yourself and your life purpose. But they would argue that if everyone lived according to the best of their nature and the common good, that would improve the whole world. Marcus Aurelius repeatedly stresses that we're all connected and the good we do benefits all. He's remarkably tolerant of human nature: 'Whenever you are offended by a man's shamelessness, ask yourself immediately, is it possible then for the shameless not to be in the world? It is not; do not then ask for the impossible, for he, too, is one of the shameless who must exist in the world. And have the same ready also for the rogue, the traitor and every kind of wrongdoer; for directly you remind yourself that the class of such persons cannot but be, you will be gentler to them as individuals.'

Marcus Aurelius was, in his time, probably the most powerful man in the world. Easy for him to be tolerant, perhaps, and to argue for acceptance. But another of the great Stoics, Epictetus, came from a very different background. He was born into slavery and his famous work *The Enchiridion*, which more or less means the handbook, teaches the same thing. And it was his teachings that gave US Vice Admiral James Stockdale the courage to face nearly eight years as a prisoner of war in Vietnam. He was tortured 15 times and in solitary confinement for more than four years. But Epictetus was with him and taught him how to let go of all that he didn't have control over and to focus on that which he could control – how he dealt with prison life and the constant humiliation, how to stay true to what was important to him and try to ignore the conditions he was in. Things that are within our control are, according to Epictetus, 'Opinion, pursuit, desire, aversion and, in a word, whatever are our own actions.' We don't fully control what happens to us, what happens to our bodies or our reputation, our property, etc. If we spend too much energy worrying about everything outside our control, we become unhappy and prone to making unwise life decisions.

Epictetus was once asked what the use of all his doctrines was. He answered with three sharp words: 'Tranquillity. Fearlessness. And freedom.' Solzhenitsyn blessed his prison because he found his freedom and the meaning of life in it, and Stockdale blessed his experience as a prisoner of war because it taught him about himself. Again, this isn't the same as saying you should wish to be made a sufferer, a slave, a prisoner or a victim of torture, or inflict that suffering upon others. But it shows that even in the darkest of experiences, there's a kind of courage and meaning to be found – but you have to find it and make it yourself.

On a much smaller scale, I've done the same. As I mentioned, my father died when I was 12. It remains a tragic event but I think my life changed for the better because of it. I was destined to grow up in a tiny countryside community and eventually become a merchant or a trader. Instead, I was sent to the European School of Brussels, Belgium, which gave me a European baccalaureate and introduced me to a multicultural life I could only have imagined. This turn of events has undoubtedly made my life much more rewarding and fascinating than it would otherwise have been. In that way, I can bless my father's death in the same spirit that Solzhenitsyn blessed his prison, not as a happy event but as something that has given my life a different meaning. Fortunately, most of us face much less severe and life-threatening adversity than death, prison and torture. But the Stoics' approach towards it can teach us to focus on the essential things and let go of the rest. This also makes it easier to find a 'have it both ways' solution to your dilemmas – perhaps what you found important turned out not to be so crucial after all: the enviable address, car and job title. It can teach us tolerance towards others and their struggles and make it easier for us to reach out and ask for help.

Lasse Rich Henningsen stresses that his relationships turned out to be vital. During his crisis, he heard from numerous people who offered emotional support; some did so repeatedly and some were people he hadn't heard from in years. But now they were ready to help him through: 'When I looked at myself in the mirror, I saw not only myself reflected there. I saw all those people behind me, supporting and loving me. I wasn't alone; I was loved and appreciated. Sometimes, I felt it was undeserved but people kept telling me I'd done the same for them. I believe that you reap what you sow. Be certain that you sow the seeds of friendship.'

Stress can be beneficial

The ability to suffer stoically may seem extremely aloof and philosophical. However, to some extent, both psychology and neurology have validated this approach. Cognitive psychology is a branch of psychology that gained traction in the 1950s and 1960s. Contrary to traditional psychoanalysis, it focuses on mental processes such as perception, memory and reasoning, whereas psychoanalysis is mainly concerned with the unconscious. Cognitive psychology has provided evidence of specific cognitive strategies and techniques, such as learning to face your fears (rather than just understand them), mindfulness and acceptance-based therapies. According to cognitive psychology, we can change how we interpret and respond to events. As with the Stoics, the idea is that you can't change what has happened but you can change how you think about it. Both fields look to reframe events in a way that allows you to grow from adversity and make meaning of even adverse life events.

In neurology, adversity will usually be understood as stress – a response to a perceived threat or challenge, which triggers a cascade of physiological and psychological changes in the body. These days, stress is usually framed negatively. People suffer from depression triggered by stress; people leave work because of stress. However, a certain amount of adversity can be good for you. Back in 1991, a small group of scientists and ecologists shut themselves in a huge, dome-like structure, the Biosphere 2, in the town of Oracle, Arizona. Biosphere 2 (our planet is Biosphere 1) was an attempt to create a complete, self-sustaining ecosystem that could, for instance, provide valuable lessons on how to build colonies in space. Not everything went well but the scientists made valuable observations. One of the most surprising things was the trees. In the beginning, they grew fast. However, long before they reached maturity, they toppled over and died. They had plenty of sunlight, the soil was nutritious and they had access to water. So, what happened? It turns out that trees need wind. The wind stresses the young trees, forcing them to grow stronger and develop what's sometimes called 'stress wood', particularly at the base. Without the wind, the trees didn't produce stress wood and withered away at a young age. This process is known as hormesis and is defined as a phenomenon in which a harmful action gives stimulating and beneficial effects to living organisms when the quantity of the destructive action isn't overwhelming.

While chronic stress accelerates biological ageing, hormetic stress improves ageing because it activates protective mechanisms all over your body that have anti-ageing biological effects. Your body reacts the same way as the trees, as any person who has spent even just a few weeks immobilised in a hospital bed or otherwise has been bedridden will know. Muscle atrophy sets in and limbs lose their strength. They need the stress of daily tasks to stay strong and healthy. I've illustrated this below. To the left, you'll find a cross-section of the thighs of a 40-year-old triathlete. The white dots in the middle are femurs, surrounded by muscle in the dark and fat in the white. To the right, you'll find the same cross-section of a 74-year-old sedentary person and recognise that muscle has been substituted by fat. The femurs have also reduced in size. However, below these you'll see that this ageing process is neither automatic nor irreversible. A 74-year-old triathlete has the same muscle-to-fat ratio as a 40-year-old triathlete. Uplifting.

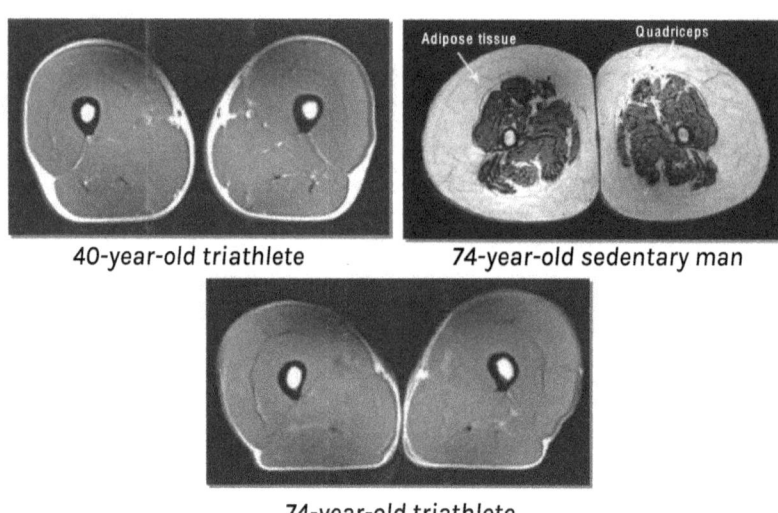

40-year-old triathlete   74-year-old sedentary man

74-year-old triathlete

Figure 13: The impact of hormesis: cross-sections of thighs. Source: Wroblewski et al 2011

Regular exercise both decreases the risk of falling and reduces the negative impact should you fall. If this isn't a good reason to perform physical activity such as squats and running, then I don't know what is. Now, bodily stress is one thing but science shows us that the mind isn't that different. Chronic stress can have adverse effects on physical and mental health. It's considered a danger to your wellbeing and I've had clients who have suffered from acute and life-threatening reactions. The brain plays a crucial role in the stress response by releasing stress hormones such as cortisol and adrenaline. These hormones activate the body's fight or flight response, which increases heart rate, blood pressure and glucose levels, among other things.

Suppose you're constantly in this state of alert. In that case, you're at increased risk of a number of adverse health outcomes, including an increased risk of cardiovascular disease, depression, anxiety and cognitive impairment. Research has also shown that chronic stress can alter the structure and function of the hippocampus, a brain region involved in memory and learning, which may contribute to cognitive impairments. Many people suffering from prolonged periods of stress complain that their short-term memory has practically gone, and it's often the last thing to switch back on after a stressful period. Some people feel as if they'll never return to the same state as before. They call it 'brain fog'.

Chronic stress has also been linked to immune dysfunction and chronic inflammation, which could contribute to developing certain neurological disorders such as multiple sclerosis. However, it's equally important to underline that moderate stress levels can be beneficial. Just consider the excitement many people feel before an important interview, an exam or a sports game. Stress hormones kick in and help to increase focus, motivation and performance. Research has shown that stress can also enhance the immune response, which can be beneficial in fighting off infections or illnesses – and it can also build mental and physical resilience.

Mark Seery, an American psychologist at the University of Buffalo, published a controversial paper in 2010, 'Whatever does not kill us'. He challenged the belief that traumatic events always increase our risk of illness, depression and anxiety. His study showed that people with a history of adversity and adverse life events will sometimes be protected against those outcomes because they have a certain amount of resilience. However, there's a sweet spot. Too little and too much adversity harms the quality of life. It may seem counterintuitive but the people who have lived a life with minimal struggle are less happy and healthy than those who have faced a certain number of stressful events and periods. Based on the famous saying, Seery concludes that 'these results suggest that, in moderation, whatever does not kill us may indeed make us stronger'.

> Moderate stress levels can be beneficial

Acute stress can also be a positive experience, such as the rush of adrenaline felt during a thrilling adventure, which can be exciting and enjoyable. You may have experienced it at work, during a challenging project or task where everything was happening at speed and with the sense of electrifying excitement that your adrenaline rush will provide. Additionally, moderate amounts of stress can help to challenge and push us out of our comfort zones, leading to personal growth and development. Stress can also be an opportunity for learning and developing coping mechanisms.

The effects of stress vary from person to person and you can probably also recollect times when you found it easier to cope with stress than others. Sometimes, small and seemingly inconsequential things can stress us out; sometimes, we'll walk through turmoil and still feel a certain calm. It depends on the circumstances. Stress management techniques draw from the same coping techniques as cognitive psychology and stoicism. Behavioural therapy, mindfulness and physical activity effectively reduce stress and its adverse effects on the brain and body. However, it's also necessary to consider the workload and the stress factors you're exposed to.

Questions to ask yourself

- What do you long for? And why isn't it in your life right now?
- If you want to be your own hero in ten years' time, what must you do?
- How do you find the resilience to get through hard times?
- How do you discover when to recharge your energy and care for yourself?

Part 3
Going further

Chapter 7
Navigating the wider perspective

Some of the people I speak to feel that the world is falling apart and don't understand the changing cultural currents and shifting paradigms. It fuels the confusion and sense of meaninglessness that some already experience, especially when you doubt your priorities and future. It can seem self-indulgent to improve your own life when so many others live in appalling conditions and the climate crisis threatens to end humanity as we know it. But the 'end times' have always been with us, looking different for each generation, who nevertheless survived. And times and paradigms have constantly been changing. To understand yourself and to find meaning and clarity, you need to see yourself from a wider perspective. The philosophers help us to do that.

When the twin towers fell in New York on 11 September 2001, I was in an office in Copenhagen, Denmark, immersed in a complicated Excel sheet – probably one that felt dreadfully important at the time. Somebody behind me said a plane had just crashed into one of the towers. I imagined a small two-seater hitting the building like a tiny mosquito on an arm. And, figuratively, I just brushed it off. While I did that, the world changed.

I think of this episode whenever people, especially middle-aged men like me, brush something off as unimportant – something life changing. We're so used to a default dismissal of new, disturbing facts or ideas that it takes a conscious effort to take in new information that might challenge our understanding and self-perception. As the author Mark Manson (2016) puts it, 'The more something threatens your identity, the more you will avoid it.'

We can learn from history but the future doesn't fit into the containers of the past. We must be able to adjust our way of thinking, and neurology teaches us that this is possible, regardless of age. But we don't have to forsake the wisdom we have accumulated. We must find new ways to apply it. Why is all this relevant in a book about your existence? Because none of us exists separately from our times. You may be uncomfortable with some of the societal shifts but being aware of them and your values makes it easier to navigate. You don't have to embrace new paradigms as your own but when you begin to understand them and keep an open mind about them, it becomes easier to engage with them instead of feeling threatened – as many of us do when we face change. Slow down and look your monsters in the eye. As the saying goes, 'Wisdom has been chasing you, but you have always been faster.'

Cultural changes

How we think about ourselves, others and society changes constantly. Sometimes in profound and ground-shaking ways, at other times as small but persistent steps that eventually change the culture and the established way of thinking. This also means we must adjust our sense of how and where we belong in this world. The original definition of a paradigm shift was solely reserved for the natural sciences – the concept was coined by the American physicist and philosopher Thomas Kuhn in 1962. He described how science develops and a paradigm shift is a fundamental change in a scientific discipline, a revolution. In this definition, the new paradigm always replaces the old one and is considered an improvement, not just a change. When Charles Darwin developed his theory of evolution, the paradigm of natural selection replaced the one that all species had been created by a godly power. However, the concept has also entered the social sciences and is now used to describe how society progresses when we change how we understand or think about our world and how it should be. With paradigm shifts also comes a change in perceptions, ideals and values.

When we talk about paradigm shifts today, we often mean cultural ones.

To name but one example, once it was acceptable to keep people as slaves. Today, in most societies, it's considered unthinkably cruel. That change, of course, is about more than just slavery. It's also about more subtle changes, about recognising human dignity in all, regardless of situation and background, and it's a step towards realising that colour and ethnicity shouldn't matter when assessing another human being. The right for women to vote is another example. That right was the legal change, just as it took legal action to abolish slavery. But behind it are other changes: how we think about gender and the expectations and roles we attribute to them.

We casually use the term paradigm shift for small developments and changes. However, for something to be a true paradigm shift, it must be a fundamental change – a point of no return, at least in the natural sciences. In the social sciences, it may be more likely that colliding paradigms thrive side by side. Today's identity politics imply as much. But there's rarely any going back within the individuals, the groups and organisations that have adopted a new paradigm. Once you've agreed that slavery is cruel and misogyny unacceptable, that's it. Even in the unlikely event that slavery was once again made legal, your values would likely prevent you from finding it acceptable to keep enslaved people.

Some paradigms shift through many small changes that accumulate until they become sufficient to bring about a major change

Significant events can bring on paradigm shifts. The medieval Black Death not only wiped out perhaps half of Europe's population but was also a cause of fundamental cultural change. If you could die suddenly and without warning, a legacy was important. However, some paradigms shift through many small changes that accumulate until they become sufficient to bring about a major change. While we're part of the change, it may be challenging to identify what will eventually become a paradigm shift, not just a trend or a development. Still, I think that the

#MeToo movement had the power to lead to fundamental changes in how we talk about sex, gender, gender equality, equity and consent. The rapid rise in the acceptance of homosexuality and the LGBTQ+ debates in many countries also reflect minor changes that add to a paradigm shift, but not always everywhere and rarely at once. Cultural paradigm shifts can be flimsy and don't always withstand the test of time.

Last but not least, I'll leave you with an image. Do you know how a tightrope walker uses her balancing pole to keep balance? By carrying a pole horizontally in her hands, the tightrope walker increases her moment of inertia, ie she minimises her body's 'rotation' around the rope. The length of the pole also plays an important role: the longer the pole, the better it is for stability. Now then, do you know what happens when a tightrope walker slips and falls? There's ample evidence that the tightrope walker instinctively clings to her balancing pole even when falling to her death. Why? Well, because it's her safety guarantee. Just like your paradigms. If nothing else works, you'll instinctively cling to your paradigms, your safety guarantee, even when they don't serve you anymore.

A chance to do better

Paradigm shifts are almost always difficult to wrap your head around. Darwin's theories have been the subject of heated disputes, and cultural shifts towards or away from secularism are hard fought. As I write this, the debate about gender and identity seems to be as heated as ever and progress can never be taken for granted, as several backslides into a more conservative and authoritarian agenda demonstrate.

Paradigm shifts often feel personal. If your values are rooted in a paradigm that's challenged, a shift can feel like a personal attack on your identity. I hear many people express confusion at some of the current cultural changes and feel it myself when I debate with my children, their friends or my students. For the same reason, my wife and I make it a priority to have friends who are younger than us. They challenge our perspectives and views. They keep us on our toes and force us to reconsider assumptions that we'd comfortably stored in the 'that's just how things are' drawer of our daily lives. If you ever find yourself opposing an idea with the words 'that's just unnatural', you could well be facing a paradigm shift. We tend to defend the current cultural state of our worldview with what we consider to be natural.

However, if you think about it, your paradigms and views have probably also shifted numerous times throughout your life. You can adapt to new ways of thinking while using your experience to cut through and neglect what's just a fad or less critical. But be honest with yourself. It's easy to dismiss new ideas and thoughts with 'been there, tried that, didn't work' or 'that goes against logic'. You must stay open and curious.

Being trained as an economist, I saw growth as the foundation for business and how to do things. If there was economic growth, sustainability could then be added. However, my children, their partners and colleagues abide by different values. They see sustainability as the foundation on which growth can be built. They think more fluidly and circularly; they think of networks rather than hierarchies and find value in collaboration rather than competition. They have no problem reaching out for or giving help, something that I've had trouble with (at least the former) and I know from my conversations with clients that the same goes for many of them. We've adapted to a paradigm where striving to be the best is worthy. This usually also means coming across as somebody strong, somebody who can make decisions, beat others and is rarely in doubt. Otherwise, you're probably not the best. This is a rough and somewhat parodic description of a more nuanced reality but if you consider your life to be a staircase where you must get to the top, there are only two directions: up or down. There's a shift here, as expressed to me by my children. They and their peers think differently. And so it has been throughout human history. Different generations have different ideas, values and perceptions, but at least to me, it feels as if something profound is going on right now. We're in the middle of paradigm shifts that could shape our future and – if used constructively – make way for a more just and benevolent society.

You must stay open and curious

This may all sound overly optimistic. When you look around or read the news, it's easy to feel a kind of despair. Climate change is looming and we must still deal with pandemics. Russia has invaded Ukraine, adding millions of new refugees to the already staggering number of displaced people around the world. Israel has declared war on Hamas, which attacked Israel. Nuclear war is no longer a thing of the past but a real danger looming in the headlines. The gap in opportunities is widening, stock markets are on a rollercoaster of seemingly unpredictable ups and downs and more countries are sliding away from democracy into something less liberal and enlightened. It is indeed a time characterised by unpredictability, limitlessness and structurelessness. We're part of a new era in which change has become systemic. What was right yesterday may already be questionable today and wrong tomorrow.

According to James Crutchfield (1996), distinguished professor of physics at UC Davis, 'Our brains have a certain capacity for detecting regularity. To the extent that the world matches these characteristics of ours, we can see structure and pattern. To the extent that behaviour in the world exceeds our capacities, the excess amount of sophistication in the stimulus is lost on us and turns into randomness, into apparent structurelessness that we can't represent.' From a motivational point of view, one may say that obstacles are the things you see when you take your eyes off the target. Very often there's more noise than signal.

> What was right yesterday may already be questionable today and wrong tomorrow

My take on this is that we need to develop a 'pattern recognition' mind, creating collective meaning out of individual perceptions. To me, it represents higher-order thinking. A brilliant example of this is Elon Musk, who uses Aristotle's 'first principles thinking', a mode of enquiry that relentlessly pursues the foundations of a problem. In an interview with *Business Insider* (Baer 2015), he said: 'The normal way we conduct our lives is we reason by analogy. We are doing this because it's like something else that was done, or it is like what other people are doing. With first principles you boil things down to the most fundamental truths... and then reason up from there.' The results of this way of thinking are Musk's ground-breaking companies Tesla, SpaceX (and perhaps his transition of Twitter to X?). So much for conventional wisdom! A second reason behind Musk's visionary achievements is that he performs sequential multi-tasking, meaning that he fully focuses on one problem at a time before going on to the next, only interrupted by computer games. A third reason for Musk's breakthrough results is perhaps his negotiation style. He's known for saying, 'A yes is a yes. A maybe is a yes. A no is a conditional yes.'

In times like this, how do we make sense of what's happening? Why even bother? I speak with a worrying number of people who seem to expect this to be the end of the world as we know it. Newspaper headlines are all gloom and doom. Enjoying yourself can feel almost sinful when the world around you seems to be dissolving. Thriving can look like a selfish luxury. Even time for inward reflection and searching for meaning may seem self-indulgent. Shouldn't you be doing something worthwhile instead of contemplating how to make your own life better? It's a false dichotomy. There seems to be an artificial opposition between the bonds of community and individual freedom. Indeed, doing something worthwhile and working towards making the world a better place will help most people thrive. At the core of thriving is a deep sense of meaning: what you do is meaningful. As we're a social species, this will frequently involve helping others in one way or another, as I mentioned earlier. So, there's no real dilemma here. You can make thriving and a meaningful life noble aims without being selfish. Self-interest can be a common interest.

Short downs, long ups

However, I question that the times are as dark as they seem to many people. I'm not talking about people who are personally going through a crisis or suffering from poverty, diseases, injustice, war or oppression. Their suffering is real and shouldn't be neglected or waved off as unimportant. I'm talking about people who generally feel that society and the world are heading in the wrong direction. The problems we're dealing with globally and nationally need urgent attention. And yet, when you look beyond the immediate challenges and issues and consider the broader perspective, there's a lot to celebrate.

It may seem banal, but there have always been ups and downs

throughout history. And yet, when you look at it, the overall trend is hugely positive. The world is in so many ways a better place now than 100 or 1,000 years ago. Things don't move up and down from a fixed baseline. The curve moves upwards and setbacks don't usually last long. We tend to catch up and then progress reasonably fast. In his 2018 masterpiece *Factfulness*, Hans Rosling clearly demonstrates this.

The stock market, of course, isn't proof of anything apart from the investment climate. Economists often remind people that the stock market is not the economy. Low unemployment and rising real wages have much more relevance to most people's lives. However, the stock market has been pretty good at reflecting the overall tendencies and new highs rapidly replace huge dips. Even severe economic crises such as the one we experienced from 2008 until 2012 don't cause lasting damage to the overall development. They can be devastating for individuals and groups and the current levels of polarisation and turns towards populism and social unrest are at least to some extent rooted in the sense of being deprived of opportunities that many experienced in the early 2000s, the so-called 'lost decade'. But it's essential to keep the overall upward trend in view.

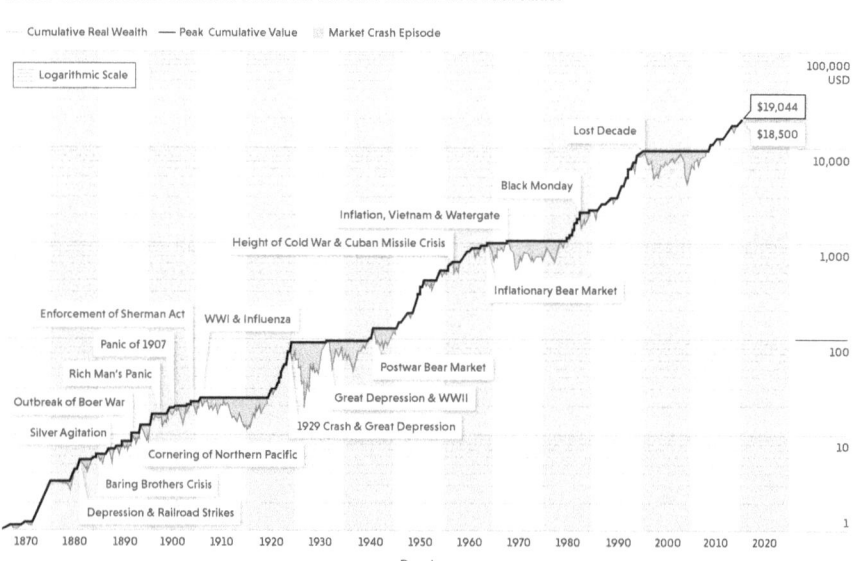

Figure 14: Market crash timeline: the growth of $1. Source: Kaplan (2020)

In this figure you may recognise some seismic events: the Second World War, the oil crisis of the early 1970s, the end of the Cold War and China opening towards the West at the end of the 1980s. In the 2020s, we're experiencing a fourth seismic event combining the wars in Israel and Ukraine, the Covid-19 pandemic, high inflation and China's new role, with decreased growth. The word of the day is 'permacrisis'. Historians call this an open historical situation. One of my clients described it as running in quicksand. Russia's invasion and war with Ukraine is also highly unusual. Since the Second World War, conflicts between nations in Europe have dwindled remarkably. So has the number of people killed by war, both directly and indirectly. The world isn't necessarily more peaceful but the conflicts tend to be less deadly and nations generally solve their mutual disagreements with means other than war.

Death by communicable diseases has fallen dramatically and so has infant mortality. As a result, more people die at a ripe old age. When we debate the so-called overpopulation, we often overlook that the global birth rate has more than halved in a few decades. In 2022, the medical journal *The Lancet* published a study that showed that the global population could fall below the current level by the end of the century because the birth rate has fallen so significantly in most countries. One of the fundamental differences between today and the world 100 years ago is that we live to be so much older. Almost half of the nearly 60 million people who die annually across the world are over 70 years old. In a century, the global life expectancy has doubled and is now around 74 years. And no country in the world has a lower life expectancy today than the highest 100 years ago.

One of the fundamental differences between today and the world 100 years ago is that we live to be so much older

Malnourishment is still a global challenge but it has changed. Famines are becoming rare and more people die from conditions stemming from obesity and poor diets than from hunger. Nearly all children go to school and get some degree of education, regardless of gender, and while inequality in opportunities has risen, poverty is decreasing. And despite recent setbacks to democracy, the world is still more democratic now than it was 50 years ago.

While it's true that climate change is a looming disaster that's already negatively affecting millions of people, the world is also making progress when it comes to a transition into a carbon-neutral society. There has never been more of us to deal with the problem, nor have we been so well connected to pool our shared knowledge and ingenuity.

We're exposed to adverse events

So, how come so many people feel that the world is falling apart? One reason is that we're preoccupied with what's harmful. It's a survival mechanism to scan our environment for dangers and developments that could threaten us. The media enhances this. The news reflects events that are sudden and unusual. Progress is not. As the Canadian psychologist and author Steven Pinker has noticed, progress rarely happens on a Monday in October. It's ongoing, with setbacks and jumps forward, but usually, there's so little to report on that it goes unnoticed by the media. Accidents, murder, wars, famines – all of these are much more likely to make headlines because they represent a deviation from the norm.

Pinker, who wrote the book *The Better Angels of Our Nature* (2011) about how the world has progressed, stresses another point. Western intellectualism prides itself on being sceptical and critical. Optimists are generally considered naïve, whereas intellectuals emphasising what's wrong with society and humanity are considered wise. And yet, the optimists have the facts on their side. The world is progressing, just not in an even way. Neither should we take progress for granted. We've become accustomed to the West shaping most of the past couple of centuries, with liberal democracy being the gold standard of rule and enlightenment. But empires and civilisations have dwindled before and they don't usually disappear with a bang and a flash but with a slow and painful whisper. Progress is something that must be nurtured.

You undoubtedly know the expression 'This, too, shall pass'. You may also know the story behind it. A king asked his wise counsellor to find him a quote that would cheer him up when he was feeling down and remind him to be humble when things were going well, which would always be true. The counsellor pondered the task but then gravely presented the king with this sentence: 'This, too, shall pass.' The king was so pleased that he had the words engraved in a ring. It remains a wise sentence. The current catastrophes will one day be history, hopefully sooner rather than later. But the same goes for all the privileges we enjoy. The world is a far better place today than it was 50 years ago but not for all and not by any law of nature. It's something that we must fight for. And though we can all feel the occasional sense of despair over current developments, perhaps it's wise to remember that this has been the case throughout human history. Prophets and doomsayers have endlessly declared the end of times.

However, there's no doubt that we're entering a new era. From a geopolitical, political and economic perspective, we're leaving behind three decades characterised by integration, free markets and deflation and moving into an uncertain future of fragmentation, trade wars and inflation. The main cost of these paradigm shifts stems from three factors: rewiring the global supply chain, moving from maximum efficiency to maximum resilience, and massive investments in decarbonisation. China, aspiring to become the most significant game player on the planet, is on the rise. It seems as if the recent past is already a couple of light years ago.

Progress is something that must be nurtured

Many younger leaders have never tried navigating this kind of adversity. It isn't a cyclical but a structural break. We're moving away from a period of extraordinary harmony. And now, we're experiencing a transition from strong, sustained growth to limiting factors and supply constraints. Just look at the workforce situation. Let's push despair aside. We have a chance to make the world a better place and current paradigm shifts could contribute if we understand them and handle them wisely.

Philosophy is also a work in progress

These changes are also reflected in different schools of thought among philosophers and vice versa. How the dominant thinkers view Self, relationships and society also enables and enhances paradigm shifts. My professional and academic careers have led me to define three schools of thought: the rational school, the emotional school and the existential school. Throughout the book, I've tried to synthesise how thinkers within philosophy, psychology, neurology and strategy have cross-fertilised each other through the past century. For the reader wanting to get into more detail, it's perhaps helpful to have an overview of the different schools of thought here. Though they're philosophical, they both influence and are influenced by other academic disciplines and sciences.

The key table opposite summarises some trends and gives an indication of where we're headed. This isn't a snapshot but rather a metaphorical scenario that should provide inspiration and provoke new associations.

Seen from an epochal perspective, the pendulum has swung back into the middle position. First, the extreme point was external focus (the rational outside-in school). Then the opposite extreme became internal focus (the emotional inside-out school). My synthesis is that now both points of view are on the way to becoming integrated into an inside and outside point of view with velocity and collaboration as central concepts. A new existential era has begun – a more balanced era with due respect for past paradigms. As Aristotle puts it, 'It is the mark of an educated mind to be able to entertain a thought without accepting it.'

One defining paradigm shift came courtesy of Descartes. Mathematics was central to his method of inquiry. He connected the previously separate fields of geometry and algebra into analytic geometry and introduced scepticism as an essential part of the scientific method. The rational school can be described in terms of hardware. My interpretation is that in postwar Western societies, there has been a strong reaction against this rational thought pattern. Taken too far, it doesn't allow for emotions, mystery, wonder. This reaction was perhaps most vividly represented by the student revolts in the 1960s and the ensuing youth rebellion, which to some extent morphed into the New Age movement with its distrust of authorities and conventional wisdom.

	The rational school	**The emotional school**	**The existential school**
Maxim	I think, therefore I am	I feel, therefore I am	I act, therefore I am
Focus	Object	Subject	Self
Approach	Thesis	Antithesis	Synthesis
Lens	Outside-in	Inside-out	Holistic
Perspective	Top-down	Bottom-up	Both-and
Attitude	Hard	Soft	Pragmatic
Measure	Quantity	Quality	Impact
Brain	Left brain	Right brain	Third eye
Preference	Deductive	Inductive	Abductive
Goal	Product	Process	Mastery
Slogan	Doing things right	Doing the right things	Doing the right things right
Radiation	Seriousness	Passion	Relaxed readiness
Success	Results	Relationships	Role model
Contribution	Management	Leadership	Service
Intelligence	IQ	EQ	Meta

Table 4: Three schools of thought: rational, emotional and existential

Lately, the general rejection of new public management, with its focus on strict measurement and output, underpins this development. And in more sinister ways, so does the rise of conspiracy theories and the rejection of science. The American science fiction author Isaac Asimov – who wrote the *Foundation* books and theorised on robots and conscience – lamented this in an essay from 1980: 'The strain of anti-intellectualism has been a constant thread winding its way through our political and cultural life, nurtured by the false notion that democracy means that my ignorance is just as good as your knowledge.'

The trend towards the emotional school ('I feel, therefore I am'), focusing on social justice, animal rights, empathy and collaboration, can be explained in terms of software. There's also a spiritual element to this. A longing, perhaps, for an understanding of ourselves and our existence that goes beyond whatever can be explained in terms of scientific formulae and rationality. A meaning that's defined not only by rational explanations but also by a sense that values matter and that we aim for something higher and not only for ourselves: a longing for the wondrous. My perhaps overly optimistic synthesis is that we're now primarily dealing with the existential school ('I act, therefore I am'). Amid complexity, data overload and the looming global crisis, it's no longer sufficient to think or to feel. It takes a long time to finish something that you're not working on. If something is important to you, then focus on it, and if not, then don't. But don't say that something is important to you if you don't do anything about it.

As individuals, we all need to act. We need to choose and take responsibility for our actions. However, we shouldn't discard rationality or emotions as valid reasons to act. Instead, we should go beyond rational and emotional in our quest for meaning. We gain integrity and the agency to act by integrating hardware and software. This is why existentialism is the main philosophy in my practice.

For ease of understanding, let me introduce some key characteristics from the above table, school by school.

The rational school: 'I think, therefore I am.'
Object, thesis, outside-in, top-down, hard, quantity, left brain, deductive, product, doing things right, seriousness, results, management, IQ.

The emotional school: 'I feel, therefore I am.'
Subject, antithesis, inside-out, bottom-up, soft, quality, right brain, inductive, process, doing the right things, passion, relationships, leadership, EQ.

The existential school: 'I act, therefore I am.'
Self, synthesis, holistic, both-and, pragmatic, impact, third eye, abductive, mastery, doing the right things right, relaxed readiness, role model, service, meta.

There's no doubt that my business school education had me solidly anchored in the rational school. However, experience has taught me that it's OK to trust my intuition. So, for some time I've adhered to the emotional school. Even though intuition isn't always 100 per cent correct, it always takes me in the right direction and creates a better position to act from. The existential school appeals to me because it emphasises action. I've interviewed and coached so many competent people, masters of communication, and have grown tired of all the words. You can't talk yourself out of a situation that you've behaved yourself into. I need to see the end result in the form of action to judge the quality of the thinking and the argument. And that's where I am now.

Why not stay in La-La Land?

Undoubtedly, the rational school is the most austere, the emotional school the most comfortable and the existential school, with its emphasis on choice, action and responsibility, the most demanding. So why not stay in La-La Land? After all, it's a nice place to be. However, after some time, it becomes less satisfying. In order to thrive, we all need challenges – both physical and mental. Remember that the right amount of stress can be beneficial and indeed necessary to help us grow. The law of diminishing returns also works in this context. And let's not neglect the fact that emotions can also be damaging. Dictators and populists know how to use fear, hatred and rage to stay in power. Adding to this, the climate, biodiversity and social justice crises all demand action. Few of us will be morally inclined to ignore those crises to stay comfortable, even though it sometimes seems the obvious answer. We can all become exhausted when things get tough and the tasks seem infinite.

Words have many meanings and I could've chosen other characteristics to describe these three schools of thought. However, I've worked on these characteristics for more than ten years and they've passed the time test in my practice.

So far, I've mentioned the overarching schools of thought but we also see shifts on a smaller scale – trends rather than schools, although they certainly influence and are influenced by the existing paradigms and values. Notice, for instance, the way we nickname some decades, such as 'the Roaring Twenties', 'the Swinging Sixties', or 'the Greedy Eighties', to summarise the dominant cultural themes of different periods. It is with a sense of curiosity that I observe the recent changes in the economic cycle. In the 2010s, we discussed a renaissance of the Roaring Twenties. Everything was set for a new growth era. Then came Covid-19, the war in Europe and the energy crisis. Everything changed. And undoubtedly, it will change back to a period of progress and optimism sometime in the future. Under these and other challenging future circumstances, the characteristics mentioned above will serve you well and help you find solid ground in changing paradigms.

In order to thrive, we all need challenges

You'll find a more thorough timeline of what preceded the existential school in Appendix 2 (page 203), which presents a timeline of existential thinkers by school. This is the academic foundation upon which I've based my three schools of thought. Now, let's have a look at how our four disciplines underpin my three schools of thought.

Neurology in its present form is a relatively young science but humanity has been curious about the brain for centuries. In the 16th century, thinkers and scientists became interested in our nervous system. Descartes was interested in the mind and our ability to think and he also pondered the connection between a stimulus and our reaction towards it and whether this was created by way of nerves. Throughout the 18th and 19th centuries, scientists made progress in discovering and describing aspects of the brain and the nervous system, including visualisation of neurons and brain cells, as well as understanding how brain segments deal with different parts of the body. The Russian physiologist Ivan Pavlov famously developed the principles of conditioning by demonstrating that dogs could be trained to behave in a specific way by stimulating them. The dogs would begin to salivate at the sound of a bell after having learned that the bell meant food.

In the late 19th century, brain science received so much attention that several hospitals and universities founded schools and centres to study the brain and nervous system. In the early 20th century, different aspects of neurology received the Nobel Prize, among them the work of British neurophysiologist **Charles Scott Sherrington**, who defined several aspects of neuroscience and was particularly interested in the nervous system and its function. He coined the word synapse – the connection between brain cells or neurons. Still, thanks to the German-British physician and biophysicist Bernard Katz, it wasn't until 1962 that it was proven that neurotransmission between neurons is due to synapses. The 1960s were, in many ways, the decade when neuroscience took off. Scientific progress in other fields such as medical imaging allowed a closer study of the brain and nervous system. Neuroscience became an academic field at top universities.

You may notice the near absence of women in Appendix 2. It seems that philosophy, psychology, neurology and strategy since antiquity have been Caucasian men's worlds, meaning that most thinking has been seriously biased. One notable exception is the feminist **Simone de Beauvoir** – the high priestess of existentialism – born in 1908.

You may also notice that there was a fresh start in all four disciplines at the beginning of the last century:

- **1905**: The philosopher Jean-Paul Sartre was born; he published *Nausea* in 1938. Though he became famous during the tumultuous 1960s, Sartre remained a simple man with few possessions. He also remained committed to causes. During the student revolution of May 1968, he was arrested for civil disobedience. However, President Charles de Gaulle intervened and pardoned him, commenting, 'You don't arrest Voltaire.' Throughout his life, Sartre remained fiercely independent. In 1945 he refused the Légion d'Honneur and in 1964, he was the first Nobel Prize laureate to decline the prize voluntarily.

- **1905**: The psychologist **Viktor E Frankl** was born; he published *Man's Search for Meaning* in 1946. As opposed to the French existentialists, Frankl thought that the meaning of life resulted from a discovery and not a choice. So, the purpose of life is life itself. Each one of us has a specific task that needs to be done – a calling or a mission. Frankl writes that the reason he survived Holocaust was his determination to write a book describing his theory of logotherapy, or 'healing through meaning'.
- **1906**: The political philosopher **Hannah Arendt** was born; she published *The Origins of Totalitarianism* in 1951. In this seminal work she describes and analyses Nazism and Stalinism as the major totalitarian political movements of the first half of the 20th century. In *The Human Condition* (1958), Arendt explains how 'human activities' should be and have been understood throughout Western history. She distinguishes three sorts of activity (labour, work and action) and discusses how they have been affected by changes in Western history. We'll return to this in Chapter 8.
- **1908**: Another notable psychologist, **Abraham Maslow**, was born. He created his hierarchy of needs, a theory of psychological health predicated on fulfilling innate human needs in priority, culminating in self-actualisation. Maslow defined self-actualisation as achieving the fullest use of one's talents and interests – the need to 'become everything that one is capable of becoming' – much in line with Frankl's thinking.

All in all, there's a significant alignment between these schools of thought. Frankl would see the meaning of life as an intrinsic dimension to be discovered and Sartre would see life as an extrinsic dimension to be chosen. Both work under the umbrella of potential to be realised or to be chosen. Maslow coined the term self-actualisation, which has been a driver for much of the personal development arena ever since. As Clayton Christensen advises, 'Don't reserve your best business thinking for your career.' Warren Buffett puts it this way: 'Ultimately, there's one investment that supersedes all others: invest in yourself.' And Hannah Arendt put all of this in a political context, emphasising the role of the state as opposed to the activities of the individual.

- **1909**: Turning to strategy, **Peter Drucker** was born in Austria in 1909 and later moved to the United States. He's often considered to be the father of modern management for his ground-breaking business and organisational theory. Drucker was influenced by various streams of thought, including Austrian economics, existentialism and his observations of the human condition within organisations. It's no coincidence that individual development correlates with organisational development. After all, individuals make up organisations. Drucker was among the first to recognise the importance of 'knowledge workers' in the economy, anticipating the shift from an industrial to a knowledge-based society. He also consulted for major corporations and nonprofits, further extending his influence. Drucker wrote numerous books but his first, *The End of Economic Man: A Study of the New Totalitarianism* from 1939, was among his most important.
- **1909**: The neurobiologist **Rita Levi-Montalcini** was born; she was later awarded the Nobel Prize for her discovery of nerve growth factor (NGF), primarily involved in the regulation of growth, maintenance, proliferation and survival of certain target nerve cells. All living organisms are made of cells. A cell is the basic unit of life that's responsible for the functioning of organisms. So, our lives depend on it. Fun fact: on 22 April 2009, Levi-Montalcini became the first Nobel laureate to reach the age of 100.
- **1918**: Neurology took a new turn with the birth of **Brenda Milner**, who's considered to be the 'mother of neuropsychology'. As described earlier, neuropsychology is a branch of psychology concerned with how a person's cognition and behaviour are related to the brain and the rest of the nervous system. Professionals in this branch of psychology often focus on how injuries or illnesses of the brain affect cognitive and behavioural functions. Milner focused on the study of

memory and other cognitive functions in humankind. Fun fact: at the time of writing, Milner is still alive.

The only thing that separates all these seminal works is the Second World War, so one may argue that they are parallel. This is at least how I see it in the greater historical perspective.

In this light, I've always been fascinated by wave theory. The idea was conceived by Russian economist Nikolai Kondratiev and later popularised by Austrian economist **Joseph Schumpeter**. From an epochal perspective it's possible to document some overall long-term economic waves of approximately 30 years' duration with, for example, the following peaks and valleys: La Belle Époque, the crisis of the 1930s, the cool 1960s and the digital 1990s. Perhaps we're now in the sustainable 2020s.

In the medium term, it's possible to describe waves of approximately ten-year durations, such as the oil crisis of the 1970s; the conservatism and free market economics 'new questions' era of the 1980s; the postmodernism of the 1990s; the big tech, globalisation, terrorism and financial crisis of the 2000s; the mobile revolution, social media, climate activism, rise of AI and #MeToo of the 2010s; and the Covid-19, remote work, war in Europe and deglobalisation 'decisive decade' for climate action of the 2020s.

In the short term, it's possible to identify a few buzzwords, which last approximately three years and are replaced by the next (according to the management consultants) eternally blissful concept. Among many other examples we can mention disruption (2017–19), digital transformation (2018–20), remote work (2019–21), sustainability and ESG (2020–22), the metaverse (2021–23), and hybrid work (2022–24). Each of these concepts builds on a long research tradition but on each occasion is presented as news. My teaching experience has clearly shown me the volatility of these buzzword cycles. My students at Copenhagen Business School invariably think they're truly original in their choice of master thesis subject. However, with my outside-in perspective, it becomes evident that their choice is governed by the buzzwords of the day. As the social scientists Maxwell McCombs' and Donald Shaw's agenda-setting theory (1972) puts it: 'Media don't tell us what to think. Media tell us what to think about.'

Let's now move on from wave theory to work theory. The work domain is undergoing tectonic changes, blurring the boundaries between private and professional. Being centred on your values and understanding that change is natural, unavoidable and a chance to grow will help you when everything else seems in turmoil. You can still be connected and present, finding the ground to stand on and a lever long enough to move the Earth.

Questions to ask yourself

- Is the world, as you see it, better or worse today than in your youth? List three ways it is better and where you see it as worse.
- Consider what makes you feel that way – write down key words next to each subject.
- Do you remember to reserve sufficient time regularly to reflect on your life and actions? How about dedicating two hours every week to this?
- How are you trying to improve the world around you?

Chapter 8
How to thrive at work

We're seeing a massive shift in how and why we work. AI will transform work and is seen as both an opportunity and a threat. Young generations demand meaning and purpose, not just a pay cheque. All ages are discovering that there's more to life than work, especially if your job feels trivial, meaningless, unethical or unhealthy. This, in turn, is causing a shift in our leadership expectations. Values and authenticity, credibility, understanding human nature and how to engage people rather than boss them around are becoming sought-after qualities. As new leadership paradigms evolve, so does the idea that leadership isn't a title but an intrinsic responsibility for all of us, both inside and outside work. This chapter explores cultural shifts, how they align with your desire to reinvent yourself and how you can lead a meaningful life. It also introduces my new model of leadership, the Nordic Leadership Model.

Are you listened to and respected because of your hierarchical position or because you're you? Quite a few of my clients are grappling with this question. They fear that losing their position will also cause them to lose whatever makes them valued and respected by others. That could make it difficult to reinvent yourself. You have something to lose, not just a lovely home, car and school for the children. Feeling valued and appreciated is crucial to our wellbeing and sense of belonging and we tend to tie that value and appreciation to our formal position.

However, it doesn't have to be that way. I know a man in his early fifties who used to be the CEO of a big international company.

Eventually, he quit. He took a break for a couple of years, trying to figure out what he wanted to do next while sharing his knowledge with start-ups and entrepreneurs, nurturing their ambitions. He had many thoughts about what makes society work and eventually, he wrote a book about it, which was very well received. It began a new phase for him: he's now a respected board member and keynote speaker. 'People used to call me and wanted to talk to me because I was the CEO. Now they call me to hear what I have to say. Not from any position of power but because they find my views interesting. It's liberating,' he says.

I'm using this example because most of us feel that our value to society is in our workplace work, in other words, our job. The visible proof of our value is the money that flows (or trickles) into the bank account regularly; the pay cheque and the feeling of being valued have been enough to make many of us put up with many struggles that would otherwise have made us quit. Increasingly, it's not enough. The paradigm shifts I mentioned in the previous chapter also hit companies and organisations hard. More and more people expect their work to provide meaning and purpose and align with their values and priorities. A young freelance IT supporter told me that she wouldn't accept work from the weapons industry or betting companies. Organisations that are actively and credibly supporting the sustainability agenda are finding it easier to attract talent.

Your work has to move the future in the right direction

Work is no longer enough in and of itself. Your work has to move the future in the right direction. If you remember my guiding principle from earlier in the book, work can become a kind of lever to help you move the world. An increasing number of people expect work to be organised in a way that doesn't prevent you from having a meaningful personal life with family and friends and the things you care about. The post-Covid phenomenon of 'quiet quitting' is an example of what can happen when people find their jobs meaningless. Some people quit outright; others stop doing more than is absolutely necessary. They aren't engaged, sparing their energy and focusing on things outside work that matter more to them.

The other colossal shift is artificial intelligence, or AI. It seemed like a far-off science fiction idea until suddenly it seemed to be everywhere, accessible and human-like in its ability to perform and communicate. Margrethe Vestager, the Danish executive vice president of the European Commission for A Europe Fit for the Digital Age, puts it this way: 'I have never experienced anything more significant. It's difficult to compare with something else because it's so pervasive. It will affect all sectors and everything we do; the way we live and work, the way we educate ourselves, the way we produce. I don't think any area will be left untouched.' (Kildegaard & Lekfeldt 2023).

In a conversation with the former executive chairman of Google, Eric Schmidt (Luscombe 2021), former US Secretary of State Henry Kissinger compared the impact of generative AI to the impact of the atomic bomb. AI can potentially transform society as thoroughly as the agricultural or industrial revolutions did. As digital models and software robots take over increasingly complex tasks, why we work becomes even more acute. If machines and algorithms can take over tasks that don't require a unique human touch, what constitutes a singularly human quality? And how do we nurture that at work? How do leaders learn how to lead people in a way that brings out the best of their humanity?

If machines and algorithms can take over tasks that don't require a unique human touch, what constitutes a singularly human quality?

As you begin to reinvent yourself, you may also want to reinvent your relationship with work. And if you're a leader or have an ambition to hold a leadership position, you need to lead in a way that engages people and allows them to find meaning. This goes hand in hand with writer/illustrator Tim Urban's definition of leadership (2023): 'Leadership is the ability to move things in a direction that the cultural forces are not already taking things.'

Working steady hours

As I mentioned, humans have been hunter-gatherers throughout at least 98 per cent of our history. Our bodies and brains are adapted to a life where we pursue food, safety, leisure and pleasure in nature, depending on the circumstances. When we became farmers and built civilisations centred around food production, work took on a different aspect with a much more predictable structure. But even on the kind of sustenance farm that has been the dominant model and remains so in large parts of the world, work will be fluid and highly dependent on the seasons. And the value of hunting-gathering and farming is measured by the output rather than the number of hours going into it.

It is in that sense both strange and, though I use the word hesitantly, unnatural for humans to have their work lives divided into rigid structures measured in hours, but this has been the case since the industrial revolution. In the most rigid model, you have eight hours of work, eight hours of sleep and eight hours for everything else. Work is something that takes place away from your home and you get paid for the number of hours you deliver. Even when there isn't much to do – and let's face it, those times are not too rare – you still have to at least look busy. However, it would probably make more sense to both you and your employer that you left your desk and did something more worthwhile and then put in the effort at a time when the workload demanded it. And you generally have to be at the office, even when your work might as well be done from home, because you're getting paid by the hour and it isn't easy to measure whether you're putting in the promised hours if you're not present under the watchful gaze of your superior.

The Industrial Age model has secured a steadily increasing output and wealth that has allowed the majority of people to become well-educated or at least literate; it has expanded our life expectancy by decades and removed the dangers of food scarcity because good planning, skilled labour and automation have enabled us to be largely shielded from natural fluctuations such as seasons and the weather. It has, in other words, been meaningful. However, it has also had its costs. We've had to allow people to retire because they've been physically and frequently mentally worn out. We have high levels of stress and burnout and, globally, we're seeing inequality on the rise, increasing social tensions in large parts of the world. We've overexploited the planet to a degree that threatens our existence as a species.

At the same time, we've invented digital technologies that fundamentally change how we work. We can now produce, despite not being physically present at the workplace. We can talk and collaborate in real time across endless distances. Programs and machines replaced jobs that once were dependent on manual labour. People are increasingly employed because of their human qualities – ingenuity, innovation, empathy, perspective, caring and communication – rather than their manual labour. And yes, also that very human quality of unpredictability – because something marvellous may arise from the unexpected. This change has enormous implications for how we work. Most of all, it forces us to reconsider what work is and how we work to stay connected to ourselves and our relationships. Did anybody say regenerative leadership?

Work is identity

In the most straightforward possible terms, work is what you get paid to do. But it doesn't take much scrutiny to tear that definition apart. Billions of people do things that need to be done without getting paid. Any parent can testify to the work it takes to bring up children or care for an elderly relative, not to mention all the daily chores of cleaning, keeping tabs on the family calendar or growing and weeding the garden. We do heaps of demanding tasks without getting paid. And yet, if we want others to do them for us, for instance, gardening or babysitting, we have to pay. So, a definition of work can't simply be about whether you're getting paid. What kind of work we pay for is a political decision rooted in history, tradition and gender, to name a few factors, and a lot of very busy people choose to work voluntarily as well. They may engage themselves in charities or NGOs, being mentors and educators, coaches for sports teams or chairing the local association of homeowners. All these go beyond the bare necessities. They speak of something more profound. Work goes beyond something you do because you get paid to do it; maybe not for all, but for many people.

In my experience, it frequently baffles people new to a country like Denmark when one of the first questions they're asked is 'And what do you do for a living?' To Danes, it's such a natural question that they find it difficult to comprehend why it could be considered almost rude in other cultures. When Danes are asked to present themselves, they usually begin with their jobs, even when the presentation doesn't occur in a professional context. Work is more than money: it is identity. *Laboro ergo sum* – I work, therefore I am, could be the existential essence of many people.

Hannah Arendt and the difference between labour, work and action

The German-born American philosopher Hannah Arendt was one of the leading political thinkers of the 20th century. She was born in 1906 and was highly influenced by the atrocities she witnessed during the Second World War. She wrote extensively on subjects such as totalitarianism and moral and political life. But most of all, her concern was with what she called 'the human condition'. This led her to examine work as well. Arendt distinguished between labour, work and action. According to her, they're all aspects of the same fundamental human need to live an active life or *vita activa*, as she called it, as a contrast to the life of contemplation that both Greek and Christian philosophers have favoured. All three – labour, work and action – are necessary and present in our lives.

Concepts	Basic condition	Attitude	Metaphor	Existential perspective
LABOUR	Nature	Endurance	Body work	**SURVIVE**
WORK	Our material world	Result focus	Hand work	**LIVE**
ACTION	Dialogue and community	Ideas and values	Soul work	**THRIVE**

Table 5: Arendt's key concepts: labour, work and action. Source: Adapted from Tommy Kjær Lassen's Philosophy for Leaders (2020, in Danish)

Labour is that which is necessary to survive – finding food, finding shelter. Animals do this as well. Labour, in this sense of the word, produces nothing material. It's a question of taking care of life and reproducing it. You're hungry, you find food, you eat, repeat. You have to be persistent and resilient. Work is what's necessary to live, what we do to maintain and improve a world fit for humans – what we create, how we use our knowledge and our hands to change the world around us. This is something more substantial – our houses, tools, poems, paintings, all the artefacts that make us share the world. It takes focus and a wish to see results to get this kind of work done.

Action is what's needed to thrive: what we do, how that defines us and shapes our identities, and, not least, how that affects other people; it's the dialogues and communities we share. Action is what you choose to do, a constant rebirth of society from new ideas and choices. You can only choose if you have the freedom to do so, and your actions only resonate and become manifest when they affect others. In that sense, action is a political thing that impacts society and shapes the values and ideas we share.

> *Action is what you choose to do, a constant rebirth of society from new ideas and choices*

This is a simplified version of her thoughts and ideas on labour, work and action. Still, the way she distinguishes between the three aspects of an active life is unique and, I believe, useful in this context when we debate what it is to be human and how to lead a meaningful life. According to Arendt, we've put too much emphasis on work. The result is endless consumerism. We need to focus more on action, to engage and enable people to act and think more about how our actions define us and our world. In that way, I see it as an existentialist point of view: choice, action and responsibility are at the heart of it. When we distinguish between what we usually label work in this way, we become more attuned to our evolutionary history and the life we've adapted to. We've done a lot of labour and work and both are necessary. But we must act to live the active life that Arendt saw as the ideal. Action is connected to purpose and perhaps the increasing emphasis on purpose reflects this. We don't just want to produce and reproduce; we want meaningful action.

Another kind of freedom

Again, this is a perspective from a somewhat privileged point of view. Throughout history, there has been plenty of meaning to be found in sustaining yourself and your family, and this is still the case in large parts of the world. However, it's evident in our society that the Industrial Age, with its emphasis on labour, no longer resonates. We want more from life.

Some find it in what Arendt would call action. They nurture parts of themselves that they may have neglected. They begin to play the piano or learn how to paint. They may seek calm and contemplation because there has been little time for that. And although Arendt sees an active life as the ideal, sometimes contemplation is necessary. The freedom to act in Arendt's sense of the word is not just a question of having freedom in the usual understanding of the word. You have to be able to act – to have the relevant knowledge and skills – and you have to consider how that affects others; the plurality, as she called it.

An active life isn't a life of incessant action

This kind of ability or empowerment to act needs nourishment. There are things we can't do, either because they're beyond our capabilities or because we choose not to act because the effects of our actions would be unacceptable; for instance, if they harm other people. So, an active life also needs times of inaction and quiet reflection, of learning and doing simple things. Many of my clients haven't had time for this since childhood and youth. An active life isn't a life of incessant action. Instead, it's about meaningful action. Arendt celebrated new beginnings and how all humans were equal yet unique. Our relationship with work changes when we begin to look for meaning, purpose and being connected to our values and feelings. We won't simply be producers and consumers. We want to work in a way that benefits both ourselves and others.

The current focus on sustainability and the UN Sustainable Development Goals is a visible sign of this, not least in the private sector. And from all corners, we hear about young people who want to work in a place where they can make a positive difference. They're not only looking for labour; they're looking for meaningful action.

Reaching out

I used to see shifting paradigms as opposites: crystallised vs fluid, control vs trust, planning vs innovation, hierarchy vs networking and linear vs circular. But the more I think about it, the more they seem to be coexisting layers. There are times when fluidity and 'try as we go along' aren't the right choices (consider a journey by plane with a pilot happily leaving it to experiments to get you there safely), just as other processes must be tightly controlled. In contrast, trying to plan and control every detail in a rapidly changing environment will hamper innovation and efficiency. It will frequently frustrate workers when they can't use their skills and creativity to take advantage of an unexpected chance or deal with an equally unexpected emergency.

We see shifting paradigms in many places: the changing concept of power; strength in unity vs strength in diversity; and formal equality vs social justice. Perhaps these changes have, to some extent, something to do with how we've created value in our societies. Value creation and organisation tend to mirror each other. The industrial revolution was founded on linear thinking and economy of scale. Those at the top decided and those further down did what they were told. In the organisational flow chart, input equalled output.

The absence of such hierarchy can be seen as the definition of anarchy: in an anarchy there is no hierarchically superior, coercive power that can resolve disputes, enforce law or order the system. This leads me to ask the following question: is our unconscious fear of anarchy the hidden psychological background for maintaining hierarchies?

In contrast, the digital era is dominated by network thinking and phenomena such as crowdfunding, crowdsourcing, co-creating, sharing and contributing. Hierarchies don't work well in this context and there's no perceived weakness in asking for help. Reaching out is an opportunity for others to contribute and, through that, they increase their status and value in the network. And, perhaps most importantly, they want their contributions to be meaningful. They should be a force for good.

If you're firmly grounded in the linear, hierarchical way of thought, the networkers may come across as less ambitious or spoiled. They aren't as eager to fight for a place at the top, and there are kinds of work they don't want to do. This can cause some of us to be surprised and even dismayed. Have the younger generations become too spoiled to put effort into what needs doing, as the accusations sometimes imply? Hardly. If you look deeper into their view of the world, it simply doesn't make sense to talk about being on top. There's no top in a network, but you can make yourself valued and central by contributing and collaborating. New generations – as well as some from older generations – are striving for something other than a place at the top. They're striving for meaning, for doing something beneficial to them, their relationships and society. They want to be valued and have a life that doesn't force them to choose between career and relationships. Everything is connected.

So far, these two different paradigms exist side by side. My prediction is that the latter will come to dominate, and while there will be situations where hierarchies are still relevant, they may not be as strict and crystallised as today. I once saw the following graffiti: 'If I was meant to be controlled, I would have come with a remote.'

The Nordic Nine

The Nordic countries – Norway, Sweden, Iceland, Finland and Denmark – share many similarities, one of which is an emphasis on trust, collaboration and community. As societies, they're generally considered safe, efficient and well run, with healthy and stable democracies and a work–life balance that allows for time with friends and families and participating in civil society. The Nordic Nine is a set of transformational leadership and organisational capabilities developed by Copenhagen Business School for their students, to which I've contributed in my role as associate professor. Specifically, the Nordic Nine consists of nine transformational capabilities:

KNOWLEDGE
- You have deep business knowledge placed in a broad context.
- You are analytical with data and curious about ambiguity.
- You recognise humanity's challenges and have the entrepreneurial knowledge to help resolve them.

VALUES
- You are competitive in business and compassionate in society.
- You understand ethical dilemmas and have the leadership values to overcome them.
- You are critical when thinking and constructive when collaborating.

ACTION
- You produce prosperity and protect the prosperity of the next generations.
- You grow by relearning and by teaching others to do the same.
- You create value from global connections for local communities.

Table 6: The Nordic Nine

The framework explores the principles fundamental to Nordic leadership, reflecting those of Nordic societies and building on a foundation of trust.

Please consider that although these principles characterise the different Nordic societies at large, there are differences between and within the countries and the principles will sometimes be more like an ideal than an absolute reality. However, all the Nordic countries share an egalitarian culture emphasising collaboration and a strong appreciation of individual rights and contributions. And they (in combination with Scandi chic) have been a driving force behind the success of Nordic organisations and societies.

These Nordic leadership principles include:

- **Equity** – treating everyone fairly and respectfully, regardless of background, gender or ethnicity. Nordic leaders believe that diversity is a strength and embrace inclusiveness in all aspects of the organisation. Diversity strengthens decision making and innovation.
- **Trust** – building relationships based on mutual respect and openness. Nordic leaders believe trust is essential for creating a culture of engagement where everyone feels heard and valued and no one is afraid to suggest improvements or radical changes.
- **Collaboration** – working together towards a common goal. Nordic leaders believe collaboration is essential for creating a culture of innovation where everyone feels free to share their ideas and opinions.
- **Innovation** – finding new and better ways of doing things. Nordic leaders believe innovation is essential for staying competitive and adapting to changing market conditions.
- **Sustainability** – taking responsibility for the environment and society. Nordic leaders believe that sustainability is fundamental and should be implicit in all strategies, all business models and all value chains.
- **Pragmatism** – adapting to circumstances, handling unexpected events and grabbing unexpected opportunities instead of insisting on sticking to a goal that may no longer be the right one.
- **Simplicity** – removing organisational clutter and empowering people to get things done without having to consult with several managers or bureaucratic procedures.
- **Openness and transparency** – these are fundamental for building trust. In a psychologically safe environment, it's possible to acknowledge mistakes and learn from them. Values and priorities should be clear, as should chains of responsibility.
- **Responsibility and accountability** – are also fundamental for trust and for building a work environment where people can count on each other and their leaders.

My work with the Nordic Nine has sparked the creation of the new Nordic Leadership Model, which I've developed through a synthesis of my experience as a marketeer, a leading executive search consultant, a top executive coach and my academic work at Copenhagen Business School and as an associate at Møller Institute, Churchill College, the University of Cambridge. It offers a unique approach to engagement that combines various dimensions and perspectives, not least fundamental values. Let's explore how leaders can apply the model to engage more effectively in the workplace.

The new Nordic Leadership Model

Over the years, I've refined my new Nordic Leadership Model, synthesising many of the dynamics I've previously mentioned. In some ways it's my capstone model.

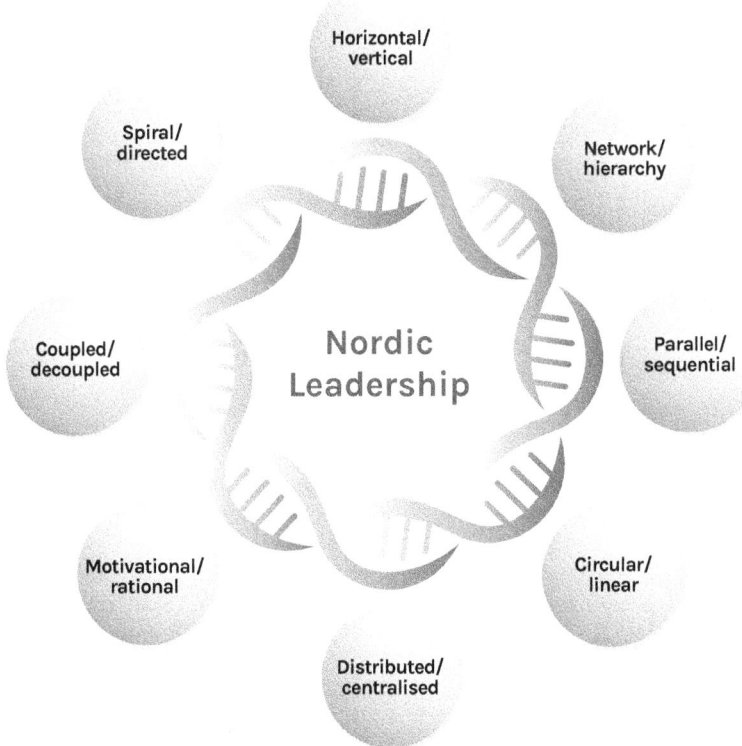

Figure 15: The Nordic Leadership Model (NLM)

This model is all about finding the sweet spot in specific situations without compromising your fundamental values as a leader or risking the future of the organisation. My work has resulted in identifying the following eight dimensions:

1. Horizontal/vertical

Definition: This refers to the structure of an organisation. Horizontal structures are characterised by a flat hierarchy, where decision making is decentralised and employees have a large degree of autonomy. Vertical structures are designed to work top-down; decision making is centralised and employees have less autonomy.

Required action: Depending on organisational needs and the specific job at hand, leaders need to find the right balance between horizontal and vertical. The vertical dimension should be limited to what's necessary in order to ensure a clear strategy and alignment across the organisation.

Desired outcome: Leaders will operate more effectively by providing employees with the necessary autonomy and clear boundaries within which to make independent decisions, while still maintaining control over the organisation. A hybrid culture will allow for flexibility, agility and collaboration while also ensuring accountability and efficiency.

2. Network/hierarchy

Definition: This dimension refers to the way in which information flows within an organisation and how decisions are made. In a networked organisation, information flows freely between employees and decisions are made collaboratively. In a hierarchical organisation, information flows top-down and decisions are made solely by senior management.

Required action: Depending on the situation, leaders need to engage with both network and hierarchy to create an equilibrium between bottom-up engagement and top-down governance.

Desired outcome: Information flows freely and everyone's opinion is heard. Leaders will empower local decision making where appropriate, while key strategic decisions remain the responsibility of senior management and the board.

3. Parallel/sequential

Definition: This refers to the way in which tasks are completed. In a parallel system, tasks are completed simultaneously by different teams or individuals. In a sequential system, tasks are completed one after another, in a specific order.

Required action: Depending on the organisation's needs, leaders need to consider both parallel and sequential systems. Some tasks are better suited to a traditional sequential system with a high level of control and security, while others can benefit from an agile or beta approach in which different teams or individuals can experiment their way towards a solution. Leaders must weigh up which approach will be the most relevant to the job at hand.

Desired outcome: Leaders will ensure that tasks are completed efficiently and results are achieved while still allowing for collaboration, creativity, experimentation and innovation.

4. Circular/linear

Definition: This refers to the way in which communication and decision making works within an organisation. In a circular system, there's no set hierarchy and communication flows freely between employees. In a linear system, there's a set hierarchy and communication flows from the top down.

Required action: Leaders need to engage with both dimensions to create a culture that allows for continuous learning, adaptation and transformation while also ensuring stability, predictability and control.

Desired outcome: A culture that incorporates a more circular approach – one that opens up alternatives, is more flexible and invites input, while also allowing a more directive, linear approach, according to the task at hand.

5. Distributed/centralised

Definition: This refers to the way in which decision making is handled within an organisation. In a distributed system, decision making is decentralised and employees have more autonomy. In a centralised system, senior management makes all the decisions.

Required action: Leaders need to find a way of balancing these dimensions by providing employees with the necessary autonomy to make decisions while still maintaining control over the organisation. In times of crisis, power needs to go peripheral. Think of the way in which the Covid-19 pandemic necessitated local decision making and how it was handled in different regions. When business becomes more 'as usual', centralisation tends to reappear.

Desired outcome: A culture that allows for diversity, local context and empowerment while ensuring coherence, consistency and alignment.

6. Motivational/rational

Definition: This refers to the way in which employees are motivated and engaged and to what degree decisions should be based on data and facts or values and ideals.

Required action: Leaders need to acknowledge that even rationality depends on basic values. If the purpose of a given organisation is to maximise profit (which is a motivational idea), it becomes rational to use cheap labour. However, if the values are based on sustainability, using cheap labour would be completely irrational. Leaders need to ensure that decisions are based on both emotions and data, and for the right reasons. Values and ideals aren't necessarily irrational but contrary to purely rational decisions they hinge less on data and more on what feels like the right thing to do.

Desired outcome: A culture that balances intuition and analysis – one that allows for purpose, meaning and passion while honouring logic, evidence and facts. Leaders will be transparent about what motivates them to make particular decisions.

7. Coupled/decoupled

Definition: This refers to the way in which tasks and goals are connected within an organisation. In a coupled system, they're interconnected and the success of one task or goal depends on the success of another. In a decoupled system, the success of one task or goal doesn't depend on the success of another.

Required action: Leaders need to engage with both dimensions by ensuring that tasks and goals are interconnected and the people within the organisation can count on others while still allowing for individual flexibility and adaptability.

Desired outcome: A culture that balances interdependence and independence – one that allows for collaboration, empathy, accountability and social responsibility while encouraging autonomy, self-reliance, integrity, authority and differentiation.

8. Spiral/directed

Definition: The directed dimension is about getting from A to B in a planned and predictable manner. It's ideal for existing practices where nothing fundamental needs to change and decisions about optimisation usually come from the top. The spiral dimension allows for continuous improvement and learning, with people collaborating and sharing knowledge along the way. Often the spiral dimension has a longer time perspective.

Required action: Leaders need to ensure that, where appropriate, teams can make their own decisions. Think in terms of the directed dimension being similar to single loop learning (making adjustments to correct mistakes or problems) and the spiral dimension being similar to double and triple loop learning (understanding what caused the problem and taking action to correct it, then going deeper to understand why decisions are made and the purpose and values that underpin them).

Desired outcome: A culture that's built for continuous improvement and learning, while giving leaders leeway to apply the directed dimension where necessary. Think evolution rather than revolution.

A useful illustration to help visualise the new Nordic Leadership Model is the DNA helix – look at Figure 15 again. In its inherent beauty, DNA symbolises life itself, while in this context it represents an organisation in its form as a breathing organism – eg centralising and decentralising over time, being dynamic instead of static.

Even if you can't immediately see them all, the eight dimensions are all present in the helix. If you flatten it out and make it two-dimensional, you can easily see the horizontal/vertical and spiral/directed dimensions. Imagine the other dimensions connecting into them like the 'rungs of the ladder' (base pairs) on a helix. The traditional organisational diagram represents flatland; it is two-dimensional and static. The new Nordic Leadership Model is spherical and dynamic.

Bear in mind that, when you look at an organisational chart, it's only one side of the coin. If you follow the new Nordic Leadership Model, you're less likely to follow the path of least resistance (the hierarchical path). Your perception of reality is dependent on your filters. If you accept an organisational chart with a formal structure, you also accept all the limitations inherent within it. The more organic, integrated structure of this new model will therefore influence your behaviour, your beliefs and your ideas, so that you'll be able to use your creativity when seeking solutions. The aim is always to find a balance between the two matching dimensions – rather like the tightrope walker's pole, which I mentioned earlier. My hope is that the Nordic Leadership Model will create a paradigm shift in the way you look at how organisations are run – in practice, not in theory. After all, we're all inherently flawed human beings.

I want to leave you with this image of the DNA helix, just as I left you with the image of the tightrope walker clinging to her paradigm, even when it was no longer of use. These two images will help you notice – and react – when you instinctively opt for a well-known perception that fits into your existing paradigm. Please challenge yourself and look out for convictions that no longer serve you well. Not only will it make you a more interesting conversation partner, it will also help you to experience some of the clarity and relaxed readiness that I've previously mentioned.

A new kind of power

This paradigm shift will also affect the way in which we define power, because nobody can be on top of a network. In that sense, we're all leaders, whether it's our formal position or not. This is why I believe that being aware of the responsibilities of leadership is a responsibility for everyone. You may not yourself hold a formal leadership position or aim to have one. But you will be a leader in numerous other ways, for briefer or extended periods. It could be of your family, friends, a football team – or yourself. Self-leadership is, to some extent, what this book is all about. There will be situations in which you have power over others or situations, and with power comes responsibility. To free up leadership energy, you must be able to observe and listen to the surroundings without letting too many emotions come into play. You may compare it to observing an empty bowl. The bowl is the object or the task and the emotions are what you put in the bowl. In other words, it's not the problem that's the problem; what you mean or feel about the problem is the problem. Be conscious of the fact that you can choose to attribute greater or lesser importance to any event. It's fundamental to be able to choose not to be affected by outer circumstances.

When I grew up, you took or were given power because you deserved it. It was a formal position of authority – the right to decide how others should act. To some extent, that's still part of the concept. In some situations, decisions won't be up for debate and somebody has to be in charge. But power has also been about knowing more than others and using that information for your benefit. There can be power in withholding information. Anyway, AI has created instant availability of information, so power has increasingly become about sharing knowledge and influence and enabling and empowering others. At the centre of this are two challenging dilemmas:

1. giving away power
2. losing control.

Giving away power involves delegating decision-making authority to others and trusting them to make the right decisions. This can be challenging for leaders who are used to making all the decisions themselves and feel unsafe and perhaps less like leaders when not doing so. After all, isn't leadership all about making hard choices? Actually, it isn't. It's mainly about ensuring that the whole organisation and everyone in it can make the right decisions and execute the strategy to the best of their abilities. Simply put, strategy is structured common sense.

In a world that's usually difficult to predict, it makes little sense to plan everything in detail and make every decision according to that plan. The danger of doing this is that you become great at following the plan but it may turn out to be the wrong plan, especially with the increased speed and complexity of operating in today's world. You certainly need to possess the skills to successfully navigate the twists and turns, dead ends and detours. The leader is no longer the person with the most accurate picture of what's happening across the organisation or how a given service or product can be improved. Employees are. Chances are that the leader will make the wrong decisions based on an outdated or incomplete picture of the situation. It makes much more sense for leaders to spend energy on the crucial decisions on strategy and which values should define the organisation while empowering the people to make relevant and competent everyday decisions that align with the overall strategy and values.

In order to create a culture of empowerment, it's necessary to give away power. Everyone needs to feel responsible and accountable for the organisation's success and be able to use their best capabilities and judgement, which is part of what engages people. This is Hannah Arendt's definition of action. Losing control is closely associated with giving away power. It involves letting go of the need to control every aspect of the organisation and trusting others to take charge – and for the same reason. This can be challenging for leaders who are used to micromanaging and controlling every aspect of the organisation. However, losing control is necessary to create a trusting culture where everyone feels valued and respected. This is a central debate in leadership these days. How do you lead when you can't do it simply by ordering people around? You may ask why this is no longer viable. The brief answer is that people are no longer putting up with it. If they feel underappreciated or unable to stay connected to their humanity, dignity and relationships, they'll find other places to work. They'll quit quietly or, if they continue to work even though they find it stressful, become ill. And again, AI will take over the tasks that don't require specific human qualities. People will be employed because of their humanity, and to unfold that human potential, you'll need other leadership skills than bossing people around.

You have to inspire people to follow you. You'll attain power not from knowing everything but from being somebody who can ask and listen, invite the right questions, or be somebody worth following. It's not a question of staying on top, preventing others from reaching the same spot. It's a case of growing together. In some instances, leadership will look more like a catalyst; in some cases, it will look like traditional leadership; in others, it will look like being a facilitator and enabler. It depends on the situation and the organisation's needs, understood by the people who are part of it.

In order to create a culture of empowerment, it's necessary to give away power

Power in service of the greater good

The term 'servant leadership' has been around for decades but has recently gained traction. It was coined by Robert K Greenleaf in 1970 in the essay *The Servant as a Leader*. He was inspired by a story, *Journey to the East*, written by German-Swiss poet and novelist Hermann Hesse. In the story, a group of prominent men set out on a mythic journey. With them is Leo, their servant, who nurtures and encourages them. When he disappears, everything goes wrong and the expedition falls apart. It turns out that Leo was the true leader.

Greenleaf used this to write about a different concept of the connection between leadership and power – the seemingly lowly servant can be a leadership role model by working towards a higher meaning and prioritising serving the greater good rather than the group's objectives. The team and the organisation come first. As the name suggests, servant leadership works by providing support to others. It's about building influence by inspiring rather than deploying control orders and traditional leadership tactics. Greenleaf didn't see servant leadership as a leadership tactic. The servant can become a leader but the instinct to serve the greater good comes first. Greenleaf's ideas were generally well received, if not exactly put to use. But lately, they've received more attention as the stronger emphasis on meaning, the greater good and collaboration is challenging traditional and linear understandings of how power should work.

In the past couple of years, the power paradigm shift has also been visible in other frameworks, both in the business world and outside it. The United Nations agreed on the Sustainable Development Goals in 2015, a roadmap to a future where no one is left behind and people can live in dignity on a healthy planet. This, in turn, has given rise to the Inner Development Goals, an open-source initiative with prominent members such as IKEA and Google and hubs worldwide, which tries to advance the transformational skills for sustainable development. The founders believe that we can only become sustainable through developing ourselves in five ways.

1	**Being**	Relationship to Self
2	**Thinking**	Cognitive skills
3	**Relating**	Caring for others and the world
4	**Collaborating**	Social skills
5	**Acting**	Driving change

Table 7: The Inner Development Goals. Source: innerdevelopmentgoals.org

As you've found throughout the book, I share some of the same ideas. You need to understand yourself, improve your cognitive skills, connect, collaborate and relate, and you need to want to drive change and know how to do it. The framework and the network behind it are constantly growing and can be viewed in detail on the initiative's home page. It's yet another example of how power is increasingly about inner growth rather than formal positions. We must remain in a state of permanent beta: always a work in progress, acknowledging that we have bugs and need to adapt and evolve. It's a lifelong commitment to continuous personal and professional growth.

Questions to ask yourself

- What makes somebody a good leader, in your opinion? List between five and seven qualities.
- Why have you chosen those particular qualities? Explain it in a way that a young, ambitious person would understand and appreciate.
- What does your own ideal work life look like?
- Are you living it? If not, why not? And what will you do about it?

Chapter 9
Lessons for transformation

Moments of existential doubt can be full of anxiety, doubts, cloudy perspectives and a feeling of being buffeted by heavy winds seemingly coming from all directions. Or they can lead to what's known as analysis paralysis. Faced with almost endless possibilities, we lose the ability to decide for fear that we'll make the wrong choices. But – as I hope I've made a case for – once you emerge from those moments, they can also bring clarity and give you a sense of serenity, a stronger sense of yourself and what matters to you, who you are, who you have been and who you want to become. This chapter summarises the advice from each of the four disciplines in the book: how to know yourself (philosophy), how to understand yourself (psychology), how to expand yourself (neurology), and how to transform yourself (strategy).

Throughout the book, I've used knowledge from the four academic disciplines: philosophy, psychology, neurology and strategy. My original thought was to go through them individually – a kind of 'the meaning of life according to...' approach. But the whole point of bringing them together is that they're interwoven and, even though they're original fields of research, they're very much their own entities and tackle the big questions from different perspectives. They also share a purpose, aiming to understand our existence and to use that understanding to improve our lives.

Each discipline has its advice on how to thrive, grow and find that meaning, which enables us to find an island of quiet in the whirlwind of life. So, at the end of the book, I thought it would still be helpful to look at them separately to see which perspectives and advice each specific discipline has to offer and how we can apply it – not only at inflection points in our lives but as a new awareness that we can build on, a new level of understanding that will empower us to move not only forward but upwards and, at the same time, deeper into ourselves. Or perhaps more precisely, our *Selves*. It will allow us to choose, act and respond knowingly, based on a solid sense of our virtues and meaning.

We're each shaped by different genes, experiences and conditions. We're not the same but we can all assess whatever we're shaped from and use our awareness to aim for a more meaningful life positively connected to ourselves, to others and to society. So I decided to summarise some of the perspectives each of the disciplines offer in their own right. They ask different questions but frequently arrive at remarkably similar answers.

Philosophy invites you to answer 'Who am I?' and 'What is the meaning of my life?' Psychology asks related questions: 'What motivates and drives human behaviour? How do I see myself with others? How do I live a rich and meaningful life?' Neurology deals with our existence and thriving from the perspective of our brains and neural systems. In which way do they contribute to how we perceive and behave? To what extent do they shape our personalities, our abilities to perform, to learn, to grow? And finally, strategy is focused on the how: how do you apply all of this knowledge? How do you become successful in your life in a way that's meaningful to you? How do you set meaningful goals and how do you reach them?

So, let us look at them individually to see what they have to teach us.

Know yourself (philosophy)

No one knows the origin of the phrase 'know thyself' but it's the first of the three maxims written above the entrance to the ancient temple of Delphi, and different Greek philosophers often quoted it. It's the essence of philosophy but different philosophers have addressed the challenge in different ways and various schools of thought have emerged. They keep appearing as we learn more and strive to integrate new scientific knowledge into our understanding of ourselves and our relationship with others and the world.

As discussed in Chapter 4, the Self is often defined as the individual consciousness or the subject of our experience. We have our thoughts, feelings, values and understandings of the world and how we relate to it. Though others may share them to some or sometimes even a large extent, our individual experiences are inevitably shaped by our experiences. Although we're all human, no two humans are the same. This 'otherness', the personal traits that set us apart and make each of us unique, can be characterised as a Self but it's not something we're born with. It's a process constantly shaped by our experiences and choices. Some values may remain constant throughout our lives but many people will find that their Self is more like a slowly evolving web than a solid core.

Greek philosophers such as Plato and Aristotle focused on knowledge, reason and the pursuit of wisdom. Much later, in the Age of Enlightenment, French philosopher René Descartes of *cogito, ergo sum* fame built upon that foundation and incorporated the growing body of scientific discoveries into his work, which was a renewal of rational thinking and the emphasis on reason and knowledge, intellectual curiosity and the role of systematic doubt – still very much present in the modern scientific method. However, he would also influence the later school of existentialism with his teachings on the individual condition and responsibility. And he was occupied with the body as well as the mind. Descartes defined the existence of the Self as a thinking, doubting entity separate from the body. The mind was immaterial, capable of thought, perception and reason. The body was physical and subject to the laws of physics. He saw body and mind as two distinct substances interacting with each other but felt that while the mind influenced the body, the opposite wasn't true.

Kierkegaard went a step further. Like Descartes, he perceived the body and mind as separate entities but found that the connection between them was even closer. The body is the source of physical sensations and impulses, able to feel pain and pleasure and shape some of our experiences, an unavoidable aspect of our human existence and a way to understand ourselves in the world. The mind is the source of thoughts, feelings and beliefs, and though body and mind are interdependent in their thinking, the mind is vital to understanding the true nature of what it means to be human. One of Kierkegaard's main contributions to philosophical existentialist thinking was his emphasis on choice, and he found that the body is a source of impulses, temptations or fear of physical pain that can lead us to make choices that aren't in line with our true selves and our sense of responsibility. In other words, we should listen more to our minds than obey our bodies, even if our bodies are closely connected to our minds and an essential aspect of human existence.

Meanwhile, psychology was emerging as a discipline and, with it, new understandings of the mind, which influenced later existentialists such as Jean-Paul Sartre and **Martin Heidegger**. As existentialists, they were primarily occupied with individual freedom and choice and the inherent meaninglessness of life – it's your job to make meaning of your life; nothing is a given. However, these existentialists were influenced by the psychological concept of self-actualisation – the idea that we as individuals can become our true selves. The psychological concept of anxiety has also found its way into existentialist thinking. We experience anxiety as a result of our freedom to make choices. And 'existential guilt' – the feeling of guilt that arises when we realise that we haven't fulfilled our full potential or even that we've wasted our lives – is also evident in later existentialist thinking, as are the psychoanalytic theories of Freud and Jung with their emphasis on the importance of the unconscious mind.

It's your job to make meaning of your life; nothing is a given

Sartre and Heidegger bridged the philosophical gap between body and mind. They found that it's through our physical experiences that we come to understand ourselves in the world. Body and mind are mutually dependent. At the same time, they were influenced by the ideas of social constructivism – that our perception of reality isn't necessarily founded in irrefutable facts but rather in how we make meaning of our experiences. Sartre emphasised the freedom and agency of the individual in shaping our identity and purpose. Heidegger emphasised the role of the social and cultural context in how we understand ourselves and the world. Both agreed that we're not fixed entities but are constantly constructing ourselves and being constructed by others and our interactions with them and our environment.

The French philosopher Paul Ricoeur (the mentor of French President Emmanuel Macron) went even further in integrating body and mind. He believed that our experiences, including our perceptions, emotions and actions, are rooted in our bodily existence, and he sees our gestures, postures and facial expressions not just as body movements but as ways to communicate what's going on in our minds. His work is deeply concerned with how we make meaning of our world, which, in his view, isn't so much through individual choice and action but through our interpretations of whatever we experience.

As science has evolved, so has philosophy. I've already mentioned psychology as a source. In later years, neurology has changed our understanding of mind, memory and consciousness, among others. Modern philosophers such as David Chalmers, **Antonio Damasio** and Alva Noë have studied the relationship between consciousness and the brain and how the brain affects decision making. Through his neurophilosophy field, Paul Churchland has sought to integrate insights from neuroscience into philosophy, just as neuropsychology seeks to integrate neurological science into psychology.

Philosophy has long been considered irrelevant, not least to leaders in the business world. As money became the pivot point, cost efficiency became the dominant ethic. When the Cold War was over, many took it as a clear demonstration that capitalism won. The market would provide. Philosophy became something obscure that many associated with old men in white robes surrounded by marble pillars. There was lots of talk, minimal action and very little relevance to the real world. Many didn't realise, or they forgot, that philosophy has kept up the pace. As is evident, philosophy didn't stop with Aristotle or even Kierkegaard or Sartre. With the onset of the financial and economic crises in 2008–9 and movements such as Occupy Wall Street, it gradually became more apparent that capitalism and the power of the market wouldn't bring prosperity and justice to the world. The financial crisis was experienced as a walk in the park: Jurassic Park!

At the same time, both leaders and employees increasingly felt frustrated and prone to exhaustion and stress. And problems such as tax evasion, whitewashing, pollution, child labour and dreadful working conditions in sweatshops demanded answers and different ethics. Outside the business world, it also became more evident that inequality – economic as well as social disparities – couldn't be solved by business as usual. Even if money and efficiency were part of the answer, they couldn't be the only answer. Apart from profitability and economic growth, something would have to be the guiding principle in business and society.

This is, by the way, something that has made me adjust my thinking. I no longer believe in the trickle-down effect. We need better answers to the question of how to ensure a sustainable future that's just and equitable. I think this is one of the reasons that philosophy has become essential. We're looking for meaning in our personal lives, but we're also trying to determine what values and meaning should guide our societies. We have old questions that need new answers – and philosophy can help us with that. After all, above everything else, philosophy is about meaning.

> I no longer believe in the trickle-down effect

This is a brief example of how an old philosopher can become hugely relevant in these times. I've mentioned Descartes several times throughout the book as an example of the rational school of thought. We usually stress the 'think' of the sentence 'I think, therefore I am'. However, there's something else at stake. If you highlight the 'I' instead, you'll see it. According to Descartes, we can't be confident that anyone else beyond ourselves is conscious; we can only judge ourselves. We may feel it and be convinced that it's so – and we do – but we have no way of proving it. This is gaining new relevance today as we debate whether AI can become truly intelligent and sentient. How will we know? If we can't even prove that other people are conscious – though we assume they are – how will we know if computers become intelligent? Maybe sentience and personality can exist without the body after all but in a program of some form?

We still don't know. Conscience hasn't been definitively defined and philosophers still debate the nature of conscience, emotions and intelligence. The American philosopher and cognitive scientist Daniel Dennett argues, for instance, that our consciousness is, to a large extent, an illusion created by the brain and that we're highly complex biological machines that we may one day – once we understand ourselves well enough – be able to replicate in a kind of artificial intelligence where 1s and 0s replace the biological and evolutionary programming that defines humans.

Some scientists even deny that we have anything resembling free will; we're products of our roughly 100 billion neurons and the trillions of synapses between them. What we think are deliberate actions are beyond our conscious control. The brain is way ahead of us and has already determined what we should do. Stanford neuroscientist Robert Sapolsky (2023) said, 'What we call free will is simply the biology that we haven't understood well enough yet.'

As I believe in the existentialist school of thought, I don't see it this way. I believe in personal choice, action and responsibility. Fortunately, other scientists support the concept of free will. And I'm vindicated in one sense: studies show that people who believe in free will feel more meaningful and content in their lives. The science may not be conclusive but the philosopher's view is to make the most of what we can.

Philosophy constantly adds to an already vast body of philosophical insights that offer us different perspectives on what it means to be human. The basic questions are as old as humankind. I find it strangely comforting that it continues to fascinate us and that it can't be reduced to a simple formula.

But let me offer a few lessons from philosophy, as I see it.

- Know yourself. This doesn't mean you must know every little corner of you or spend the rest of your life contemplating your inner motives. It means you should know what drives you, your virtues, your priorities, and what's holding you back.
- Your Self is evolving and capable of growth. We're not born with a fully formed or even predestined Self. Our choices,

actions, responses and responsibilities shape us. So do our relationships and our interactions. And so do our experiences in life. You may be predisposed to a particular disposition, sunny or grumpy, to use a caricature. However, you'll still be able to evolve and grow, especially when you embrace this growth with a larger sense of awareness. You can become your own hero.

- Your Self is both body, mind and brain. Science tells us that we can't separate body and mind and that our brains and personalities evolve through physical experiences. This means you should take good care of your body and brain.
- To know good is to be able to choose, act and beneficially take responsibility. 'To know good is to do good' is one of the points that the ancient philosopher Socrates made. He thought that if people knew what virtues were, they would naturally be virtuous. That seems to have been too optimistic but I firmly share his belief that awareness is key. When we know what's good for us and others, we tend to let that guide our choices and actions. And if we make choices and act in ways that don't comply with that knowledge, we have to accept responsibility.

Understand yourself (psychology)

Psychology has explored how we live and thrive (as well as what makes us miserable) since it emerged in the late 19th century. As a discipline, it has deep roots in philosophy, sharing the interest in questions about the nature of the mind and consciousness. But from the beginning, it also included physiology, trying to study and structure the workings of the mind as you would study and structure the workings of the body. One of the earliest pioneers was Wilhelm Wundt, a German physiologist and philosopher frequently called the father of psychology. He established the first experimental psychology laboratory at the University of Leipzig, where he researched sensory perception, attention and consciousness. He wasn't alone in his interest. Other researchers began to establish psychology as a distinct

Lessons for transformation

scientific discipline, among them the American psychologist and philosopher William James. In 1890, he wrote and published *The Principles of Psychology*, a book widely considered the first modern psychology textbook.

These early psychologists used self-reflection or deep introspection and self-observation to discover how the mind works and is structured. They were also interested in how the mind adapts to different environments and circumstances. They were trying to break the structure of the mind and mental processes down into their smallest components. It was an important beginning but one that was challenged almost from the beginning. The mind, some argued, was different from the body and the subconscious was of greater importance than the conscious mind. Enter Sigmund Freud and Carl Jung, two of the most influential psychological thinkers. Their works differ and are widely challenged today but they're also frequently quoted.

Freud emphasised the role of unconscious conflicts and repressed emotions in shaping behaviour and mental health. He divided the mind into three parts: the id, the ego and the superego. The id represents all that we desire and do unconsciously. According to Freud, it's the most primitive part of our brain, constantly seeking gratification and pleasure. On the other side of the spectrum is the superego, which constantly internalises society's morals and ethics. You may feel like taking the biggest slice of cake on the table and beating others to it. Still, your superego will restrain you, reminding you that it will be unacceptable behaviour.

You can become your own hero

To some extent, you can visualise the id as the little devil on one of your shoulders, telling you to give into temptation, and the superego as the sanctimonious angel on the other, informing you of all the shame that will befall you if you do. The ego, then, your conscious and rational Self, will constantly mediate between the two. Freud's division of the mind is deemed too simplistic today but it remains highly influential – even if the id nowadays is more frequently (and even less precisely) referred to as our reptile brain.

Jung is best known for his work on analytical psychology and the collective unconscious and archetypes in shaping our behaviour and mental wellbeing. He saw universal thought patterns across cultures and emphasised symbolism, dreams and spirituality. Though his ideas are also contested, they are, like Freud's, still influential. You may have tried the ubiquitous Myers–Briggs Type Indicator personality test. It's based on Jung's theories of archetypal behaviour – for instance, whether we're introverted or extroverted, sensing or feeling, judging or processing, and so on.

In the early 1900s, behaviourism emerged as a significant departure from the introspective and psychodynamic approaches that had dominated psychology up to that point. Behaviourists found the mental processes and emotions way too flimsy for scientific observation. They suggested that our behaviours and reactions towards specific situations and opportunities, rewards and punishments are a better measurement of how our minds work and set about studying that rigorously.

This school of thought became hugely popular but critics found it too mechanical, not allowing for the role of cognition and mental processes in shaping our minds. It began to lose traction in the second half of the 20th century. It was gradually replaced by different approaches such as humanistic psychology, which emphasised the importance of our experiences, abilities and inherent drive for personal growth. You could call it a more optimistic approach, championed by psychologists such as Carl Rogers, Abraham Maslow and Viktor Frankl.

At the same time, cognitive psychology emerged and has remained one of the most influential schools to this day. It focuses on mental processing, attention, problem solving and memory and how these influence our wellbeing. Like behaviourism, it emphasises being measurable and has proven successful in treating an array of conditions such as PTSD, anxiety, depression and phobias. When applied, it aims to break negative thought patterns and replace them with positive actions. While humanistic psychology is focused mainly on the growth and development of the individual, including their emotional and spiritual wellbeing, cognitive psychology is more concerned with understanding and changing patterns of thought and behaviours. They're not necessarily opposed. The Swiss psychologist

Jean Piaget, who has greatly influenced how we view how children develop, grow and learn, drew from both humanistic and cognitive psychology. Meanwhile, both evolutionary and social psychology have emerged. The former is preoccupied with how our mental processes have evolved, and social psychology focuses on social factors and how they influence how we think and respond.

One of the latest and frequently most influential schools is positive psychology. While psychology evolved from a wish to understand what makes us suffer mentally, positive psychology aims to understand what makes us thrive and flourish, such as positive emotions, strong relationships to others and society and a sense of personal strength and advocacy. It has, to some degree, been abused and misrepresented. One of the most significant misconceptions is that it focuses on individual happiness. While happiness is one aspect of positive psychology, it's not the end goal. Positive psychology promotes wellbeing in a much broader sense, concerned with positive relationships, meaning in life and resilience.

Neither is it just about the individual. Positive psychology recognises the crucial importance of social and cultural factors and relationships. According to positive psychology, community involvement is one of the elements of wellbeing. Positive thinking is another commonly misunderstood concept. It's not a cure-all. You can't think all of your problems away. Some should be handled and positive thinking won't magically whisk all obstacles aside, nor do the positive psychologists suggest that it will. It's not a 'don't worry, be happy' kind of psychology. It's not about ignoring the difficulties of being human or the harsh realities of life but rather about cultivating emotions and strengths that will help you cope with adversity and conflicts and build resilience.

Like philosophy, psychology has evolved and continues to do so. And increasingly, our knowledge about the brain influences psychological thinking and theories. There are also valid objections to accepting psychology as Western thinkers have defined it as the sole

> While happiness is one aspect of positive psychology, it's not the end goal

scientific base. People from other cultures and backgrounds have different experiences, even if humans share a common biological and evolutionary history. For instance, a lot has been made of the classic psychology of sexual repression. However, this experience may differ significantly across cultures and individuals, just as family relationships and dynamics vary, which means how they influence our experiences and lives will also vary. But we've come a long way, and despite differences and inevitable disagreements, we know a lot about what will provide us with a feeling of meaning and wellbeing.

Here are my takes on psychology.

- Stay in touch with what matters to you. This is closely related to the 'know yourself' of philosophy. It's easy to get caught up in seemingly essential matters that later turn out to be of only superficial significance.
- The smallest social entity is two. We're shaped by and shape the people we meet and who become part of our lives, however briefly. As a species, we're hardwired to be social. Take good care of the people in your life – including yourself – and make sure that you have people you can depend on and who can depend on you.
- Prioritise what energises you and brings you happiness. It could be playing with your children, cooking or meeting with friends for a walk. It's meaningful and will help you build resilience.
- Stay playful. We also feel a meaningful connection to life and others when we play and laugh. Playfulness will help you grow and learn, which is excellent. When you approach new things with a playful attitude, you'll find it easier to accept that you can fail and have fun simultaneously. But first, being playful will give you happiness, even if there's no point beyond playing and laughing. In her memoir, the actor Barbra Streisand (2023) states, 'I haven't had much fun in

Take good care of the people in your life – including yourself

my life, to tell you the truth. And I want to have more fun.'
- Nurture a growth mindset. When you focus on your potential for growth and development and accept that you can improve your intelligence and abilities if you dedicate yourself to it, you'll be able to see challenges and failures as opportunities for learning and personal development.
- Talk kindly to yourself. A lot of us have a negative inner conversation, the kind of voice that keeps bringing us down. Replace it with a kinder and more constructive dialogue – much as you'd talk to a trusted friend. It doesn't mean glossing over mistakes or making self-aggrandising statements. Instead, it allows you to accept mistakes and setbacks – they don't define you.

Expand yourself (neurology)

When I went to school, we were taught that the brain doesn't change. Brain cells can't regenerate, so the common wisdom was that once they were lost, that was it. In the middle of the 20th century, the concept of neuroplasticity was evolving but didn't gain wider recognition until the 1990s. Neuroplasticity is all about how the brain can change and adapt to new conditions and circumstances. While brain cells don't regenerate, the brain can often rearrange itself to compensate for the loss. The brain isn't fixed; it's plastic and constantly changing to allow for new experiences.

The human brain consists of 100 billion cells, neurons, which differ from other cells. They have a unique structure that allows them to communicate through specialised connections called synapses, and each cell can both transmit and receive signals from other cells. Each neuron has, on average, about 6,000 synaptic connections with other neurons. That puts the synapse count in the hundreds of trillions. Brain cells can form complex networks that enable the brain to process and store information. The cells also communicate through electrical and chemical signals and neurotransmitters. When a signal is sent, it triggers the release of chemicals such as dopamine, serotonin and acetylcholine, which in turn regulate or influence, among other things, motivation, movement, mood, sleep, muscle control, learning and memory. When we damage or lose brain cells, the brain can often reorganise the networks. It will try to use the synapses to create new pathways – much as you would build a bridge or a new road if the old road is lost due to a flood. It may not always be as fast and efficient but it will do the job.

The stronger and more complex these networks are, the more likely the brain will be able to reorganise itself to compensate for damages and losses. Fortunately, today, we know how to help these networks grow. I'll get back to that a bit later but the discovery of neuroplasticity has been one of the game changers in neurology and how it's applied to thriving and wellbeing.

Neurology, of course, goes way further back than the 20th century. The brain always seems to have fascinated us, and even ancient civilisations such as the Greeks, Egyptians and Romans had some idea of how the nervous system worked. However, it wasn't until the 18th century that systematic studies of the brain began. In the late 18th century, the German physician Franz Gall promoted the idea that the shape and size of the skull could reveal a person's personality, criminal tendencies, potential and intelligence. At the time, it was known that different brain regions were responsible for different mental functions. So, the theory went that if you could measure these parts of the skull correctly, you could also judge a person on those measurements. This field of brain studies became known as phrenology and it was influential in the 1800s and considered a legitimate scientific field. It was, however, without empirical evidence and reliant on racial and gender stereotypes. Women and people of colour would almost always be shown to be less intelligent and have less potential than white males.

The discovery of neuroplasticity has been one of the game changers in neurology

In the 19th century, the Italian physician **Camillo Golgi** developed a technique to visualise individual nerve cells or neurons. Spanish neuroscientist **Santiago Ramón y Cajal** used Golgi's method to draw neurons and their connections in detail, making it possible to understand it better. With the development of different visual techniques in neurology – first X-rays, later the electroencephalogram (EEG), CT and MRI, it became possible to visualise brain activity and diagnose neurological disorders. In the latter half of the 20th century, the study of neurotransmitters led to new treatments for neurological and psychiatric disorders, including serotonin reuptake inhibitors (SSRIs) for depression and certain OCD-related disorders.

Lately, the field of neuroscience has evolved a better understanding of the genetic and molecular mechanisms underlying certain disorders, including Alzheimer's disease, and new fields are constantly being studied, including neuromodulation, where you alter brain activity with electric or magnetic stimulation to treat certain disorders. Another emerging field is the study of the microbiome gut–brain axis. Recent research has highlighted how the billions of microorganisms living in and on our bodies help regulate brain function and behaviour. The axis is a two-way link between the gut and the central nervous system. Researchers are trying to find out if and how we can manipulate the microbiome to improve brain health.

With the growing understanding of the importance and plasticity of our brain, we're also encountering several ethical concerns regarding the study of it and the treatments available. There's still a taboo surrounding brain research, prohibiting certain studies and treatments because changing your brain may also mean changing yourself and perhaps in ways that aren't always foreseeable. An acquaintance on the autism spectrum was asked if he wished for treatment for his condition. He looked shocked. 'But then I wouldn't love trains as much,' he protested. They've been his lifelong passion. Would that passion be rendered meaningless or disappear by a treatment? Or would he keep it while being able to improve his social skills?

While we debate the ethics and morals of brain science and how to apply it, we know today that we can help ourselves to develop solid and complex neural networks. This will help us feel better and improve our chances of having good brain health well into late age – to become one of the 'super agers', as they're known. First, learning new things changes the brain and helps it develop new synapses. So does physical exercise, which has been proven to strengthen the growth of synapses, especially in the hippocampus, which is essential to learning and memory. Sleeping and eating well is important too.

A growing number of studies emphasise the importance of strong social connections. Not only do you help your brain when you have positive social relationships and close friends; it's also associated with an overall increased likelihood of remaining healthy and happy.

As you'll see in Appendix 2, neurology is a surprisingly old scientific field, but recently it's been expanding rapidly and has some excellent results to show. And while neurology is all about the hardware of our mind, it also concerns how that hardware influences our minds, wellbeing and behaviour. So here's some advice on how to take good care of your brain and improve its chances of staying healthy well into old age.

- Stay curious. The brain loves learning and experiencing new things. Learn a new language, travel in new ways or to new places and practise new skills such as playing the piano or painting. It reduces your risk of cognitive decline and is also great fun. You may also make new friends and become a more interesting person to your old friends and family.
- Exercise regularly. Regular physical activity has been shown to improve brain function and your ability to focus and increase neuroplasticity – which will increase your ability to learn new things and adapt to unique circumstances.
- Spend time in nature. We know that this reduces stress, boosts your mood and improves cognitive abilities. It also helps lower your blood pressure and boosts your immune system, which benefits the brain.
- Maintain a healthy lifestyle. Sleep well. Eat a balanced diet rich in vegetables, legumes and fruit and don't smoke or drink alcohol. This advice is usually provided for keeping your body fit but is also excellent for your brain. After all, it is – together with the heart – your motor, and to keep running smoothly, you have to provide it with the best fuel and keep it away from harm.

- ⊗ If you cycle, wear a helmet. Like most Danes, if you ride a bike, you should wear a helmet. It may not look sexy or smart but it protects the brain. The same goes for any sport where your brain may be at increased risk. We know today that some sports are way more damaging to the brain than was previously believed. Protect your brain.
- ⊗ Stay socially connected. Neurology agrees with psychology on a lot of things. This is one of the most important. You need other people. Social interaction is essential for cognitive wellbeing and reduces your risk of cognitive decline.
- ⊗ Manage your stress and workload. Chronic stress can negatively affect brain function and influence your general wellbeing in a harmful and sometimes potentially life-threatening way. Stress management techniques such as deep breathing, exercise and mindfulness can help you reduce stress. But remember to look at your workload. If you're constantly overworked, no amount of mindfulness can help you stay happy and healthy.

Transform yourself (strategy)

Strategy is, in its briefest description, how to set a goal and make a deliberate plan about how to achieve it. Initially, it was mainly applied in warfare but has evolved into all spheres of our lives – business, politics, economics and personal success. Strategy is an ancient discipline, which no doubt goes much further back than our first known source, *The Art of War*, written by Chinese general and strategist Sun Tzu, probably around 2,500 years ago. The ancient Greeks and Romans also theorised extensively about war, strategy and tactics. Theories of military strategy seeped into other fields. The classical philosophers considered strategic skills of vital importance in governance. In *The Republic*, Plato stressed that the ideal leader had to balance short-term needs with long-term goals and adapt strategies in response to changing circumstances.

In his work *Politics*, Aristotle emphasised the importance of strategic thinking in achieving political goals. However, he did caution against 'the end justifies the means' dogma and advised against deception or unethical tactics. The same could be said about the Roman philosopher and statesman Cicero, who argued that successful leaders must be able to anticipate and respond to threats to their authority while maintaining a sense of integrity and ethical conduct.

No such scruples bothered the Italian Renaissance thinker, author, diplomat and historian Niccolò Machiavelli, who wrote his most famous work, *The Prince*, during the last years of his life in the early 1500s. It was published in 1532, five years after his death. It can be considered the first work that discusses a systematic and pragmatic use of strategy in state-building and power, and while many people to this day consider it a masterpiece, the term Machiavellian has also come to describe an unscrupulous leader who uses any means necessary to stay in power, including manipulation and deceit. His view of politics as a strategic power game was and remains controversial and highly influential.

These days, another old strategic theorist is gaining new-found fame, namely Carl von Clausewitz, a Prussian general and military strategist who wrote extensively on military strategy in his unfinished work *Vom Kriege* (in English, *On War*), mainly written just after the Napoleonic Wars and published by his wife after his death, between 1832 and 1835. Many of his military theories are still being taught and debated in military academies. Some of his ideas are also highly relevant in other fields, including his thesis on friction. To Clausewitz, friction means all the unforeseen things that can happen despite the best of plans. The weather can make a road slow or even impossible to travel, communication can break down and people can behave unpredictably. For most of us, the instinct is to try to plan even better, considering more possibilities. Clausewitz argued that this would be a highly inefficient and unrealistic way of dealing with friction. Instead, you have to prepare yourself to encounter obstacles and opportunities you hadn't planned for and be ready to deal with them as they come. One of his solutions was to suggest that soldiers and units should have knowledge of the overall strategic goal and its importance and then be given agency to make their own decisions and use their abilities to reach it.

This approach is highly relevant today when things change fast and frequently unpredictably. It also applies to setting a personal goal and defining personal success. Suppose you try to plan every step along the way. In that case, you risk that friction, in the Clausewitz sense of the word, will deter you and you may miss otherwise obvious opportunities along the way, too intent on following a specific plan.

You need to set goals that aren't so specific that everything hinges on you achieving a position as, say, the CEO of a particular company. Instead, ask yourself what kind of life you want – and not least why – and then accept that there are more ways than one to get there. The same goes for how to define personal success. As I wrote earlier, I've met many people who'd achieved exactly what they'd dreamt of – but remained unhappy because the goal wasn't the right one or their definition of success was too narrow and not centred in their sense of meaning.

However, neither Clausewitz nor I would advise just going where the wind takes you. Strategy is important. By setting goals for your life, you can focus your energy and resources on the activities that will help you reach those goals. Remember, where attention goes, energy flows. Devising a strategy can also help you identify your strengths, weaknesses, opportunities, threats and critical factors for your results. Most people in the business world will know this as a SWOT analysis and the purpose is to make you aware and conscious of what works for you and what works against you so you can consider that when you set your goals and draft a plan.

> *Ask yourself what kind of life you want – and not least why – and then accept that there are more ways than one to get there*

One of the fundamental principles of strategy is to use your resources effectively. How you spend your time, your energy and your finances all play into your chances of achieving your goals. You must prioritise the activities and investments that will most likely help you achieve your goals – these need not be financial; it could also be the time you invest in building your networks. And, as Clausewitz stresses, you need to be able to adapt to changing circumstances. Stay open to new ideas and possibilities and be ready to adjust your goals and plans. A short-term failure can become a long-term win if you learn from experience and transform that learning into something valuable.

There are many ways to apply lessons from strategy. I've done so in my coaching and my book *The Personal Business Plan* (2013) so let me summarise some of the key points.

- Find the right goals. This involves knowing your virtues and what gives you meaning in life. The goals may differ from what you initially expected – less about success in a traditional way and more about feeling a sense of meaning and being valued for who you are, not for material success. You should find goals that excite you and make you realise that you must stretch yourself to reach them.
- What is success to you? Define success in a way that's meaningful to you. Imagine how you'll feel when you reach your goal. Does the thought of it make you truly happy? Is it in line with the person you've decided you want to be and does it allow you to prioritise the people and things in life that are important to you?
- Confide in others when you set your goals. That way, you'll feel more accountable – and you'll also find that people are willing to help you reach your goals and remind you when you move in the wrong direction.
- Remember that goals are big decisions. Execution is all the small everyday decisions that will get you where you want to be. Define shorter-term targets and be ready to evaluate whether you're going in the right direction. If not, ask yourself whether it's the goal (the big decision) or your execution (all the small decisions) that are stopping you.
- Keep a log of your progress and the small things. It's easy to feel that you're getting nowhere. A record can help you see positive changes that you might otherwise forget.
- Learn how to be persistent in the face of adversity. See failures and obstacles as opportunities for growth and learning rather than fiascos that should be avoided. Write

Lessons for transformation

down your lessons each time you either succeed or fail.
- Celebrate your victories.

As you can see, regardless of the field of science, there are remarkable resemblances. Our social connections with and to other people are of the utmost importance. They are part of us; we are part of them. Curiosity, openness and playfulness, in the sense that we can do things just for the joy of them and without fear of failing, also give us a sense of wellbeing and meaning.

I hope this book has given you an awareness of how much knowledge we already have about human thriving. I also hope that you'll be able to put it to use and live a life that you find meaningful and rewarding. To live that life, you need awareness of who you are, who you want to be to yourself and others and what it will take to get there. To reach that point is, I believe, freedom in the truest sense of the word. In my previous book, I coined the term 'freedom systematised'.

Freedom isn't just the absence of coercion and external control but freedom *from* something. We can think and act for ourselves and feel responsible for our actions, feeling free to do something. As Hannah Arendt argued, freedom is our ability to act and create something new in the world. We can only do so if we have a sense of agency and a force of agency. Arendt also stressed the necessity of plurality, of diversity in opinion and experiences. We have to allow others their freedom and we need to acknowledge our responsibilities towards others.

> See failures and obstacles as opportunities for growth and learning

Remember the first three questions in the book? Try to answer them now. Hopefully, the answers will give you this kind of freedom, a relaxed readiness and existential clarity that will allow you to navigate the unknown future waters with a sense of meaning and adventure. Permit yourself to be magnificent.

Questions to ask yourself

- What is my next existential choice?
- What is my next existential act?
- Which existential responsibility do I still need to address?
- What is keeping me from choosing, acting and being responsible?

Epilogue
Ten existential hacks

This is the 'fridge door' version – ten pieces of advice to hang up in a prominent place. To implement the hacks, use the scorecard in Appendix 1 (page 201) to track your progress. The scorecard also offers further examples.

1. Reach out
You're not alone. Your relationships are vital and define you. Nurture them. Reach out to others to ask for help and give help and support. Plenty of research and studies confirm that having good relationships and people you can rely on and who can rely on you is vital to thriving, regardless of age. I've explored this throughout the book, so there's no need to elaborate here but if you want only one piece of advice for leading a better life, this is it.

2. Expose yourself to awe
Gaze at the starry sky on a winter's night. Become overwhelmed by the music and atmosphere at a live concert or an act of courage. Feel humbled by the craftsmanship exhibited by our forefathers in ancient buildings, artefacts and pieces of art, and feel the thrill and the terror of huge waves crashing onto the shore on a stormy day... Awe provides us with perspective and humility that isn't obeisance but joy in our diminished focus on Self and feeling connected to something bigger, to a heightened sense of meaning. Research shows that this kind of awe benefits our mental health, healing us and putting our lives into perspective.

3. Play and have fun

Adult life is frequently depicted as serious, which makes it seem almost frivolous to have fun and play. So, we dress it up as competition or try to suppress our inherent love of games and laughter. Playing eases stress, whips up beneficial hormones, gives you energy and is frequently a social connector. People who know how to have a good time are more fun. Your social life will benefit if you allow yourself to play. If you think you should work hard first, think again. A fun break can give you the energy you need to finish your tasks. Lego's creed in the 1960s was 'work hard, play harder', which remains relevant today.

4. The right time is now

I sometimes wear a badge that states: 'It's Time'. In this book, I've explained that when people ask 'Time for what?', I answer, 'Time to reinvent yourself.' But that isn't the only answer. There's a quote attributed to several people: 'If not you, who? And if not now, when?' There's always a better time and somebody better made for the task. Or, to quote the wise and ancient wizard Gandalf in J R R Tolkien's The Lord of the Rings, when the hobbit Frodo sighs that he wishes the challenging times ahead hadn't happened in his time: 'So do I, and so do all who live to see such times. But that is not for them to decide. All we have to decide is what to do with the time that is given us.' The less lofty character, the indomitable Sam Gamgee, says it in a different way: 'It's the job that's never started as takes the longest to finish.' Most of us are brilliant procrastinators and adept at finding excuses. But the right time is now, and the right person is you.

5. Practise courage

Courage is about doing what you're afraid to do, not about being fearless. It isn't a struggle if you do something you're unafraid of. Nevertheless, it may be praiseworthy but courage demands something different of us. Courage can be learned and practised. Do something you're afraid of doing at least once a week. Of course, don't do something physically dangerous that you're unprepared for. But for most of us, courage is more about emotions than the imminent danger of death. Say yes to something you want to do but are afraid of doing. Say no to something that you don't want to do, even if it seems that it could backfire. Walk up to a stranger at a party and begin to chat. Give a speech even though you hate being in front of many people. Share your doubts and ask for advice. Ask yourself, 'What's the worst thing that could happen?' Most of the time, when you think about it, the answer isn't terrible. Yes, you may make a fool of yourself. So what? You won't be the first nor the last; chances are that others have done the same. You may even find yourself admired for daring to put yourself out there.

6. Be someone rather than something

Status tends to lure us into prioritising short-term goals and neglecting what would give us meaning and fulfilment. There's nothing wrong with status in itself. Most of us would like an influential and well-paid job, a beautiful home in a nice place and enough money not to worry about them. But you risk getting so fixated on being a CEO, prosperous homeowner and board member that you forget where your fundamental values and worth lie. If you strip away titles, the home that's the envy of your acquaintances and the membership of prestigious clubs, what can you contribute? If you're valued and value yourself for who you are rather than what you are, it'll be far easier to let go of titles and objects that may not give you the feeling of meaning you're looking for. Pay attention to what matters to you and invest your time and attention in that. It all comes back to the question of how you define success.

7. Relearn how to learn

As you get older, you become accustomed to being good at something. The downside is that you get bad at being bad and that makes learning new skills or new ways of thinking more challenging. Your brain likes what's predictable. The brain is a high-maintenance and energy-consuming ball of jelly, so it's looking to cut corners when it can. Besides, you get comfortable with your abilities and what you already know. Learning something new means that you must accept that you'll be making unpredictable mistakes and feel frustrated by your lack of skill, which is the opposite of comfort. But with it also comes a sense of triumph when you eventually manage the task. If you've ever seen a baby learning to crawl and then walk, you may recognise the range of feelings on their face, from red-faced frustration to radiant success. It has always taken time to learn new skills, and you can teach an old dog new tricks. It's a lot easier if you know how to laugh lovingly rather than derisively at yourself as you make the inevitable mistakes.

8. Shake things up

There are a lot of unhealthy polarisations in today's societies. We're continually seeking out peers and like-minded people, which is putting a brake on one of our most precious human qualities: empathy. By the way, this is one of the most sought-after working skills and is predicted to become even more valuable. Expose yourself to different views. Listen more to people you disagree with and put energy into doing so with an open mind. Listen actively behind the words to the thinking and what's not being said. You don't have to agree but begin to understand where they're coming from. Get used to ambiguity and the horrible notion that you might be wrong. It's called ambiguity tolerance. Challenge your assumptions. Seek out new experiences and learn to appreciate the unknown. It will teach you empathy and enable you to be creative and innovative, which also happen to be highly valued skills.

9. Stay physically active

Whether you stretch, dance, run, walk, kayak or lift weights, staying physically active is crucial to your wellbeing. It helps you focus; it will make you sleep better, give you energy and it can prevent depression. The scientific evidence on the benefits of staying active is overwhelming. It doesn't have to be anything ambitious; just move that body! If you do so in nature, it's even better. Surrounding yourself with nature comes with a myriad of benefits, enhancing those you already get from being physically active.

10. Believe in free will

With the superpower of AI unleashed, heralding a new direction for society, the question of will, mind and soul acquires a new urgency. What is human? What is intelligence? And is free will an illusion? Some brain experts think that we're nothing but biological processes that occur without us even noticing. However, whether or not they're correct, there's a case to be made for believing in free will. It makes you happier with life, which isn't only my belief, as studies have shown it too. I think it will also make you kinder towards others. If you are free to act, you must assume responsibility for your actions. Choice, action, responsibility are key to your existence.

Appendix 1

Scorecard for a meaningful life

When I introduced my 'ten existential hacks' (page 197) to a client on my 'Personal Business Plan' programme, he suggested having a scorecard to keep track of the commitments to self-improvement he was making.

You can use the scorecard over the page to keep track of your own progress. I've listed actions as examples to inspire you. Score yourself every week, every month, every year, or every decade! It's up to you how and when you want to live a truly meaningful life.

As another practical way to bring existentialist ideas into your daily life, think back to Figure 2 (page 27), my four-leaf clover model. The two eternity symbols are like the figure 8. As a way to connect this image with my own life, I like to find health-related targets which are based on the figure 8. For example:

- 8 hours of sleep a day
- 8 hours of exercise per week
- I stopped drinking alcohol in 2008
- I will run a marathon when I'm 80.

And as a happy coincidence, I gave myself 10 years to complete this book, but I made it ahead of schedule in... 8! How could you bring the power of 8 into your own life?

Scoring:
3 = To a great extent
2 = Somewhat
1 = Not at all or to a limited extent

Existential hacks	Examples of actions	Q1	Q2	Q3	Q4	...
1. Reach out	Ask for help: contact three friends Join a club or an association Pay a family visit					
2. Expose yourself to awe	Trek Go to a live concert Read a literary masterpiece					
3. Play and have fun	Play a board game Go to the movies Travel					
4. The right time is now	Make a bold decision Take a risk Start acting instead of procrastinating					
5. Practise courage	Say yes to something you want to do Say no to something that you do not want to do Let go of the risk of ridicule					
6. Be someone rather than something	Pay attention to what matters to you Praise yourself and have a positive inner dialogue Invest your time and attention in meaningful acts					
7. Relearn how to learn	Unlearn something old Learn something new Place yourself in uncommon situations					
8. Shake things up	Listen to people you disagree with Challenge your assumptions Follow first principles					
9. Stay physically active	Move that body Get out in nature Start an exercise routine					
10. Believe in free will	Choose Act Take responsibility					

Appendix 2
Standing on the shoulders of giants

Every philosophical idea builds on the thinking of many people in the past. In this appendix I would like to pay respect to the thought leaders of the past and present the families of ideas which have fed into mine, through a series of timelines.

Existential philosophy

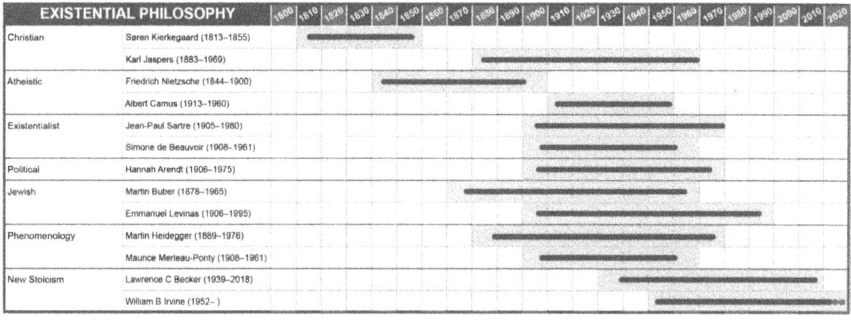

This chronology shows that Søren Kierkegaard (1813–1855) as a Christian philosopher is followed by:

- ❀ Friedrich Nietzsche (1844–1900) atheistic
- ❀ Martin Buber (1878–1965) Jewish
- ❀ Karl Jaspers (1883–1969) Christian, and
- ❀ Martin Heidegger (1889–1976) phenomenology.

Most of these thinkers can be characterised as existential philosophers with Germanic roots. Then follows a batch of philosophers of primarily French and later British origin:

- Jean-Paul Sartre (1905-1980) existentialist
- Emmanuel Levinas (1906-1995) Jewish
- Hannah Arendt (1906-1975) political – and the first woman on the list!
- Simone de Beauvoir (1908-1986) existentialist – the second woman on the list.
- Maurice Merleau-Ponty (1908-1961) phenomenology
- Albert Camus (1913-1960) atheistic
- Lawrence C Becker (1939-2018) New Stoicism
- William B Irvine (1952-) New Stoicism.

But then something less obvious emerges. A whole school of existential psychologists materialises in parallel:

Existential psychology

EXISTENTIAL PSYCHOLOGY		1800 1810 1820 1830 1840 1850 1860 1870 1880 1890 1900 1910 1920 1930 1940 1950 1960 1970 1980 1990 2000 2010 2020
Psychoanalysis	Sigmund Freud (1856-1939)	
Analytical psychology	Carl Jung (1875-1961)	
Dream and existence	Ludwig Binswanger (1881-1960)	
Man's Search for Meaning	Viktor E Frankl (1905-1997)	
Self-actualisation	Abraham Maslow (1908-1970)	
The Meaning of Anxiety	Rollo May (1909-1994)	
The Divided Self	Ronald D Laing (1927-1988)	
Existential psychotherapy	Irvin D Yalom (1931-)	

- Sigmund Freud (1856-1939) psychoanalysis
- Carl Jung (1875-1961) analytical psychology
- Ludwig Binswanger (1881-1960) dream and existence
- Viktor E Frankl (1905-1997) logotherapy and *Man's Search for Meaning*
- Rollo May (1909-1994) humanistic psychology and the meaning of anxiety
- Abraham Maslow (1908-1970) hierarchy of needs
- Ronald D Laing (1927-1988) *The Divided Self*
- Irvin D Yalom (1931-) existential psychotherapy
- Mihaly Csikszentmihalyi (1934-2021) flow

- Martin Seligman (1942–) positive psychology
- Emmy van Deurzen (1951–) happiness – only the third woman on the list.

Most of these thinkers are existential psychologists with American Jewish roots. Many of their parents fled authoritarian regimes in greater Europe (including Russia). Fun fact: Sigmund Freud, the founder of psychoanalysis, was initially a neuroscientist but abandoned neuroscience completely after he made a last attempt to link both in his book *Project of a Scientific Psychology* in 1895.

Neurology

Turning to neurology, I found – much to my surprise – that the list already starts in 1824 with Paul Broca's work on language disorders, followed by the work of Jean-Martin Charcot (born 1925) on neurological disorders. When I started writing this book, I could have sworn that neurology was a more recent discipline.

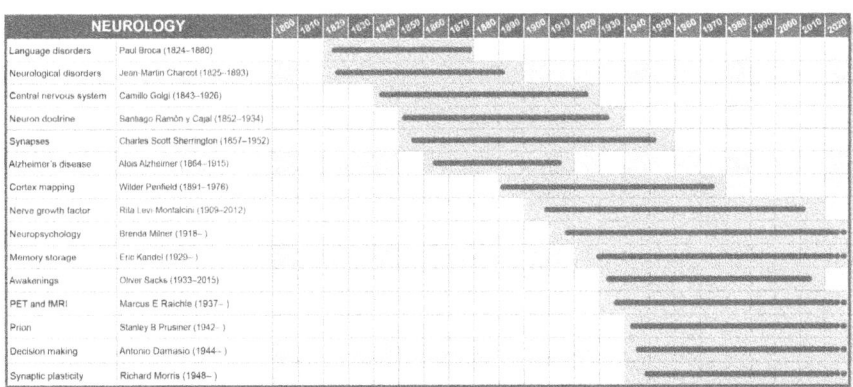

- Paul Broca (1824–1880) language disorders
- Jean-Martin Charcot (1825–1893) neurological disorders
- Camillo Golgi (1843–1926) central nervous system
- Santiago Ramón y Cajal (1852–1934) neuron doctrine
- Charles Scott Sherrington (1857–1952) synapses
- Alois Alzheimer (1864–1915) Alzheimer's disease
- Wilder Penfield (1891–1976) cortex mapping
- Rita Levi-Montalcini (1909–2012) nerve growth factor – the fourth woman on the list

- ⊗ Brenda Milner (1918–) neuropsychology – the fifth woman on the list
- ⊗ Eric Kandel (1929–) memory storage
- ⊗ Oliver Sacks (1933–2015) *Awakenings*
- ⊗ Stanley B Prusiner (1942–) prion
- ⊗ Antonio Damasio (1944–) decision-making
- ⊗ Marcus E Raichle (1937–) PET and fMRI
- ⊗ Richard Morris (1948–) synaptic plasticity.

This means that neurology is indeed an old science. The pioneers of neurology lived in the same era as Kierkegaard! Then, of course, neurology continued to develop fast due to technological developments in the form of, among others, PET and fMRI.

Strategy

In parallel, the domain of strategy developed. It goes way back and has its origin in warfare but it took on a broader meaning and began to influence businesses in the late 1800s and early 1900s.

STRATEGY		
Planning	Igor Ansoff (1918–2002)	
	Bruce D Henderson (1915–1992)	
	Michael E Porter (1945–)	
	Russell L Ackoff (1919–2009)	
	Kim W Chan (1952–)	
	Renée Mauborgne (1963–)	
	Roger Martin (1956–)	
Execution	Peter Drucker (1909–2005)	
	Robert B Kaplan (1940–)	
	Ram Charan (1939–)	
	Stephen Bungay (1954–)	
	Jeroen De Flander (1972 –)	
	John Doerr (1951–)	
Adaption	Henry Mintzberg (1939–)	
	Tom Peters (1942–)	
Concentration	C K Prahalad (1941– 2010)	
	Gary Hamel (1954–)	
	Richard Normann (1943–2003)	
	Birger Wernerfelt (1951–)	
	Jay B Barney (1951–)	
	Herbert Simon (1916–2001)	
	Karl E Weick (1936–)	
	Daniel Kahneman (1934–2024)	
Change	John Kotter (1947–)	
	Peter Senge (1947–)	
	Rosabeth Moss Kanter (1943–)	
Black swan	Joseph Schumpeter (1883–1950)	
	Clayton M Christensen (1952–2020)	

Appendix 2

In chronological order, the leading thinkers within the strategy domain are:

- Joseph Schumpeter (1883–1950) business cycles and creative destruction
- Peter Drucker (1909–2005) management by objectives
- Bruce D Henderson (1915–1992) BCG (Boston Consulting Group) matrix
- Herbert Simon (1916–2001) bounded rationality and satisficing
- Igor Ansoff (1918–2002) Ansoff matrix
- Russell L Ackoff (1919–2009) systems thinking
- Daniel Kahneman (1934–2024) System I and System II
- Karl E Weick (1936–) sensemaking and mindfulness
- Henry Mintzberg (1939–) emergent strategy
- Ram Charan (1939–) getting things done
- Robert S Kaplan (1940–) balanced scorecard
- C K Prahalad (1941–2010) core competencies
- Tom Peters (1942–) *In Search of Excellence*
- Richard Normann (1943–2003) service management and mission
- Rosabeth Moss Kanter (1943–) change management – the sixth woman on the list
- John Kotter (1947–) change management
- Michael E Porter (1947–) value chain and Porter's five forces
- Peter Senge (1947–) *The Fifth Discipline*
- John Doerr (1951–) objectives and key results (OKRs)
- Birger Wernerfelt (1951–) resource-based view of the firm
- Clayton M Christensen (1952–2020) disruption and *How Will You Measure Your Life?*
- W Chan Kim (1952–) *Blue Ocean Strategy*
- Stephen Bungay (1954–) *The Art of Action*
- Gary Hamel (1954–) core competencies
- Jay B Barney (1954–) VRIO (value, rareness, inimitability and organisation) and sustainable competitive advantage
- Roger Martin (1956–) *Playing to Win*

- Renée Mauborgne (1963–) *Blue Ocean Strategy*
- Jeroen De Flander (1972–) strategy execution.

Of course, I could have chosen to include other existential thinkers but these thinkers constitute my ultimate frame of reference. To the best of my ability, I've tried to understand their thinking, build on their concepts and cross-fertilise their ideas.

I can't help noticing what I see as relay batons:

- Kierkegaard dies in 1855 and Freud was born in 1856 (Christian philosophy)
- Nietzsche died in 1900 and Camus was born in 1913 (atheistic philosophy)
- Schumpeter (creative destruction) died in 1950 and Christensen (disruption) was born in 1952.

Last but not least, I'm perfectly aware that there's a serious gender and ethnic bias in the list. Only 10 per cent of these existential thinkers are female and all are Caucasian. To be honest, this unfortunately also goes for my expert panel, which only consists of Caucasian middle-aged men. My apologies!

Appendix 3
Three existential models
The WHY, the HOW and the WHAT

Returning to the four-leaf clover image again (see Chapter 1 and Appendix 1), I have used it to encapsulate three levels of connections (refer back to the stages of life and Self explored in Chapter 4) – each of which also relates to my own journey through life.

They also connect with my own journey as a writer and thinker:

1. My first book was about **Career**: *Your Next Career: The Headhunter's Guide to Lifelong Success* (in Danish)
2. My second book was about **Happiness**: *The Personal Business Plan: A Blueprint for Running Your Life*
3. This, my third book, is about **Meaning**: *The Existential Playbook: How to Survive, Live and Thrive*.

So the book that you have just read completes my trilogy and synthesises my key learning for a life well lived.

I recommend you use the four-leaf clover symbol in the figure below to explore the stages of your own life and how your Self opens up to new possibilities over time.

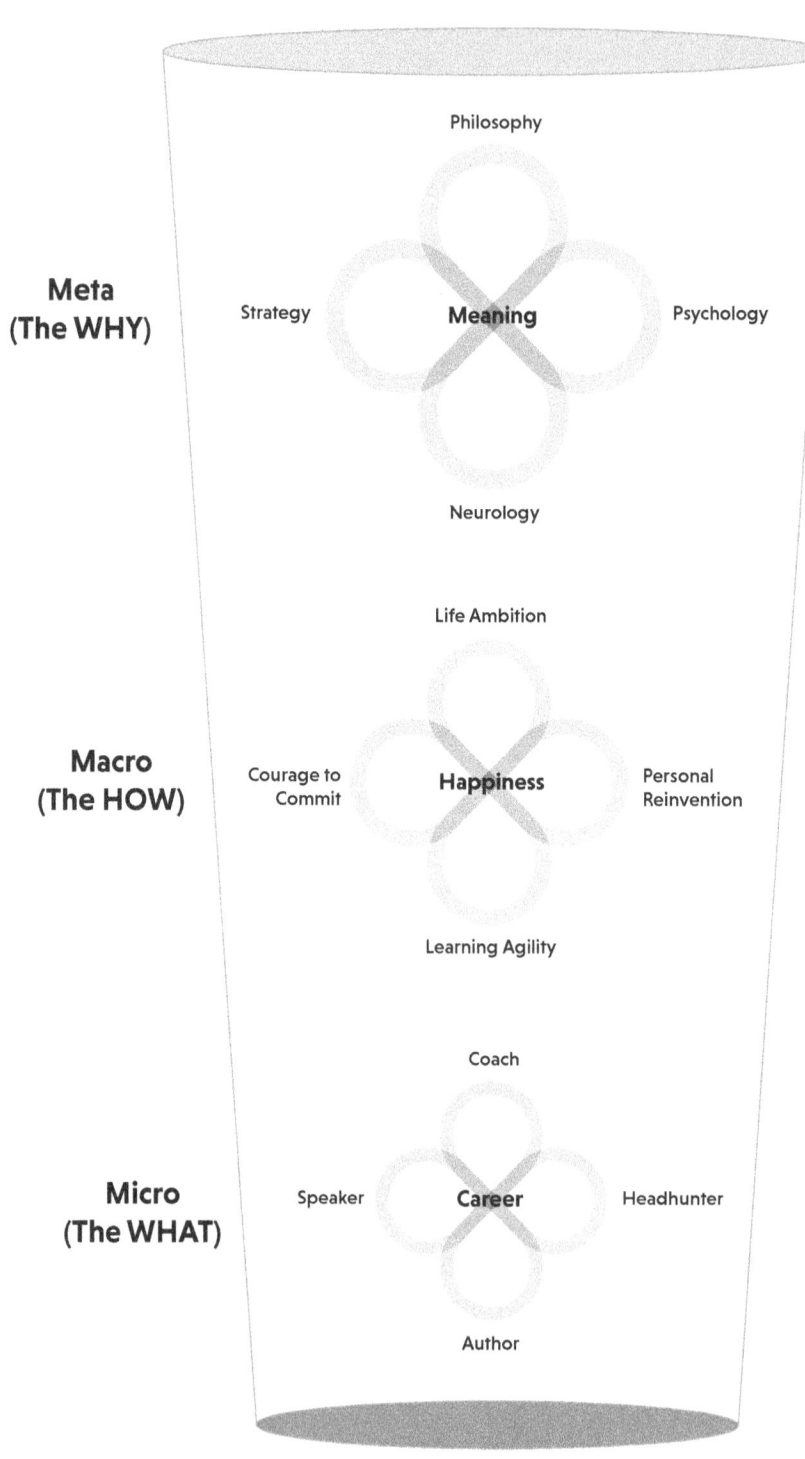

Top ten recommended reads

The amount of existential literature is overwhelming. Dealing with the four different disciplines of philosophy, psychology, neurology and strategy makes the picture even more complex. In this top ten, I've tried to accommodate all schools of thought and picked representative works. By reading these books and applying the insights you will find meaning in life and become an even better person.

1. Arendt, H (1958) *The Human Condition*. University of Chicago Press.
2. Bakewell, S (2016) *At the Existentialist Café – Freedom, Being & Apricot Cocktails*. Penguin.
3. Christensen, C M, Allworth, J, Dillon, K (2012) *How Will You Measure Your Life?* Harper Business.
4. Drucker, P (1939) *The End of Economic Man: A Study of the New Totalitarianism*. The John Day Company.
5. Frankl, V E (1946) *Man's Search for Meaning: An Introduction to Logotherapy*. Beacon Press.
6. Kahneman, D (2012) *Thinking, Fast and Slow*. Penguin.
7. Kierkegaard, S (2023) *The Sickness unto Death: A New Translation*. Liveright.
8. Rogers, C (1989) *On Becoming a Person: A Therapist's View of Psychotherapy*. Houghton Mifflin.
9. Sartre, J-P (2007) *Existentialism is a Humanism*. Yale University Press.
10. Yalom, I D (1980) *Existential Psychotherapy*. Yalom Family Trust.

Bibliography

Aqel, I (2019) 'One point of view does not show the whole picture'. URL: youtube.com/watch?v=Dmc3mQ87GiQ

Arden, P (2003) *It's Not How Good You Are, It's How Good You Want to Be.* Phaidon Press.

Arendt, H (1958) *The Human Condition.* University of Chicago Press.

Aristotle (1968) *On Poetics.* Oxford University Press.

Asimov, I (1980) 'A cult of ignorance'. *Newsweek*, 21 January.

Aurelius, M (2014) *Meditations.* Penguin Classics.

Baer, D (2015) 'Elon Musk uses this ancient critical-thinking strategy to outsmart everybody else'. *Business Insider*, 5 January. URL: businessinsider.com/elon-musk-first-principles-2015-1

Bakewell, S (2016) *At the Existentialist Café: Freedom, being and apricot cocktails.* Penguin.

Brønniche, V, Vogel, A, et al (2018) 'Psychometric properties and reference data for Danish versions of free and cued selective reminding test, category cued memory test and logical memory'. *Scandinavian Journal of Psychology.* URL: pubmed.ncbi.nlm.nih.gov/29999180

Bruyant-Langer, S (1999) 'The competition concept of the future – an epochal theory' (in Danish). *Leadership Today.*

Bruyant-Langer, S (2012) *Your Next Career – The Headhunter's Guide to Lifelong Success* (in Danish). Lindhardt & Ringhof.

Bruyant-Langer, S (2013) *The Personal Business Plan: A Blueprint for Running Your Life.* Wiley.

Bruyant-Langer, S (2022) 'How Does Hybrid Working Rhyme with Nordic Leadership?'. The Møller Institute, Churchill College, University of Cambridge, 12 July. URL: mollerinstitute.com/insights/how-does-hybrid-working-rhyme-with-nordic-leadership

Bruyant-Langer, S (2024) 'Engagement in a Nordic Leadership Perspective'. The Møller Institute, Churchill College, University of Cambridge, 29 January. URL: mollerinstitute.com/insights/engagement-in-a-nordic-leadership-perspective

Camus, A (1991) *The Fall.* Vintage Books.

Chalmers, D (1996) *The Conscious Mind: In search of a fundamental theory.* Oxford University Press.

Changeux, P (1997) *Neuronal Man: The Biology of Mind.* Princeton University Press.

Christensen, C M (2016) *The Innovator's Dilemma: When New Technologies Cause Great Firms to Fail.* Harvard Business Press.

Bibliography

Christensen, C M, Allworth, J, Dillon, K (2012) *How Will You Measure Your Life?* Harper Business.
Churchland, P (1984) *Matter and Consciousness.* Massachusetts Institute of Technology Press.
Cialdini, R (2021) *Influence: The Psychology of Persuasion.* Harper Business.
Clausewitz, C von (1993) *On War.* David Campbell Publishers.
Colgi, C (1903) *Opera Omnia.* Hoepli.
Crutchfield, J & Kahn, N (1996) 'Turbulent landscapes'. *Complexity* 2(2).
Csikszentmihalyi, M (1990) *Flow: The psychology of optimal experience.* Harper and Row.
Cuddy, A (2012) 'Fake it till you make it'. TED talk. URL: youtube.com/watch?v=RVmMeMcGc0Y
Damasio, A (2010) *Self Comes to Mind: Constructing the conscious brain.* Pantheon.
Darwin, C (1871) *The Descent of Man and Selection in Relation to Sex.*
Dennett, D C (2007) *Consciousness Explained.* Penguin.
Descartes, R (1641) *Meditations on First Philosophy.*
Dhingra, N, Emmett, J, et al (2020) 'Igniting individual purpose in times of crisis'. McKinsey & Company, 18 August. URL: mckinsey.com/capabilities/people-and-organizational-performance/our-insights/igniting-individual-purpose-in-times-of-crisis
Doidge, N (2008) *The Brain That Changes Itself: Stories of personal triumph from the frontiers of brain science.* Penguin.
Drucker, P (1939) *The End of Economic Man: A study of the new totalitarianism.* The John Day Company.
Dweck, C S (2007) *Mindset: The new psychology of success.* Ballantine Books.
Epictetus (2016) *Enchiridion*: *Handbook of Epictetus*, written by his pupil Arrian c 125 CE. CreateSpace.
Erikson, E H (1950) *Childhood and Society.* W W Norton & Company.
Flander, J de (2018) *The Art of Performance: The surprising science behind greatness.* Performance Factory.
Frankl, Viktor E (1946) *Man's Search for Meaning: An Introduction to Logotherapy.* Beacon Press.
Freud, S (1895) *Project of a Scientific Psychology.* Hogarth.
Frost, R (1914) 'A Servant to Servants'. URL: poetryverse.com/robert-frost-poems/a-servant-to-servants
Gall, F J (2018) *On the Functions of the Brain and of Each of Its Parts: On the organ of the moral qualities and intellectual faculties, and the plurality of the cerebral organs.* HardPress.
Goleman, D (2005) *Emotional Intelligence: Why it can matter more than IQ.* Bantam.
Greenleaf, R K (2002) *Servant Leadership: A journey into the nature of legitimate power and greatness.* Paulist Press.

Hanaway, M (2019) *The Existential Leader*. Routledge.
Hawkins, J (2007) *On Intelligence: How a new understanding of the brain will lead to the creation of truly intelligent machines*. Times Books.
Heidegger, M (2008) *Being and Time*. Harper Perennial Modern Thought.
Hesse, H (2022) *Journey to the East*. General Press.
Holt-Lunstad, J, Smith, T B et al (2015) 'Loneliness and social isolation as risk factors for mortality: A meta-analytic review'. *Perspectives on Psychological Science* 10(2). URL: pubmed.ncbi.nlm.nih.gov/25910392
Homkes, R (2024) *Survive, Reset, Thrive: Leading breakthrough growth strategy in volatile times*. Kogan Page.
James, W (2017) *The Principles of Psychology*. Pantianos Classics.
Jarden, J O, various articles: scholar.google.com/scholar?hl=en&as_sdt=0%2C5&q=Jarden+JO
Johnson, H T & Kaplan, R S (1987) *Relevance Lost: The Rise and Fall of Management Accounting*. Harvard Business School Press.
Jung, C (2014) *The Undiscovered Self: Answers to Questions Raised by the Present World Crisis*. Routledge Classics.
Kahneman, D (2012) *Thinking, Fast and Slow*. Penguin.
Kaplan (2020) 'What prior market crashes taught us in 2020'. Morningstar. URL: morningstar.com/features/what-prior-market-crashes-can-teach-us-in-2020
Katz, B (1966) *Nerve, Muscle and Synapse*. McGraw Hill.
Kegan, R (1983) *The Evolving Self*. Harvard Business Press.
Keltner, D (2009) *Born to be Good: The science of a meaningful life*. W W Norton & Company.
Kierkegaard, S (2023) *The Sickness unto Death: A New Translation*. Liveright.
Kildegaard, K & Lekfeldt, T (2023) 'Margrethe Vestager announces a new invention: We are all facing a gigantic change in our lives and society' (in Danish). *Berlingske Tidende*, 23 June.
Kim, W C & Mauborgne, R (2005) *Blue Ocean Strategy: How to create uncontested market space and make competition irrelevant*. Harvard Business School Press.
Kondratiev, N D (1925) *The Major Economic Cycles*.
Kuhn, T (1962) *The Structure of Scientific Revolutions*. University of Chicago Press.
Lancet, The (2020) 'Global population in 2100'. 14 July. URL: thelancet.com/infographics-do/population-forecast
Lassen, T K (2020) *Philosophy for Leaders* (in Danish). Samfundslitteratur.
Laozi, *Tao Te Ching* (4th century BC).
Leinwand, P & Mainardi, C with Kleiner, A (2016) *Strategy That Works: How winning companies close the strategy-to-execution gap*. Harvard Business Review Press.
Levi-Montalcini, R (1987) 'The nerve growth factor thirty-five years later'. *In Vitro Cell Development Biology* 23(4). URL: pubmed.ncbi.nlm.nih.gov/3553145
Luscombe, B (2021) 'Henry Kissinger's last crusade: stopping dangerous AI'. *Time Magazine*, 5 November 5. URL: time.com/6113393/eric-schmidt-henry-kissinger-ai-book

Machiavelli, N (2021) *The Prince*. Reader's Library Classics.
Manson, M (2016) *The Subtle Art of Not Giving a F*ck: A counterintuitive approach to living a good life.* Harper.
Maron, C & Beck, N (2023) *Promise-Based Execution: How to engage your people in strategy execution and leverage the power of promises to deliver great results.* Blue Note Consultants.
Martin, R L & Lafley, A G (2013) *Playing to Win: How strategy really works.* Harvard Business Review Press.
Maslow, A (2014) *Toward a Psychology of Being.* Sublime Books.
Masters, R D (1994) *The Neurotransmitter Revolution: Serotonin, social behaviour, and the law.* Southern Illinois University Press.
Maynard, J (2012) 'Roles of a Lifetime'. *New York Times*, October 17. URL: archive.nytimes.com/www.nytimes.com/interactive/2012/10/21/t-magazine/21well-halle.html
McCombs, M & Shaw, D L (1972) *The Agenda-Setting Function of Mass Media.* The Public Opinion Quarterly Vol 36, Oxford University Press.
Merleau-Ponty, M (2002) *Phenomenology of Perception.* Routledge Classics.
Mintzberg, H, Ahlstrand, B & Lampel, J (1998) *Strategy Safari: A guided tour through the wilds of strategic management.* Free Press.
Murakami, H (2009) *What I Talk about When I Talk about Running.* Random House.
Nietzsche, F (1961) *Thus Spoke Zarathustra: A book for everyone and no one.* Penguin Classics.
Noë, A (2023) *The Entanglement: How art and philosophy make us what we are.* Princeton University Press.
Pavlov, I P (1984) *Conditioned Reflexes: An investigation of the physiological activity of the cerebral cortex.* Dover Publications Inc.
Piaget, J & Inhelder, B (1972) *The Psychology of the Child.* Basic Books.
Pinker, S (2012) *The Better Angels of Our Nature: Why violence has declined.* Penguin Books.
Plato (2007) *The Republic.* Penguin Classics.
Ramon y Cajal, S (1893) *Manual of Normal Histology and Micrographic Technique* (second edition).
Ricoeur, P (1983–5) *Time and Narrative Volumes 1, 2, 3.* University of Chicago Press.
Rock, D (2007) *Quiet Leadership: six steps to transforming performance at work.* Harper Business.
Rogers, C (1989) *On Becoming a Person: A therapist's view of psychotherapy.* Houghton Mifflin.
Rosling, H, Rönnlund Rosling A & Rosling, O (2020) *Factfulness: Ten reasons we're wrong about the world – and why things are better than you think.* Flatiron Books.
Sacks, O (2012) *Awakenings.* Picador.

Saint-Exupéry, A de (2000) *The Little Prince*. Clarion Books.
Sapolsky, R M (2023) *Determined: A science of life without free will*. Vintage Publishing.
Sartre, J-P (2007) *Existentialism is a Humanism*. Yale University Press.
Sartre, J-P (2013) *Nausea*. New Directions.
Sartre, J-P (2021) *Being and Nothingness*. Washington Square Press.
Scharf-Hunt, D (1985) *Studying Smart: Time management for college students*. Barnes & Noble Books.
Schultz, M & Hatch, M-J (2001) 'Are the strategic stars aligned for your corporate brand?' *Harvard Business Review*, February. URL: hbr.org/2001/02/are-the-strategic-stars-aligned-for-your-corporate-brand
Schumpeter, J (1961) *The Theory of Economic Development: An inquiry into profits, capital, credit, interest, and the business cycle*. Oxford University Press.
Seery, M D, Holman, E A & Silver, R C (1999) 'Whatever does not kill us: cumulative lifetime adversity, vulnerability and resilience'. *Journal of Personality and Social Psychology* December 1999. URL: pubmed.ncbi.nlm.nih.gov/20939649
Seneca, L A (1969) *Letters from a Stoic*. Penguin Classics.
Sherrington, C S (1906) *The Integrative Action of the Nervous System*. Oxford University Press.
Sina, I (2014) *Ibn Sina's Remarks and Admonitions: Physics and Metaphysics: An analysis and annotated translation*. Columbia University Press.
Socrates, by Farnsworth, W (2021) *The Socratic Method: A Practitioner's Handbook*. David R Godine.
Solzhenitsyn, A (2018) *The Gulag Archipelago*. Vintage Classics.
Steiner, R (1996) *The Education of the Child and Early Lectures on Education*. Foundations of Waldorf Education, Steiner Books.
Stockdale, J (1993) *Courage under Fire: Testing Epictetus's doctrines in a laboratory of human behaviour*. Hoover Institution Press.
Streisand, B (2023) *My Name is Barbra*. Century.
Tzu, S (1994) *The Art of War*. Basic Books.
Urban, T (2023) *What's Our Problem?: A self-help book for societies*. Wait But Why.
Vries, M F R Kets de (2021) *Quo Vadis? The Existential Challenges of Leaders*. Palgrave.
Waldinger, R & Schulz, M (2023) *The Good Life: Lessons from the world's longest scientific study on happiness*. Simon & Schuster.
Wroblewski, A P, Amati, F et al (2011) 'Chronic exercise preserves lean muscle mass in master athletes'. *The Physician and Sportsmedicine* 39(3). URL: pubmed.ncbi.nlm.nih.gov/22030953
Wundt, W (2008) *An Introduction to Psychology*. Read & Company.
Yalom, I D (1980) *Existential Psychotherapy*. Yalom Family Trust.

Acknowledgements

This book represents an act of collaboration. I asked for help and allied myself with four experts who have contributed with wisdom and perspectives from their respective fields of expertise and their personal experiences. All through the book they act as my backing group, a sort of Greek chorus who, with a collective voice, comment on the dramatic action. This book is to a high degree due to their willingness to share and discuss ideas across academic fields.

Tommy Kjær Lassen enlightened us with his take on philosophy, ethics and existentialism. He is also profoundly concerned with how leadership and self-leadership are connected.

Mikkel Gradert thrilled us with his knowledge of psychologically safe workplaces and life quality. One of his specialities is decision-making processes, which is indeed highly relevant.

Jens Ole Jarden contributed with his extensive insight into the functioning of the brain. He brought many of our metaphysical discussions down to the laws of natural science.

Claus Maron combined the latest thinking in leadership psychology with strategy execution. He's a seasoned consultant who elegantly connects the past, the present and the future.

I'm deeply grateful for the generous and enthusiastic contribution of this expert panel. For more than two years we regularly met, presented and discussed our mutual perspectives. All the meetings were high energy and feel good. Thank you so much for your excellent company and high-level thinking.

This book would not have materialised without my top executive coaching clients. It took me eight years to write the book. All along, I bounced ideas at my clients and had countless inspiring conversations.

Specifically, I want to thank Lasse Rich Henningsen and Robert Kledal, who allowed me to share some of the outcomes of their coaching programmes in the book. Lasse, you have become a dear friend. And Robert, you are a role model – a very kind bulldozer.

Let me also thank my many colleagues and students at Copenhagen Business School. You know who you are. And my colleagues at the Møller Institute, Churchill College, the University of Cambridge, specifically Richard Leather, chief executive, and Richard Hill, director of education and leadership development.

Last but not least I want to thank you, the reader. I hope you have found the book helpful as a tool of transition. You have focused on questions and themes of identity, meaning, personal growth, choice, action and responsibility. And you have found old wisdom and new insights from a range of disciplines. I hope that the book has empowered you to make informed life choices and find peace of mind. It is in the transition phases of our life where we thrive the most. Aim for escape velocity.

Index

acceptance-based therapies 122
accountability 91, 162, 164, 167
action 15, 28, 30, 33–35, 45, 59, 66,
    86–87, 89–91, 110, 112, 115–116, 119,
    121, 146, 149, 161, 168, 170, 179, 182,
    195, 200, 202, 207, 221
    comparison with labour and work
    156–158
    conscious 55
    converting insights into 13
    deliberate 181
    destructive 123
    everyday 114
    incessant 158
    and intentions 81–82
    meaningful 13, 81, 158–159
    and responsibility 5, 33, 44, 114,
    143, 157, 181, 222
    significance of 142
Action–Responsibility Gap 89–90
active listening 200
activeness 54, 156, 157–158, 200
adrenaline 55, 82, 124, 125
adverse events 138–139
adversity 2, 107, 117–119, 121–126, 139,
    185, 194, 218
    see also stress
aestheticians 81
ageing 20–21
agenda-setting theory 148
Alzheimer's disease 61, 189
ambiguity tolerance 200
ambition 93–94
    ambitious choice 113, 114
    creeping 46
    in life 89

amygdala 59–60
analysis paralysis 24, 30, 175
anarchy 159
Andersen, Hans Christian 34
anxiety 4, 39, 52, 97, 124, 125, 175, 178,
    184
archetypal behaviour 184
archetypes 18, 184
Archimedes 70
Arden, P 17, 18
Arendt, H 146–147, 156–158, 170, 195
Aristotle 47, 54, 96, 134, 140, 177, 179,
    191–192
artificial intelligence (AI) 1, 21, 103,
    148, 151, 153, 169–171, 180
Asimov, I 141–142
attitudes 17, 35, 42, 76, 84, 110, 186
awareness 3, 6, 15, 20, 24, 28–29, 31,
    65, 80, 82, 84, 176, 182, 195
awe 98, 197

Bakewell, S 88
basal ganglia 58–59
Beauvoir, S de 145
behaviourism 184
Berry, H 43
big tech 148
biodiversity 143
biological adaptation 52
Biosphere 2 123
Black Death 131
blame-shifting *see* Action–Responsibility Gap
BMW framework 24
body and mind 65, 67, 177–179, 182
    see also mind–body dualism

bourgeois 17, 80–81
brain
    areas in 57–60
    basal ganglia 58–59
    chemicals, happiness 82–83
    cognitive functions 55, 57, 63, 147–148, 190, 191
    and consciousness 56, 60, 179, 181–182
    fear network *see* amygdala
    health and wellbeing 60–61, 65–67, 183, 189, 190–191
    neurotransmitters 67, 187, 189
    orbitofrontal cortex and amygdala 59–60
    prefrontal cortex 57–58
    scan 61, 62, 64
    and social relationships 67–70
brain fog 124–125
Brain Tuning programme 4–5, 61–65
    intelligence 64–65
    neurological assessment 61–62
    neuropsychological assessment 61, 62–63
    neuropsychological profile 63
    Z-scores and IQ performance 63
Brel, J 17
Brønniche, V E 63
Buffett, W 146
buzzword cycles 148

calling 146
the camel, the lion and the child metaphor 22
Camus, A 35, 88
carbon-neutral society 138
cardinal sins 55
cardinal virtues 44–45, 55
    see also virtues
CAR (Choice, Action, Responsibility) model 89–90
Casals, P 20
Chalmers, D 179

chemicals 82–83, 97
Choice–Action Gap 89–90
choices 5, 15, 25, 28, 31, 33–35, 39, 44–45, 66, 87–90, 112–116, 143, 146, 148, 157, 175, 177–179, 181–182, 200, 222
Christensen, C M 37–40, 42, 49, 112, 146
Churchland, P 179
Cicero 192
classical conditioning 144–145
Clausewitz, C von 192–193
climate activism 148
climate change 138
climate crisis 48, 129, 133, 138, 148
cognitive abilities and functions 55, 57, 63, 147–148, 190–191
cognitive psychology 29–30, 122, 184–185
cognitive tests and profile 62, 64
Cold War 136, 137, 179
collaboration 3, 34, 35, 53, 69, 116, 142, 160, 161, 162, 164, 167, 172
commitment 88, 89
communicable diseases 137
communication 64, 78, 143, 155, 165, 192
community 34, 39, 40, 79, 93, 121, 135, 160, 185
comparison 43
concussion 60
connectedness 24
conscience 14, 44, 85, 141–142, 181
conscious mind 183
consciousness and brain 56, 60, 179, 181–182
conservatism 132, 148
continuous growth and development, potential for 23
controllable entities 121
cortisol 97, 124
courage 44, 64, 81, 89, 121, 198–199
Covid-19 pandemic 97, 137, 144, 148, 166

creative circle, of life 18
creeping ambition 46
critical-friendly dimension, of conversation 84–85
Crutchfield, J 134
Cuddy, A 26
cultural changes 130–132
    see also paradigm shifts
curiosity 190

Damasio, A 179
Darwin, C 68–69, 130, 132
Dean, J 35
decision making 24, 57, 115, 162, 164, 165, 166, 170, 178, 179
deep breathing 83, 191
default behaviour 15
deglobalisation 148
dementia 61, 65, 78
Denmark 34–35, 49, 97, 129, 156, 160
Dennett, D 181
Descartes, R 55, 140, 144, 177, 180
design thinking 115–116
despair 17, 22, 33, 133, 139
digital technologies 148, 153, 155, 159–160
disciplines of life *see* neurology; philosophy; psychology; strategy
discovering meaning of life 146
diseases 30, 48, 52, 56, 61, 64–65, 97, 124, 135, 137, 189
disruption 37–38, 148
dopamine 83, 187
double loop learning 167–168
Drucker, P 147
Dylan, B 20

ecocentric world 48
economic crises 136, 148, 179, 180
economic cycle, changes in 144
economic waves 148
egalitarian society 34, 35, 53, 161

ego 21, 48, 183
Eliot, T S 33
emotional alchemy 44
emotional connections 33
emotional school 29, 140–143
empathy 29, 69, 86, 116, 142, 155, 167, 200
empowerment challenges
    giving away power 170
    leadership skills 171
    losing control 170–171
empty nest syndrome 20
endorphins 83
enlightenment 54, 138, 177
Epictetus 120–121
equity 21, 132, 162
Erikson, E H 16
error detection signals 59–60
ESG 148
ethicists 81
evolution 32, 52–54, 58, 59, 67, 130, 157, 181, 186
evolutionary psychology 185
execution strategies 5, 112–114, 194
exercises, physical 53, 60, 61, 65, 124, 190
existential and conscious decisions 15
existential clarity 15, 25, 27, 33, 117, 195
existential doubt 24
existential goal 94
existential guilt 178
existential inflection point 21–22
existentialism 3–4, 44–45, 46, 56, 77, 87, 88, 116, 142, 145, 147, 177, 211, 218, 221
existentialist philosophy and thinking 81, 88, 157, 178
existentialists 81
existentialist school of thought 181
existentialist thinking 178
existential psychotherapy 65–66
existential questions 14–15, 75, 86, 87, 91, 98

221

existential resilience 25, 44–45, 82, 83, 125, 185, 186
existential school 140–143, 181

failures 3, 45–46, 47, 48, 187, 194
family values 88–89, 232
famines 137, 138
fate 38, 39, 47
feelings 28, 33, 44, 55, 66, 68, 69, 76, 81, 158, 177, 178, 199
financial crisis 136, 148, 179, 180
first principles thinking 134
flow, in chemicals 82–83
fluid attention 80
fortitude 44, 55
    see also courage
four-leaf clover model 27–28, 201, 209–210
Frankl, V E 13, 146, 184
Frederik X, King 34
freedom 20, 26, 40, 44, 56, 88, 118, 121, 135, 157, 178, 195
    to act 44, 158–159, 195
    systematised 2, 195
free market economics 139, 148
free will 181, 200
French existentialism 87, 88
Freud, S 29–30, 178, 183
friction theory 192–193
friendship 69, 96, 99
frontal lobe 57
Frost, R 24
future existence 13
future Self 1–5, 87, 90, 110, 112, 113, 114
    see also Self

Gall, F J 188
Gaulle, C de 145
generativity 16
globalisation 148
global population 20, 137
goals 17, 33, 39, 40, 70, 76, 112–114, 115, 167, 193, 194

Inner Development Goals 172
    long-term 191
    meaningful 176
    seeking new goals 23, 93–94
    setting your 24–25, 27, 31, 112–114, 194
    UN Sustainable Development Goals 159, 172
Golgi, C 188–189
Gradert, M 4, 217
Greenleaf, R K 171, 172
growth mindset 187
growth-plateau-growth relationship 111
guiding principles 13, 24, 70, 80, 89, 152, 180

Hadza people 53
happiness and wellbeing 185
Harvard Study of Adult Development 68
health, WHO's definition of 56
healthy lifestyle 65, 190
heart disease 97
Heidegger, M 178, 179
helmet usage 191
help and support 99–100, 122, 159–160, 197
Henningsen, L R 75, 99–100, 119, 122, 217
Herriot, É 78
Hesse, H 171
hippocampus 124, 190
Holt-Lunstad, J 68
homosexuality 132
hormesis 123–124
HOW, the (existential model) 31, 115, 116, 176, 210
    see also strategy
human development, theory of 18
humanistic psychology 33, 184
humanity thoughts, in common 32–33
hunter-gatherer societies 52–53, 154
hybrid work 148
hygge 34

id 183
immune dysfunction 125
imperial phase, of maturity 79
impulsive phase, of maturity 79
Industrial Age model 154, 158
industrial revolution 53–54, 153, 154, 159
inequality 39, 48, 53, 138, 154–155
infancy to adolescence stages 16–21
inflection points 21–22, 25, 26, 111, 176
Inner Development Goals 172
innovation 155, 159, 162, 200
institutional/cultural level, of maturity 79
integrity 17, 79, 142, 192
intelligence 64–65, 110, 181, 188
intentions 81–82, 114
inter-individual level, of maturity 79
interpersonal level, of maturity 79
intimacy 16
intuition 80, 143, 167
IQ 63
isolation 16, 68–69
Israel, wars in 137

Jagger, M 87
James, W 183
Jarden, J O 4–5, 61, 65, 217
Johnson, H T 37
Jung, C 18, 178, 183–184
justice 44, 55

Kahneman, D 30, 58
Katz, B 145
Kegan, R 79
Kierkegaard, S 2–3, 34–35, 77, 80, 93, 177–178
kindness 12, 69, 83–86, 98, 187, 200
Kissinger, H 153
Kjær, E 117
Kledal, R 12, 41, 101, 109–111, 114, 217
Kleiner, A 31
knowledge workers 147

know thyself 54, 176, 181–182, 186
Kondratiev, N D 148
Kuhn, T 130

La Belle Époque 148
labour, work and action, difference between 156–158
Laozi 54
Lassen, T K 4, 80, 156, 223
late bloomers 21, 23
leadership 7, 26, 141–142, 151, 163, 169–172, 213
    definition of 153
    neuroscience of 66
    and power 172
    regenerative 155
    responsibilities of 169
    and self-leadership 4, 77, 169, 221
    servant leadership 171–172, 215
    values 161
    see also Nordic Leadership Model (NLM)
learning agility 88, 89, 210
learning approaches 199
Leinwand, P 31
Lenin, V 34
Levi-Montalcini, R 147
LGBTQ+ 132
life expectancy 18, 137, 154
life lessons 25
life phases 16–22, 25
    achievement in 22
    in early forties 21
    mirroring process in 19
    old aged people, changes in 20–21
    psychosocial stages in 16–17
    in thirties 21
    in twenties 21
life's path, stages on 80–81
linear thinking 95, 96, 159, 160
literature, on existentialism 211
lived body 56
loneliness 68, 69, 95, 97

lost decade 136
love 3, 16, 41, 42, 53, 83, 95, 189

Machiavelli, N 192
Mainardi, C 31
malnourishment 137
Manson, M 130
mapping network 102, 103–104
Marcus Aurelius, emperor 1–2, 119, 120
market crash timeline 136–137
Maron, C 5, 112, 217
Martin, R L 115
Maslow, A 146, 184
maturity levels 22, 79
maximising mindsets 42–43
McCombs, M 148
meaning, sense of 11, 13, 15, 23–24, 28, 31, 33, 35, 40, 49, 89, 118, 133, 135, 157, 176, 193, 194, 195
meaning 360° model 100–101
meaningful goals 112
meaningful success 40–50
   decisions and right choices for 47
   definition of 42
   failures and learning 45
   helping others 49
   mindsets and attitudes 42–43
   satisfaction and positive memories for 43
   and status 41–42
   types of 40–41
   values and rules for 44–45
meditation 60, 83
Meditations (Marcus Aurelius) 1–2
Merleau-Ponty, M 56
metacognitive therapy 30
metamorphoses 22
metaverse 148
#MeToo movement 131–132
microbiome gut–brain axis 189
military strategy 191–192
Milner, B 147–148
mind, parts of 183

mind-body dualism 54–56
mindfulness 83, 122, 126, 191
mirroring process 19
misogyny 131
mobile revolution 148
multiple perspectives 28–29
multiple sclerosis 125
Murakami, H 94
muscle atrophy 123
Musk, E 134–135
Myers–Briggs Type Indicator personality test 18, 184

Napoleonic Wars 192
natural selection 52–53, 68–69, 130
nature, spending time in 190
negative stress 95
nerve growth factor (NGF) 147
networking 96, 101–104
network thinking 159–160
neurological assessment 61–62
neurological disorders 125, 189
neurology 4, 25, 27, 28, 30, 51, 52, 144–145
   adversity and stress 117, 122, 130
   beneficial chemicals 97–98
   brain tuning programme 4–5, 61–65
   concept of Self 76
   contributors 205–206
   dimension of thriving 61, 65, 176
   expanding yourself 187–191
   neurological assessment 61–62
   neurological disorders 125, 189
   neurons and connections 57, 60–61, 67, 144–145, 181, 187, 188–189
   neurophilosophy 30, 179
   neuroplasticity 187, 188, 190
   neuropsychological assessment 61, 62–64
   neuropsychological profile 63
   neuropsychology 4–5, 30, 147, 179
   neuroscience 20, 56, 57, 59, 66, 145, 179, 189

neurotransmitters 67, 187, 189
visual techniques in 189
neurophilosophy 30, 179
neuroplasticity 187, 188, 190
neuropsychological assessment 61, 62–64
neuropsychological profile 63
neuropsychology 4, 30, 147, 179
neuroscience 20, 56, 57, 59, 66, 145, 179, 189
neurotransmitters 67, 187, 189
New Age movement 140–141
Nietzsche, F 22
Nieuwerburgh, C van 29
Noë, A 179
Nordic countries 160, 161
Nordic Leadership Model (NLM) 7, 151, 163–169
   circular/linear dimension 165–166
   coupled/decoupled dimension 167
   distributed/centralised dimension 166
   DNA helix 168
   horizontal/vertical dimension 164
   motivational/rational dimension 166–167
   network/hierarchy dimension 164–165
   parallel/sequential dimension 165
   principles 162
   spiral/directed dimension 167–168
   see also leadership
Nordic Nine 160–161, 163
now, significance of 15–16, 198
nuclear war 134

obesity 137
oil crisis 137, 148
openness and transparency 162, 195
orbitofrontal cortex 59–60
organisational theory and development 147

outside-in vs inside-out approach 78
oxytocin 83, 97

painkillers 83
paradigm shifts 59, 95, 129, 130–133, 140, 152
   adaptation 133
   factors that cost 139
   growth and sustainability 133
   Nordic Leadership Model 7, 151, 163–169
   as opposites 159–160
   pattern recognition mind 85, 134
   periodic timelines 144–148
   periodic timelines challenging 144–148
   power and challenging dilemmas 169–171
   schools of thought 29, 140–143, 176–177
pattern recognition mind 85, 134
Pavlov, I P 144–145
perfect friendship 96
permacrisis 137
Personal Business Plan 13, 46, 84, 194
personal conversations 104
personalities assessment 18
personal reinvention 88–89
phenomenology 56
philosophy 4, 25, 27, 28, 29, 31, 55, 117, 175, 185
   ancient virtues 44–45
   contemporary 35
   contemporary philosophy 35
   contributors 203–204
   existentialist philosophy and thinking 81, 88, 157, 178
   know yourself 54, 176–182, 186
   lessons from 181–182
   life's path, stages of 80
   neurophilosophy 30, 179
   schools of thoughts 140–143

Self, definition of 76
phrenology 188
physical safety 83, 98
Piaget, J 184–185
Pinker, S 138
Pinocchio model 84, 108–109, 112, 114
Plato 44, 54, 177, 191
playfulness 186–187, 198
positive psychology 185
positive thinking 185
positron emission tomography (PET) 57
postmodernism 148
Pound, E 78
poverty 39, 135, 138
power 40, 49, 108, 118–119, 132, 143, 152, 159, 166, 169–173, 179, 192, 201, 217
power paradigm shift 172
pragmatism 162
prefrontal cortex 57–58
prioritisation 6, 39, 42, 48, 70, 186, 193, 199
procrastination 90
progress record 194
promise-based execution strategy 112–114
pro-pro chart 115–116
prudence 44, 55
psychoanalysis 18–19, 122, 178
psychological safety 4, 66, 67, 83, 97
psychology 4, 5, 25, 27, 28, 29–30, 31, 145, 175, 176, 182–187
   cognitive psychology 29–30, 122, 184–185
   concept of Self 76
   contributors 204–205
   evolutionary psychology 185
   humanistic psychology 33, 184
   lessons from 186–187
   mind-body dualism 56
   neuropsychology 4–5, 30, 147, 179
   positive psychology 185

relationships, power of 67, 97, 98
SCARF model 66–67
self-actualisation 178
social psychology 185
understand yourself 182–187
psychosocial challenges in adulthood 16–17
   generativity vs stagnation 16
   integrity vs despair 17
   intimacy vs isolation 16
psychotherapy 29–30, 65

quantitative electroencephalography (QEEG) 57
quiet quitting 152

Ramón y Cajal, S 188–189
rational school of thought 29, 55, 140–143, 180
rational thinking 55, 177
reaching out to others *see* help and support
reflection points 17
reinvention strategy 20, 25–28, 107–111, 107–120
   adversity and stress 117–118, 122–126
   design thinking in 115–116
   future Self 1–5, 87, 90, 110, 112, 113–114
   promise-based execution 112–114
   Stoic approach 118–122
   strings of past, cutting 108–111
   suffering, for growth 117–118
relationships 94–98
   building and maintaining 99–100
   Ferris wheel model 100–101, 103
   and friends 95–96
   learning and teaching in 98
   versus loneliness 16, 68, 69, 95, 97, 98
   mapping network in 101–104
   quality of 100–101

Index

reinventing with work 153–155
societal connections 94
work–life balance 34, 95, 160
relaxed readiness 2, 11, 15, 82, 141, 143, 169, 195
remote work 148
respect 32, 42, 162
responsibility 28, 33, 35, 44–46, 87, 89–90, 142–143, 162, 165, 177–78, 181–182, 200, 202
and action 5, 33, 44, 114, 143, 157, 181, 222
chains of 162
existential 14, 91, 196
individual 48
intrinsic 151
of leadership 169
of senior management 165
sense of 102, 178
social 167
Responsibility–Choice Gap 89–90
retrofit story of life 26
revolution 130
Ricoeur, P 179
rites of passage 14
Robbins, T 82, 114
robots 141, 153
Rock, D 66
Rogers, C R 33, 184
Rosling, H 136

Saint-Exupéry, A de 25
Sandberg, Sheryl 42
Sapolsky, R 181
Sartre, J-P 2–3, 35, 77, 88, 145, 146, 178–179
satisfaction 39–40, 46
SCARF model of psychological safety 66–67
scepticism 101, 140
Schmidt, E. 153
Schumpeter, J 148
Second World War 137, 148, 156

seenagers 19
Seery, M 125
Self 1–5, 54, 78
communication with 78
connected to 82–85
chemicals flow for 82–83
inner voices and dialogues 84–85
relaxed readiness, sense of 82
and consciousness 55, 76–77, 183
defined as 177
definition of 76, 177
and Kierkegaard 77
monitoring and judging 81
neurological concept of 76–77
and otherness 78, 177
outside-in vs inside-out approach 78
psychological concept of 76
situational awareness 80
see also future Self
self-actualisation 146, 178
self-awareness 76–77, 108
self-interest 8, 68, 135
self-leadership 4, 77, 169, 221
self-monitoring 80
self-realisation 81
self-reflection 183
self-sustaining ecosystem 123
self-talk 187
Seneca the Younger 118
sequential multi-tasking 135
serotonin 83
serotonin reuptake inhibitors (SSRIs) 189
servant leadership 171–172, 215
Sharf-Hunt, D 112
Shaw, D 148
Sherrington, C S 145
short-term memory loss 124
short-term targets 113–114
Sim, J 48–49
simplicity 162
Sina, I 55

single loop learning 167
situational awareness 80
skin starvation 97
slavery 131
social constructivism 178
social interaction 191
social isolation 16, 68–69
social justice crises 143
social maturity, levels of 22, 79
social media 21, 70, 81, 103, 148
social psychology 185
social relationships
    guiding principle model 70
    isolation and loneliness 68–69
    meaningful connections for 69
societal connection 94
societal shifts 130
Socrates 44, 54, 182
software as a service (SaaS) business 46
Solzhenitsyn, A 118, 121
soul 54–55, 118
stagnation 16
status 41–42, 54, 69, 160, 199
Steiner, R 17, 18
Stockdale, J 120, 121
stock markets 134, 136–137
Stoicism 44, 118–122, 126, 204, 218
strategic thinking 59, 191
strategy 4, 25, 27, 28, 31, 104, 140, 145, 147, 175, 176
    adversity and stress 117–118, 122–126
    contributors 206–208
    design thinking in 115–117
    execution strategies 5, 112, 170, 194
    future Self 1–5, 87, 90, 110, 112, 113–114
    lessons from 194–195
    military strategy 191–192
    planning and execution 5
    principles of 193
    promise-based execution strategy 112–114
    reinvention strategy 20, 25–28, 107–120
    Stoic approach 118–122
    and strings of past 108–111
    suffering, for growth 117–118
    transform yourself 191–195
stress 67, 117–118, 122–126, 143
    acute 125
    bodily 123–124
    chronic 123–125, 191
    effects of 126
    hormetic 123
    hormones and chemicals 97, 125
    management 126, 191
    moderate 125
    negative 95
    neurological approach 122–125
    psychological approach 122
    stress wood 123
stroke 60–61, 65–66
Study of Adult Development, Harvard University 68
subconsciousness 76, 183
success 64
    choices and hierarchical thinking 39
    defining 194
    individual achievement and self-fulfilment as 38, 39
    long-term meaning and happiness 39
    meaningful relationship for 48
    opportunities and fate in 39
    see also meaningful success
suffering well 117–118
sufficing mindset 42–43
super agers 189
superego 183
sustainability 21, 133, 148, 152, 159, 162, 166
Sustainable Development Goals, UN 159, 172
SWOT analysis 193

symbiosis 79
symbol of life 27
sympathy 68–69
synapses 145, 181, 187–190
Systems 1 and 2 thinking 58–59

Taoism 54
TED talks 37, 38
temperance 44, 55
third eye perspective 78
threat detection signals 59–60
tightrope walkers metaphor 132
Tinggaard, G 34
totalitarianism 146, 147, 156
tragedies 47
transformation lessons 175–195
    expand yourself 187–191
    from four disciplines 175–176
    know yourself 176–182
    transform yourself 191–195
    understand yourself 182–187
transitions 16–22, 41, 86–87, 98, 111, 114
trauma 61
triple loop learning 167–168
trust 99–100, 162
type indicator personality test 184
Tzu, S 191

Ukraine, Russian invasion of 133–134, 137
unconscious mind 122, 178
unpredictability quality, of human 155
ups and downs, handling 135–138
Urban, T 153
utilitarian friendships 96

valued, being 151–152
values 119
van Nieuwerburgh, C 29
Vestager, M 153
virtues 13, 15, 44–45, 55, 116, 176, 181–82, 194

wars 52, 88, 121, 134–135, 137–138, 144, 148, 191–192, 214, 219
watershed moment 18, 31, 33, 35
wave theory 148–149
weakness, sign of 35, 63, 96, 99, 160, 193
wellbeing 124, 151, 195
    and brain health 60–61, 65–67, 183, 189, 190–191
    mental 30
    in positive psychology 184–186
    predicting 60–61
    social 56, 102
WHAT, the (existential model) 29–30, 116, 117, 210
    see also neurology; psychology
WHY, the (existential model) 29, 31, 116, 117, 210
    see also philosophy
win-win solutions 116
women, voting rights for 131
work
    comparison with labour and action 156–158
    freedom to act 158–159, 195
    as identity 155–156
    reinvent relationship with 153–155
work-life balance 34, 95, 160
workload management 191
work theory 149
Wundt, W 182

Yalom, I D 65

About the author

Stephen is a top executive coach, headhunter, economist, marketeer, author, lecturer, facilitator and keynote speaker who comes with more than 25 years of experience in executive coaching, 20 years of experience in executive search and 15 years of experience in global marketing. He has written two bestselling books and has been an associate professor in strategic market management and corporate communication at Copenhagen Business School since 1996. Stephen is also an associate at the Møller Institute, Churchill College, the University of Cambridge.

During his career, Stephen has always worked globally and with global clients. His 15 years of marketing (1982–1996) were with global market leaders such as The Coca-Cola Company and L'Oréal. His 20 years of executive search (1996–2014) established him as managing partner for Korn Ferry (Denmark), the world's leading executive search and talent management firm. His more than 25 years of executive coaching include clients such as Baker McKenzie, Deloitte, EY, Novo Nordisk, Maersk, Pandora and PwC.

Stephen describes his executive coaching work as an amalgamation of corporate, academic, entrepreneurial and consulting competencies. One effect of his strikingly varied yet coherent experience is that he has honed a pattern recognition mind. Stephen's Nordic leadership style means he is totally transparent as he values trust and respect when working with clients and colleagues.

Over the past 25 years, Stephen has built a solid reputation as a leadership expert, advising top executives and other leaders all over the world. His highly energetic and inspirational style also makes him a sought-after keynote speaker. Concurrently, Stephen has developed his top executive coaching system, The Personal Business Plan, a unique ten-step system for personal and professional development.

Stephen has personal entrepreneurial experience from running his own executive coaching company, where he – together with his wife – has built a franchise of coaching partners around the world. In

2017, they launched the Personal Business Plan system as an online toolkit, which now has users in 94 countries. Stephen has detailed the Personal Business Plan system in two bestsellers, *The Personal Business Plan – A Blueprint for Running Your Life* (Wiley, 2013) and *Your Next Career – The Headhunter's Guide to Lifelong Success* (in Danish) (Lindhardt & Ringhof, 2012). *The Existential Playbook* completes Stephen's trilogy about career, happiness and meaning respectively. You can see more at theexistentialplaybook.com.

Today, Stephen is on a dual mission. Through his executive coaching programme, he answers this fundamental question from clients: 'When I've done well, then what?' At the same time, he democratises executive coaching by making his leadership expertise and business acumen available to everyone through the user-friendly and cost-effective Personal Business Plan Online Toolkit – thepersonalbusinessplan.com

Stephen is both Danish and French and lives by the sea and the forest near Copenhagen, Denmark with his wife. Together, they have four children and nine grandchildren, who continue to build on the strong family values, which are also the foundation of Stephen's work: life ambition, personal reinvention, learning agility and courage to commit.

EU Safety Representative: euComply OÜ Pärnu mnt 139b-14 11317 Tallinn
Estonia hello@eucompliancepartner.com +33 756 90241

www.ingramcontent.com/pod-product-compliance
Lightning Source LLC
Chambersburg PA
CBHW042145160426
43201CB00022B/2414